Retail Product Management

Retail Product Management introduces students to the product management process and gives an insight into the operations and practices used by retailers to achieve their product strategy objectives. Blending theoretical approaches from a number of management perspectives, including marketing, purchasing and logistics, this text illustrates the breadth of knowledge that retail product managers need to undertake this complex managerial task.

Thoroughly revised and updated since the first edition, this important text integrates theory and practice using a broad range of up-to-date case studies and practical examples from a variety of retail sectors. This text:

- uses photos, figures, tables and conceptual diagrams to support key ideas;
- examines the practical elements of product management;
- incorporates important new chapters covering topics such as the relationship between the product range and promotional activity and retailers' response to consumer demands;
- integrates discussions on the relationship between the product and its selling environment and the overall retail brand.

Retail Product Management builds on the foundations of the highly successful last edition and provides readers with a comprehensive and accessible introduction to this important subject.

Rosemary Varley is a senior lecturer within the Department of Management and Marketing at the Huddersfield University Business School, where she teaches a wide range of retail management and marketing modules. Prior to her academic career, she worked in product management and buying in a variety of retail sectors.

Retail Product Management

Buying and merchandising

Second edition

Rosemary Varley

Routledge
Taylor & Francis Group

LONDON AND NEW YORK

First published 2001
by Routledge
2 Park Square, Milton Park, Abingdon, Oxon OX14 4RN

Simultaneously published in the USA and Canada
by Routledge
270 Madison Ave, New York, NY 10016

Reprinted 2001, 2002, 2003 (twice), 2004 (twice)
Second edition 2006

Routledge is an imprint of the Taylor & Francis Group

© 2001, 2006 Rosemary Varley

Typeset in Perpetua and Bell Gothic by
Keystroke, Jacaranda Lodge, Wolverhampton
Printed and bound in Great Britain by
TJ International Ltd, Padstow, Cornwall

British Library Cataloguing in Publication Data
A catalogue record for this book is available from the British Library

Library of Congress Cataloging in Publication Data
A catalog record of this book has been requested

ISBN10: 0–415–32714–8   ISBN13: 0–415–32714–5 (hbk)
ISBN10: 0–415–32715–6   ISBN13: 0–415–32715–2 (pbk)

Contents

Figures

FIGURES

Tables

Boxes

Case studies

Preface

Since an early age retailing activity has fascinated me, and before I reached double figures I had become something of a shopaholic. My parents tolerated this addiction through my teenage years, breathing a sigh of relief when I was old enough to earn the funds to feed my habit. Living in the country, opportunities to experience retailing on a large or sophisticated scale were restricted to occasional visits to nearby cities, and it was a visit to the Biba store in Kensington, London in the 1970s that confirmed my destiny. Founded by designer Barbara Halinuki, this huge emporium of the most delightful products, packaged and displayed as works of art, in an environment that was more luxurious and exciting than any house, museum or even dance venue I had encountered, showed me the heights to which the 'shopping experience' could be taken.

My own college training and subsequent career were geared towards finding out how the retail process worked; and in particular the relationship between the product, the selling environment and the consumer has been the focus of my attention. Time spent in commercial product management in the 1980s took me through buying offices, stores and design rooms, and gradually the fascination with retailing that I had always fostered became the preserve of the masses. The service economy boomed, people talked about shops, newspapers featured serious articles on retail companies, a career in retailing became an admirable choice, and, most importantly for my own personal development, universities began to expand the subject of retailing from the fourth 'P' of the marketing mix (place) to a specialist subject area, and then to dedicated courses.

In the transformation from practitioner to educator, my enthusiasm for retailing has not waned. Retailing is a subject that moves fast; it is interesting and fun to teach. It is an accessible subject, which most students engage well with and then find challenging in its complexity. This book is a contribution to the process of enthusing and educating retailers of the future.

Rosemary Varley

Acknowledgements

First, I would like to acknowledge the continued enthusiasm and encouragement from Francesca Heslop, Commissioning Editor for Business and Management, and the support and guidance of Emma Joyes, Editorial Assistant at Routledge. I would also like to thank Adam Gilbert and the rest of the editorial and production team at Routledge.

I would like to thank my friends and colleagues at the University of Huddersfield for their support, in particular Glynis Jones and David Harvey who could always be relied upon to make me laugh in stressful times. Thanks also go to people outside work who have helped to give me time and space near deadlines.

I am grateful for the permission granted by Debenhams, Kogan Page, Gennaro Cuomo, Alberto Pastore and Caroline Ansty to use material in this book. I would also like to thank people who have reviewed and given me valuable feedback on the first edition.

Finally, I would like to thank my family who have tolerated my distractions from them and I dedicate this new edition to my mother, Amy whose unfailing belief in me has been a life support.

Introduction

Product management has always been at the centre of a healthy retail business. In the past, traders and merchants who thrived did so because they gave their customers a better product offer than their contemporaries; intuitively knowing what the consumer market will judge to be a superior product offer is the prowess of the retail entrepreneur. In the retail environment of modern developed economies, opportunities to exploit really new products are rare, yet talented retailers manage to create the illusion of newness and freshness in their product ranges by selecting and developing innovative product variations.

The aim of this book is to combine two managerial viewpoints. It blends product marketing with retail management, exploring an often hidden and overlooked part of the retail strategy. Products are the roots from which all other retail activity stems, and as such they provide an appropriate focus for the text. However, recent retail history has highlighted the dangers of taking a one-sided view of product management. Products are managed for consumers; they are managed in order to create and respond to customer demand, to satisfy existing customers and attract potential new ones. In a crowded retail market, it is perilous to forget the close and complex relationship between products, consumers and the arena in which product exchange takes place.

In response to the physical product needs of consumers, retailers provide products where, when and however a window of shopping opportunity is created in busy lifestyles. Consumers combine these physical needs with personal aspirations and desires, and so the retailer has also to be seen as the right place to shop, to be in tune with their customers and to have desirable values. Consumers take a multi-level approach to their shopping activities, and so retailers have to take a multi-level approach to the running of their businesses. Retailers have to ensure that operations are set up to provide a smooth flow of goods to the places and at the times the buying public wants. However, operational efficiency has to be overlaid with the strategic management of retail brands to ensure that the retail arenas in which products are acquired retain their own desirability. The retail brand management process involves the creation and reinforcement of the 'branded shopping experience', being separate to but integrated with the brands attached to the product ranges within. Branding an experience requires a skilful and integrated marketing approach, blending a communication, service and location strategy to complement the product offer. This text acknowledges the contribution of these interrelated components of a retail strategy, focusing on the product range and exploring the linkage between operational and strategic product management.

Even in retail markets where consumers have seemingly endless choice, the product range retains its role as a means by which one competitor can differentiate itself from another. A retailer's product differentiation may be great, as in the case of a specialist retailer, where no other outlet matches the depth of choice within a particular category of merchandise. On the other hand, the product differentiation may be slight, for example in a supermarket, with the difference between one competitor and another being largely a perceived one, and may rely on the contribution of a handful of key items to make the difference. Alternatively, the product range may provide the link into other means by which a retailer can position themselves away from competitors, for example by using price or service differentiation.

The relationship between the product range and the position that a retailer carves out, not only in the marketplace, but also in the mind of the customer, is a recurring theme in this book. Considered by many academics and practitioners to be the most important aspect of a retailer's strategy, a retailer's positioning remains intangible and difficult to measure. However, the operational support mechanisms *are* tangible and measurable, and in order to fill a resource gap this book concentrates on these. As such, this retail textbook brings together subjects from a number of different academic subject areas in order to reflect the multi-faceted role that retail product management plays. Logistic principles, accounting and purchasing principles, and design principles are all part of the product management process, yet the overriding principles are marketing ones, concerning consumer knowledge and understanding.

The subtitle of this book, 'Buying and merchandising', reflects its operational focus. Buyers and merchandisers carry out the managerial roles within retail organisations that have traditionally had a significant involvement in the product management process. Buyers and merchandisers normally manage the interface between product and consumer, and organise the supply chain support to maximise opportunities given by that interface. However, using these managerial terms as a subtitle acknowledges that retail product management has a wider remit and is fully integrated into an overall retail strategy. The product range and the way it is managed is directly related to the ongoing levels of income and profitability, which will determine the long-term survival, and strategic development of the business.

The second edition of *Retail Product Management* builds on the strengths of the first edition. The clearly structured chapters now include learning objectives as well as introductions and summaries. Many of the examples and boxed features have been updated to provide fresh material to reflect upon. All chapters include a short case study or an exercise, as well as a set of questions. These features help to make the book a valuable resource for problem-based learning. Illustrations and diagrams are included to help students grasp academic concepts, and sources for further reading and research are provided. The new edition has given the opportunity for some reorganisation of material, which reflects the emphasis of product management in today's retail industry. Some of this is included under the new chapter (7) title 'Managing the response to sales'. Inevitably, the chapter on non-store product management (13) has been overhauled in the light of developments in electronic home shopping. In addition, a new chapter has been added on communicating the product offer.

The chapters of this book fall into four parts. The first part introduces the concept of product management in the retail organisation, illustrating to the reader how it contributes to the overall strategic positioning of the company and how product management relates to other parts of a retail business. The organisational structures and key job roles are discussed in depth to give an understanding of what retail product management entails. Traditional buying organisations and processes are compared with the category management approach to product management.

Part II of the book explores the retail product management process. It begins with a chapter on range planning and product selection, which highlights the need for retailers to satisfy consumer's product needs on a short-term and long-term basis. The next chapter introduces the various supply sources retailers might use and provides a discussion on supply base management, acknowledging the contribution that suppliers can make to the product management process. Chapter 6 introduces the principles of stock management and reviews a number of concepts that are fundamental to the understanding of how buying quantities are determined, while Chapter 7 concentrates on the theme of response as a way of introducing modern approaches towards the control of product flow into a retail organisation.

While the second part of the book is chiefly concerned with planning operations, which typically take place in a 'buying office', the third part of the book takes the reader through the aspects of product management that help to implement product plans within the retail outlet and the processes used to maximise product performance. Chapter 8 is concerned with the allocation of retail space to products; Chapter 9 explores the relationship between a retail outlet's design and the products sold within it while Chapter 10 moves into the area of visual merchandising in order to consider how products might be presented to customers most effectively. Chapter 11 contains all new material on how customer communications of various types might be used to inform customers about a retailer's product range. The section is concluded with a discussion about the various methods used to evaluate product performance in order to assess the effectiveness of retail product management. The final part of the book contains two chapters that explore particular retail product management applications, within the context of non-store retailing and international retail operations.

The intention with the new edition is to update the text with new examples and more useful cases, to bring new material to existing chapters in order to reflect the directions in which product management is moving within the various sectors of the retail industry and to provide some new perspectives. However, the main aim of this book has not changed; its purpose is to provide accessibility to a relatively under-resourced area of retail study and to take a multi-sector approach to broaden the reader's understanding of retail product management.

CHAPTER MAP

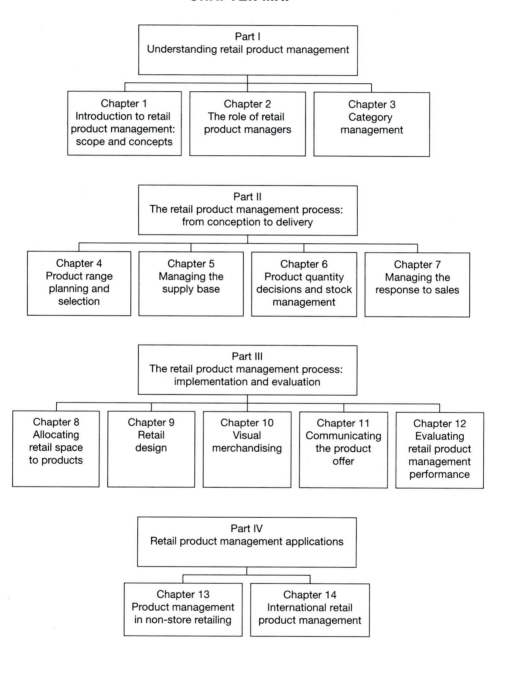

Part I
Understanding retail product management

Chapter 1
Introduction to retail product management: scope and concepts

Chapter 2
The role of retail product managers

Chapter 3
Category management

Part II
The retail product management process: from conception to delivery

Chapter 4
Product range planning and selection

Chapter 5
Managing the supply base

Chapter 6
Product quantity decisions and stock management

Chapter 7
Managing the response to sales

Part III
The retail product management process: implementation and evaluation

Chapter 8
Allocating retail space to products

Chapter 9
Retail design

Chapter 10
Visual merchandising

Chapter 11
Communicating the product offer

Chapter 12
Evaluating retail product management performance

Part IV
Retail product management applications

Chapter 13
Product management in non-store retailing

Chapter 14
International retail product management

Part I

Understanding retail product management

Chapter 1

Introduction to retail product management
Scope and concepts

LEARNING OBJECTIVES

The purpose of this chapter is to:

- Develop a definition for, and an understanding of, the term retail product management.
- Explore the scope of retail product management, through the various functions or business activities associated with it, within a retail organisation.
- Appreciate the fundamental role that product management plays within the overall business strategy of a retailer, considering the wide variation of business type within the retail industry sector.
- Introduce the concepts of general and speciality approaches to retail management, and gain an understanding of how these approaches relate to the product range or assortment.
- Understand how product range orientation is used in government classification of retail businesses, and the limitations of such a classification scheme.

INTRODUCTION

This chapter introduces the concept of product management from a retailer's viewpoint. It provides an overview of what retail product management entails, and how this relates to other management operations within a retail business organisation. Retail product management is incorporated at various levels within a retail organisation. The strategic level is where long-term product management objectives are set out and the contribution of the product range to the overall retail positioning strategy is established. The operational level is where those strategic objectives become translated into processes and operations that are carried out by product management teams and at the end of the product management process the product meets its consumer in the retail outlet.

PRODUCTS

Products are central to most organisations, whether they are in the form of tangible goods or services. Traditionally, manufacturers have been concerned with the design and production of products, whilst retailers have had the task of gathering together a relevant and inspiring selection of goods and making them available to consumers at convenient locations and times. These boundaries are becoming blurred, as we shall see throughout the book; some business organisations engage in retailing, even though the majority of their activity is concerned with some other enterprise, such as production, or entertainment, and some retailers do have their own factories. However, if a business is to be classed as a retailer, their core activity, which accounts for over half of their total revenue has to come from selling finished products or providing personal services to the final consumer. Most retailers do not engage in any other primary business activity, and so the collection of products that retailers offer to their customers is the traditional determinant of the nature of their business and the heaviest influence on all other aspects of their business strategy.

A PRODUCT DEFINED

A marketer's definition of a product is 'a physical good, service, idea, person or place that is capable of offering tangible and intangible attributes that individuals or organisations regard as so necessary, worthwhile or satisfying that they are prepared to exchange money, patronage or some other unit of value in order to acquire it' Brassington and Pettitt (2003: 268).

Most of the topics included in this text will be concerned with physical goods, even though the retailer must also concern themselves with less tangible elements of their retail offer. Alongside products, retailers might offer services that help a customer during the purchase decision (a changing room in a clothing retailer for example). The actual location, layout and design of a retailer might be considered a service, especially if those elements make the shopping process easier (by providing parking facilities, ease of access and home shopping alternatives, for example). Where a retailer's combined product and service offer lies on the product to service continuum depends on the nature of the product range and the type of retail outlet; however, the relationship between the tangible product and the less tangible retail service elements is a reoccurring theme throughout this book.

Some tangible goods are extremely durable, offer a great deal of choice in terms of specific features and benefits, and generally the purchase of them becomes complex, with a high level of involvement on the part of the consumer. Purchases such as household furnishings, cars or large electrical appliances would fit this category. Other tangible goods are consumable and convenience orientated products such as food and toiletries. These products are generally less complex, frequently purchased and being of lower value, involve less risk. Other products are information based at the purchasing stage and are consumed as they are used, such as a travel ticket or a holiday. Some service products are experienced as they are purchased and consumed, like a restaurant meal or a haircut. Service products generally have a very high proportion of intangibility and the product is not 'distributed' in the same way; the quality of a service product depends extensively on how the exchange is actually delivered with the 'product' experience being immediate and perishable. What is important to appreciate at this stage is that retailing covers all of these 'products' and that different types of products require unique sets of product management approaches in order to achieve consumer satisfaction.

RETAIL PRODUCT SECTORS

Traditionally, the retail industry has used the main type of product sold to determine the 'sector' into which a business would fall, such as the clothing sector, the electrical sector, the furniture sector and so on. This method of classification, however, is becoming less meaningful as many of the larger retailers, particularly the supermarket groups, variety stores and department stores cannot be classed in this way. Their coverage across product categories means that no one particular type of product dominates in sales value terms, and whilst the term non-specialist retailer was used for industry reporting, the sector comprising non-specialists has become so dominant, and includes retailers ranging from Tesco to Marks & Spencer to W. H. Smith, the classification system itself has become somewhat redundant. In October 2003 the UK government announced that they were going to review the production of estimates of retail sales indices for the retail industry sectors (ONS, 2003). In order to give some idea of the structure of the UK retail industry by product area, Table 1.1 shows figures issued in 2002 for both the specialist and non-specialist retail sector categories.

As in the UK, a sizeable share of retail activity in most economically developed markets is dominated by large retail organisations, although structural differences can vary from country to country and impact upon the product sector characteristics in different ways. For example, the domination of the department store in countries like the US, Japan and Germany initially slowed the progress of speciality retailers (Alexander, 1997); planning restrictions have slowed the growth of large-scale retailers in France (McGoldrick, 2002). In less developed economies, a greater percentage of per capita expenditure will be allocated to food and medical supplies with

Table 1.1 *The UK retail industry by sector*

Business type	Total retail turnover (£ billion)	%
All retailers	*230.19*	100
Predominantly food stores	*103.68*	*(45.0)*
Specialised food stores (including fruit and vegetable; meat; fish; bakery, etc.)	15.98	6.9
Non-specialised food stores	87.87	38.2
Predominantly non-food stores	*116.12*	*(50.4)*
Textiles	0.75	0.3
Clothing	29.72	12.9
Footwear and leather goods	4.37	1.9
Furniture and lighting	9.34	4.1
Electrical household appliances	11.82	5.1
Hardware/paint/glass	8.97	3.9
Other specialised non-food stores	*30.46*	
Books/newspapers/periodicals	5.26	2.3
Pharmaceutical, medical, cosmetics and toilet goods	4.18	1.8
Floor coverings	1.01	0.4
Photographic/optical/office supplies	3.83	1.7
Second-hand goods	1.35	0.6
Others	14.79	6.4
Non-specialised non-food stores	*20.75*	*9.0*
Repair	*0.55*	*0.2*
Non-store sales	*9.71*	*4.2*

Source: Adapted from National Statistics, published in WARC 2004

lower percentages in sectors like electrical goods and clothing. In addition, developing economies are likely to have a more fragmented retail structure, with fewer international players.

THE ROLE OF PRODUCT MANAGEMENT IN RETAILING

Traditionally, the retailer's role within the distribution channel was to provide suitable selections of products in small quantities, via outlets located close to viable groups of consumers. In fact, a dictionary definition of the verb to retail is 'the sale of goods in relatively small quantities to the public' (*Oxford Dictionary*, 1996).

The most fundamental role that a retailer plays then is to 'break bulk'. Until about half way through the twentieth century retailers were typically seen as 'stockists' of a particular range of manufacturer's products. However, the role of the retailer has changed significantly, from being a passive distributor to an active intermediary who controls the product range offering by carefully selecting products from manufacturers.

A historical overview

In the UK it was the abolition of resale price maintenance legislation in 1964 that accelerated the changes within the retail distribution industry: retailers were allowed to determine their own pricing strategy for their product ranges, rather than having to adhere to prices set by the manufacturers. The transfer of power allowed retailers to discount prices in order to increase volume, and thereby profits, and to reinvest the profits in more outlets, resulting in greater buying power. Manufacturers had little choice but to co-operate with the growing multiple retailers, who then wielded their power in many other areas of their business, such as developing their own brands, and improving store formats. The more recent advances in information technology have given the retailers even more power, as a result of the sales analysis afforded by EPOS systems, and the database information that can be generated by electronic trading, customer loyalty schemes and other direct communications. The result is a high level of retail concentration: an industry that is dominated by a relatively small number of extremely powerful, marketing orientated organisations (Burt and Sparks, 2003; McGoldrick, 2002).

The retailer's role has always been geared towards customer convenience. Their role in the distribution channel (see Figure 1.1) is to provide outlets that are readily accessible to consumers, to store a sufficient quantity of a product, so that consumers can buy products as and when they need, and revisit the outlet when the need arises again. For this service to the customer, the retailer adds a profit margin. The profit that a retailer makes contributes towards the costs of running the outlet(s), such as the costs of staffing, paying rent, rates and other maintenance costs and the costs of financing the stock. It also has to cover the costs incurred by the support activities of the retail organisation, such as sourcing, marketing, distribution and systems. Any profit left can then be distributed to the owners or shareholders of the business.

THE STRATEGIC ROLE OF PRODUCT MANAGEMENT

In order to carry out their traditional role in the distribution channel effectively, retailers need to offer a range of goods that satisfy the requirements of the customers who visit their outlet at the time they enter. A retailer is in the best position to know what their customers require because they have direct contact with them, either in the store or via home shopping channels. Whether knowledge is gained informally, for example in the case of a small independent owner/manager retail concern, or whether there is a highly sophisticated and complex information system, based on EPOS (electronic point of sale) data generation, retailers may need to adapt part, or all of their

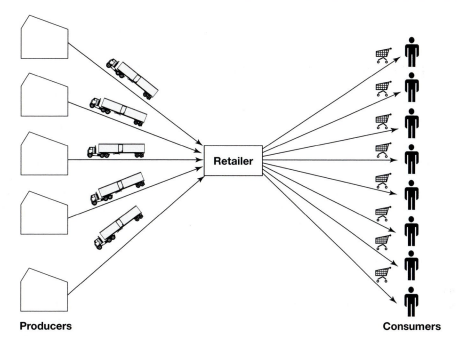

Producers   **Consumers**

Figure 1.1 *The traditional role of the retailer in the distribution channel*

product range in line with their customers' changing requirements. Retailers, therefore, need to have a good level of understanding of who their customers are, what their product preferences are and how their consumer needs and desires change over time. The time period may be through the day, within the week or according to season throughout the year. It has been found, for example, that in supermarkets, Thursday is the most popular day for buying electrical and leisure goods (Parry, 2003). Retailers also need to adapt to long-term changes in customer shopping habits, such as the deflection of shoppers from stores to home shopping.

Retailing, in its contribution to the marketing management process, offers a great opportunity to add value to the tangible product, discussed earlier in the chapter. Marketing-led organisations should not only give customers what they need, but should also identify and anticipate customer requirements. The product assortment that a retailer offers and the environment in which it is presented gives the retailer a powerful advantage over the producers of those goods, who now rely on the retailers as masters of this craft. Nevertheless, most successful retailers work in collaboration with their producers and suppliers, pooling resources to make a better job of the identification and anticipation of needs and wants, and then formulating a response to them.

Retailers have seized the opportunity to establish close relationships with customers and gain a deep understanding of their purchasing habits, manifesting their authority in the development of strong retail brand identities. The internet and other forms of direct marketing have offered opportunities for producers to fight back, by establishing a channel to take products directly from the producer to the consumer, but it is the retailers who have the greater opportunity to build on their existing knowledge and experience with consumers and use new marketing channels to their advantage (Tat Key and Park 1998; Dennis *et al.*, 2004).

BOX 1.1 CONVENIENCE RETAILING

Convenience retailing has become a very active sector of the UK retail industry. With Tesco, Sainsbury's and the Co-op all making major acquisitions of convenience retail chains and existing players like Somerfield and Morrisons reformatting small outlets to the convenience store layout, independent convenience store concerns will need to brush up their skills in order to compete. Many of the smaller convenience retailers benefit by being affiliated to symbol groups, who offer advice on various aspects of retail management as well as providing bulk-purchase 'own-branded' products.

Converting an existing product range to one geared to convenience shoppers requires subtle changes:

- A product range that offers breadth rather than depth will generally satisfy more customer needs.
- There is no point offering three sizes of a product item, when the space could be used to offer two extra different lines. One size will do for an emergency purchase; customers can be persuaded to trade up to a bigger size, or buy more than one pack if necessary.
- Focusing on well-known brands will assure customers of high product quality, even if they are paying higher prices than they would in a supermarket.
- If there is room, add more depth in the categories that will pay off; offering vast choice in home-baking ingredients for example will not generate good productivity, but increased choice in soft and alcoholic drinks, ready meals, confectionery and snacks will keep customers interested.
- Add-on service products will draw customers in on a regular basis, such as video hire, photocopying and cash machines.
- Depending on location, instant meals and coffee could be a profitable opportunity.

THE STRATEGIC ROLE OF THE PRODUCT RANGE

Retailers capture their customers' interest by the nature of their product range. It communicates to the customer what kind of retailer they are entering and therefore helps them in the search stage of their individual buying process. The nature of a retailer's business may be obvious in specialist retailers such as jewellers, but it may be less obvious in a mixed or variety store retailer like Wilkinson's, for example. The product range helps to position a retailer against its competitors within a market sector. The range may be limited but extremely specialist; it may be geared towards high quality products, or those with a strong fashion element; or alternatively the product selection may be wide, offering value for money to a wide section of the consumer market. In a concentrated and relatively saturated retail market, such as the UK, the position that a retailer etches out in the consumer mind is a vital element of its strategy. Customers must be given a good reason to shop with one retailer rather than another.

RETAIL POSITIONING

Positioning is a concept that has evolved to help a retailer to understand their own standing relative to their competition, as perceived by their customers. It can help a retail organisation that is involved in strategic planning to have a good understanding of how one retailer's offer is regarded compared to others, and the basis upon which the offer is 'measured' by consumers. Both academic and trade sources suggest that the following elements of a retail offer are important in how customers judge one retailer's offer over another:

- price;
- product assortment;
- convenient to use/visit;
- service quality.

Consumers will be expected to use and remain loyal to retailers that are closest to their 'ideal' in terms of how important these particular positioning attributes are to them personally. Most customers, however, are able and willing to make trade-offs, and so increase the number of retail outlets that they use. Circumstances that might encourage increased variety in retail outlet used are:

- *Increased disposable income*: The better off a consumer is, the more choice a consumer has in terms of where they are able to afford to shop.
- *Increased complexity within the purchase occasion*: A more complex consumer need will prompt a consumer to explore more retail outlets to find the nearest to perfect solution to their need.
- *Time and mobility constraint*: A consumer may choose a retailer that is more convenient, to make savings in travel time or cost, but this retailer may not be ideal from a pricing or assortment perspective.
- *Added value in the shopping process*: Some consumers value good quality customer service or a pleasant shopping environment as an integral part of their shopping process, and will seek out and pay premium prices at retailers that provide these aspects.

Positioning is a subjective concept, and is therefore difficult to define, but what is very apparent is that the product range itself and the way that products are retrieved by a consumer have a very strong influence on why a particular retail outlet is visited and used.

Given this important contribution to a retailer's overall positioning strategy, how can the product range be used by retailers in the effort to achieve a particular positioning within the overall retail market? An important step towards answering this question is to understand the difference between a 'general' approach to a product offer and a speciality or specialist approach.

The general retailer

A generalist approach to retailing is to provide a solution (or near solution) to as many consumers' needs as possible. It takes the view that by identifying needs that most often arise, and are most easily met, and providing non-complex solutions to such needs, a large enough proportion of consumer needs will be met to make such a product offering viable. A medium sized supermarket provides a product assortment that fits the general approach. Many mass consumer needs are met by providing a very wide range of product categories, with a limited number of (probably well-known) brands within each category. Another type of retailer that can be described as having a general approach is the variety store (for example BhS or Woolworths). Although the category emphasis is different from the supermarket, a large number of family needs can be met with the product ranges on offer within these outlets.

The speciality retailer

In contrast to the general retailer, there are some retailers who offer a product assortment that is restricted to a much smaller number of product categories, but they provide the customer with much more choice within those categories. This choice might be apparent in terms of product variation, pricing level or brand choice. This type of retailer is known as the speciality outlet, with a narrow but deep product assortment.

Although these two extremes are conceptually important in gaining an understanding of how retailers organise their product ranges in the light of their overall positioning strategy, the generalist-specialist concept might be better viewed as a continuum as opposed to distinctly opposing methods of organising a product range. Within the variety of retail formats that make up a developed retail economy like that found in the UK, it is possible to find retailers that use combinations of generalist and specialist approaches within their product offer. Indeed, finding a particularly unique blend for the product range is a way of achieving a unique or differentiated product assortment positioning. Some of the variations are illustrated in Figure 1.2. Boots, for example began as a company which specialised in pharmacy and healthcare products but have over the years, extended their range substantially. They still specialise in healthcare, pharmaceuticals and beauty products, which draw customers into the store on a regular basis. However, the additional products offer the customer the chance to purchase a much wider range of products once they are in the store, including lunchtime foods, photography items, children's clothes and gifts. As a retailer extends their product ranges, there is a danger that the initial specialism, or the core range, gets lost in the proliferation of additional products. This tendency is called 'product scrambling', and can result in a retailer's offer becoming less meaningful to customers. Woolworths is perhaps the best known retailer which 'unscrambled' their merchandise range, which at one time included food, DIY products, and clothing for all the family, to concentrate on the product categories in which they had the greatest market share: home entertainment, toys, children's clothing, stationery and confectionery (Kingfisher company report, 1999).

It is important to consider that not only will retailers differ in their approach to product assortment, some retailers will use a number of different approaches under the same retail brand. For example, a multi-channel retailer like Tesco will tailor their product assortments according to the type of retail format or outlet used. Retail formats like the transactional web site and the hypermarket provide the space needed for a wide and deep assortment. This allows the retailer to add product categories and depth within categories that would be restricted in smaller stores. A medium-sized supermarket in a typical edge of town location would have a wide and relatively shallow product range, providing as much product category variety to a large catchment population. However, some categories (in particular non-food ranges) would not be offered due to lack of space or local competition. A convenience store or small supermarket formats (such as a Tesco Express or Tesco Metro) would have a product range that was as wide as the space would allow, with more depth in some convenience orientated categories, such as pre-prepared meal components.

The worldwide dominance of powerful retailers like Wal-Mart, Tesco and Carrefour would suggest that the generalist approach to retailing is a more successful way of retailing. By offering a wide product range, the needs of a high percentage of the population can be met, with the consumer benefiting from a convenience orientated retail format (everything under one roof, free and available parking, fast transaction processing and so on). The supermarket (a term that for ease of this discussion is used to additionally refer to bigger relations in the form of the

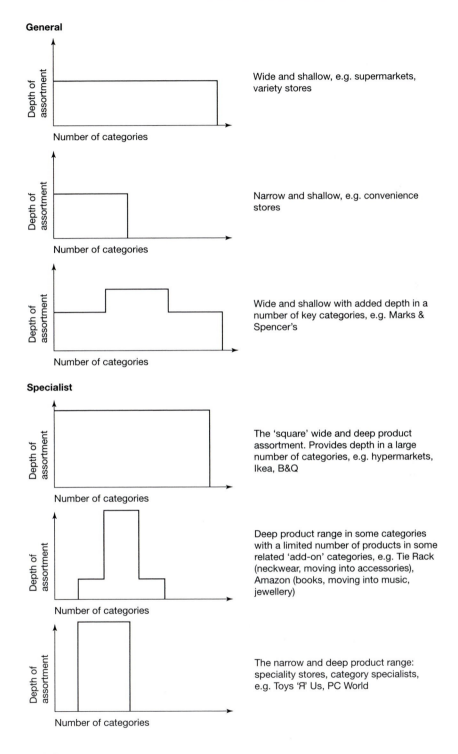

Figure 1.2 *Different product assortment strategies*

Source: Adapted from Cook and Walters, 1991

superstore and hypermarket) has been a phenomenal success in developed retail economies, allowing working women the release from the task of everyday shopping for groceries and household requisites, whilst providing ready-prepared meals and meal components to save even more valuable time. The proliferation from the grocery product base to non-food items from household cleaning products, through toiletries and healthcare, stationery, home entertainment and clothes, and finally to electrical appliances, home furnishings and gardening equipment has lured the shopper, category by category, into the habit of buying almost everything from the supermarket, leaving the more specialised retailers with a very small corner of the consumer's purse to fight over. Asda, for example has even introduced a nail bar in their new Manchester (UK) superstore.

Nevertheless, whilst supermarkets have undoubtedly taken their toll on many small and medium sized retailer businesses, there are many specialist and innovative retailers that continue to thrive alongside the superstore, and the retail industry each year awards new businesses who have found a niche which provides a distinctive product and service package to a viable group of customers (see Box 1.2).

BOX 1.2 COOK

Founded in 1999, Cook is a retailer specialising in frozen ready meals, a concept sounding neither novel nor very exciting. In spite of this the company won the UK retail industry accolade of 'Rising Star' at the Retail Week Awards in March 2004. The difference is that Cook's ready meals are hand-created and cooked in a kitchen, rather then coming off a mass production line in a factory. Fine, fresh ingredients are made into generously portioned dishes, ready for the enjoyment of customers who really like good home-cooked food, but who do not have the time or skills to cook for themselves.

To reinforce the idea that this is a different proposition to the regular supermarket offer, fixturing incorporates wood and steel, rather than the ubiquitous white plastic normally found in frozen food departments. Large-scale graphics illustrate the dishes, which are broadly categorised by main ingredient (pork, lamb or fish) or according to occasion, such as party food. The products themselves are packaged simply, while samples of the dishes are available to taste, giving the store a vibrant and interactive atmosphere. Stores are generally located in affluent catchment areas, away from main shopping centres, fostering the impression that they are a specialist and not a large chain. The company is still run on a family basis; the founder and managing director are brothers, and although they supply a number of farm shops, they only want to grow as fast as their culinary expertise will allow. Currently, Cook have nine stores, but believe the market could support hundreds; however, they do not want to rapidly expand and take on 'multiple' status too quickly. The Cook team prefer to retain their expert status and thrive in a niche where supermarkets are unable to go.

Source: Morrell, 2004

In fact, one of the problems with product range expansion and proliferation is that consumers may get confused or overwhelmed by choice. Large store formats may end up having a product range that is so all-encompassing that specific customer needs get lost, or individual customers are unable or unwilling to find the products they need and want amongst the thousands of products that they don't want. It is here that the editing service of the specialist retailer can help to fine-tune a product range to specific customer requirements (see Box 9.3, about specialist retailer MUJI). The bad news for the speciality retailer is that the general retailer is increasingly using visual merchandising and sub-branding to do this product editing exercise for targeted customers within their extended product offerings. Cross-category product ranges with sub-brands like 'good for you', 'free from', 'taste the difference' or 'no frills' are marketed using distinctive packaging and displays to help particular customer groups to fast track their way through the seemingly endless product choice (see Figure 1.3). Additionally, product categories in growth markets are given extra space to display the increase in variety given to consumers in order to clinch market share.

PRICE POSITIONING

Although product range is probably the most important factor in a retailer's market positioning strategy, the general price level of the merchandise must be a close second. Retailers can use price together with related factors like product quality, customer service quality and selling environments in order to make a very clear statement about where they belong in the market, and how they compare to competitors. Some retailers charge premium prices, for which customers get added value in the shopping process or experience, others keep their prices low, with minimal service add-on and basic store environments. Some retailers use sub-branding and category definition to pitch different product ranges at different customer groups, according to their ability to pay. Pricing therefore is an extremely valuable and effective tool to use in the creation of a viable positioning strategy.

Figure 1.3 'Free-from' ranges

Product ranges offered by retailers have to be managed within the context of an ever-changing business environment. Consumers' product preferences change according to their life-stage, lifestyle and personal wealth. One retailer's product offer is subject to scrutiny by consumers alongside those offered by many other retailers, which also are likely to change over time; therefore, product management is part of an ongoing strategic management process, which ultimately bears on the ability of a business to meet its long-term objectives.

THE SCOPE OF RETAIL PRODUCT MANAGEMENT

Retail product management is not just about making sure that the best product range is available in the store. Equally important to the customer is how products are presented to them. The way products are displayed, whether it is on a shelf in a store or on a web site, the logic of the layout, the relationship between one product group and another and the atmosphere created around the products, are all-important aspects of the retail product management process.

In a small retail organisation product management may be incorporated into the general running of the store. In a quiet moment an owner/manager may phone through an order to a supplier or stock up a depleted shelf display; but in large retail organisations product management is an extensive task, involving many different layers of management and dedicated teams of experts in massive central buying offices. Table 1.2 illustrates the scope of product management in a large multiple retailer, where many areas of product management decision-making are centralised within a head office.

Table 1.2 *The scope of product management*

Strategic product management	Product opportunities and objectives
	Market opportunities and objectives
	Sales and profit objectives
	Resource deployment
	Business environment auditing
	Integrated information systems planning
	Range planning
	Category management
Operational product management	Product development and selection
	Sourcing
	Sales forecasting
	Supply chain management
	Pricing
	Space allocation
	Store profiling
	Visual merchandising
	Promotions
Product management within the outlet	Allocate space to merchandise
	Display merchandise
	Receive and prepare stock
	Implement promotions
	Sell merchandise

Strategic product management

Product management is a strategic process, supported, in the case of a large retailer, by a complex array of operational practices and organisational structures. Strategic product management shapes the direction of growth that a retailer takes in response to changing consumer requirements, whilst carving out a market position to appeal to identified consumer market groups. Its strategic contribution is augmented by the role that product management takes in keeping operational costs as low as possible whilst generating sales volumes to maximise profitability. It is also about managing risks, identifying and pursuing product/market opportunities, whilst making realistic assessments about the resources available to do so. Introducing new products is a very good way of achieving differentiation and enhancing a retail identity in an over-subscribed retail market, but without corporate support new products may fail or go unnoticed.

Providing a relevant and interesting product range goes a long way towards attracting customers and keeping them loyal. However, customers' requirements change over time, as societal norms evolve, working patterns alter and demographic profiles shift. The product range therefore needs to be managed, extended, developed and/or rationalised according to customer needs. New product categories can provide a way of appealing to new markets, or of increasing transaction values within the existing customer base. Tailoring a product range more closely to customers who visit your outlet by removing less relevant products and expanding ranges of more popular categories or introducing a more powerful information system to track supplies and therefore improve product availability increases the productivity of the outlet and maximises 'basket values'.

Operational product management

In order to achieve strategic objectives that are tied to product range manipulation or expansion, teams of operational product managers translate the strategic objectives into feasible product related aims. These are the managers who for example find suppliers in a new product market, implement information systems to achieve availability targets, and introduce marketing campaigns to draw customers' attention to new product offerings. They also make day-to-day decisions on things like pricing, and how to display products within the retail outlet.

Product management within the outlet

Operational product management moves product planning from ideas to reality, but the completion of the product management process takes place at the outlet level where the product/consumer interface occurs. It is product managers within the retail outlets who implement space allocation and visual display plans; it is at the store level where 'availability' becomes the difference between full or empty shelves, and it is within the outlet that attention is drawn by 'in-store marketing' and customer sales service to particular products or brand offerings.

RETAIL PRODUCT MANAGEMENT: AN EVOLVING DISCIPLINE

Product management in retail organisations encompasses a wide range of functions and, as social organisational structures, many retailers have unique approaches to this area of their business. In most centrally managed retail organisations, product management, or buying and merchandising as it is frequently termed, is seen as a key functional area alongside financial, human resource and systems management. The extent to which marketing and logistics are integrated into the product management area varies from one retailer to another. To a certain extent, it is possible to trace

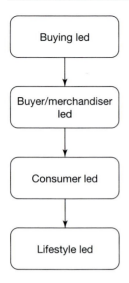

Figure 1.4

The evolution of product management

the evolutionary path along which product management has moved as the retail industry itself has changed over the years in developed economies. This is shown in Figure 1.4.

At one time buyers were considered to be kings and queens within the retail business. In some retail institutions such as department stores, buyers frequently worked their way up through the organisation, from the sales floor, through department management, then buyer's clerk, finally to make it to the ivory tower and be able to use the esteemed title of buyer, coupled with fringe benefits such as the 'buyer's cloak-room'! In modern retail companies, such as the multiple chains, buying experience is still valued highly, and although these days buyers are likely to be graduates, they still have to spend time in a kind of apprentice-ship, gaining product and supply knowledge and generally becoming familiar with the retailer's strategic and operational aims.

In the late 1970s and through the 1980s, the centralised multiple emerged as a strong force, and with it a new approach to buying, which essentially split the buying role down into qualitative considerations (product selection) and quantitative considerations (merchandising). This offered the benefit of allowing the buyer to concentrate on getting the product detail right and selecting suppliers who could meet the required price and service standard in terms of delivery, technical skill, capacity and so on. In the meantime, the merchandiser concentrated on sales forecasting, stock planning and managing product sell through.

Through the 1990s a new approach emerged, broadly termed 'consumer-led' product management. This is geared to responding to consumers, rather than forecasting what they will buy. It is a more marketing orientated approach and relies on multi-functional teams focused on the performance of narrow bands of products. In many respects, it is an adaptation of the brand management organisation found in many fast moving consumer goods producers, where teams manage the sales and distribution of an individual product, or an interrelated product group as a strategic business unit. This management approach has led to the adoption of the category management role, which is a broader role than buying or merchandising, encompassing elements of both and adding a strong marketing emphasis (Wills, 1999).

Arguably, consumer needs in the twenty-first century are becoming more complex and sophisticated. A blend of product, outlets, shopping processes, add-on services and information is all directed towards providing solutions to what might be called the 'personal process domains' (Mitchell, 2003) of the consumer. This idea converges with the concept of a 'lifestyle retailer' that provides a product and service combination for a group of consumers whose needs are determined by particular values, attitudes and choices made about how their money and time is spent.

Instead of the product being central to consumer expectation and satisfaction, the way the transaction for products is processed becomes a major part of the satisfaction; the satisfaction derived from a basket of groceries, for example, is determined not only by the quality, brands and price of the products, but also the speed, responsiveness, courtesy and friendliness received during the shopping process. Retailers have to understand that it is within this blended product/process context that customers derive value, rather than solely through the features and benefits of discrete products. They also have to understand that the same consumer may have different requirements for different types of shopping. So whilst product quality, brand and price, speediness, responsiveness, courtesy and friendliness might be important in the grocery shopping process, high levels of product knowledge, attentive service and a good atmosphere and a high level of variety might be more important for clothes shopping.

Some examples of personal process domains and retailers that might help to provide solutions:

Health and well-being domain   Boots
Home management   Tesco.com
Personal financial management   Lloyds TSB, First Direct
Personal mobility   Halfords, Easy Jet
Family leisure domain   JJB, Centerparcs
New family member domain   Mothercare, Mamas and Papas

Whether or not a retailer feels able to fully incorporate the personal-process domain as a useful way of managing products, the idea of creating overall customer value is a well-established concept. Having an understanding of what customers value, and therefore will be willing to pay extra for in terms of monetary cost or repeat custom, is very important to guide a retailer in their decisions about company risk and resource deployment. The cost of an investment to provide more customer value (such as the provision of free parking or store refurbishment) may be unavoidable because of the risks associated with not providing that investment resulting in low overall derived customer value (see Figure 1.5).

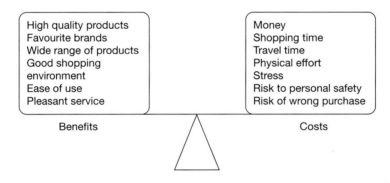

Figure 1.5 *Balancing benefits and costs to create value*

SUMMARY

Product management is central to retailing essentially because it is the product range that most effectively communicates to the consumer what the focus of the business is. The product range may be more generally orientated, offering a wide variety of merchandise, or it might have a narrower assortment, giving the consumer the chance to find specialist products. The product range contributes significantly to the strategic success of retail businesses. It is through the product range that retailers implement their pricing strategies and profitability levels, and it is through the product range that retailers maintain a consumer's interest, and adapt to their changing shopping requirements.

Product management in retailing has become wider in scope as the customer-focused orientation of retailing has grown. The product management process involves procurement, logistics, and implementation of range formulation at store level, and, as such, a new organisational structure in retailers is emerging, so that products are managed from conception to sale on a product category basis.

CASE STUDY   TOYS 'Я' US AND IMAGINE

Toys 'Я' Us is one of a group of retailers called 'category killers'. This type of retailer offers enormous depth within a restricted number of product categories. The name for them is derived from the notion that the offer is so extensive that any competitive retailer trading in this category nearby is 'killed'. Toys ' ' Us is like a toy hypermarket; having entered the warehouse-like store, the shopper is introduced to row after row of toys, from the well-known brands like Barbie, Action Man, Fisher-Price, Tomy and Vtech, to the retailer's own branded alternatives. The customer shops the store like a supermarket, moving up and down aisles and serving themselves, although friendly help is on hand to help customers if they need it. Prices are kept generally low, for customers to compare with other outlets for branded items, while the own-branded products give shoppers on a budget the opportunity to purchase similar, good quality toys at excellent price points. Although Toys 'Я' Us are susceptible to the seasonality challenges that all toy retailers face, the company has always placed good product availability as a high priority, with considerable investments in the logistical and systems support that is needed to support an outlet network that spans the globe and offers a home shopping service. Toys 'Я' Us currently have 67 stores in the UK and trade in over 20 countries worldwide. The stores are generally located in retail parks along with other large format speciality retailers and appeal to the car-borne shopper with the availability of free parking outside.

Imagine is also a toy retailer. Tucked down a cobbled street in the centre of Holmfirth, a market town in the North of England and housed in a building that was once a dour weaver's cottage, the customer is welcomed through a red door into a plethora of colour and fun. With a focus on unique, high quality products, the product range spans from party bag items to special presents. Owner and manager Caroline Ansty, who once worked as a product manager in a large mail order retailer, constantly searches out new ideas to keep the product offer fresh; the store has built a reputation for innovative interactive educational toys. The range also includes many aesthetically attractive toys including wooden items, soft toys and creative projects, which blend with the simple but bright store interior to make a lively and colourful environment. A selection of the latest products can be found close to the shop counter and payment point, and staff are encouraged to demonstrate these to customers. With the selling area being compact, but well organised so that there is room for browsing, Imagine offer a special order facility for any product a customer wishes to buy, and will even keep gifts if a customer's child curiosity level is unmanageable. Caroline keeps an index card record of all customers who join her loyalty scheme, which gives a bonus every time a customer reaches a particular level of accumulated sales value; this card details children's names and ages so that Caroline can offer suitable items. A newsletter is sent out on a monthly basis to inform customers of new arrivals and to make seasonal suggestions, including products at all levels within the price range, from 50p to £50. The staff at Imagine have built up product and customer requirement expertise, so that given a budget and a child's age, they can suggest alternative gift choices, which can then be gift wrapped, with an inclusive price for wrap and card.

Source: various, including Toys 'Я' Us web site

QUESTIONS

1   Consider the traditional role of the retailer as breaker of bulk supplies, and explain how the retailer's role has evolved in the last two decades of the twentieth century.

2   Review the scope of product management in retailing, using a chosen retailer to illustrate your discussion.

3   Explain why product management has to be part of a retailer's strategic development, upon which long-term success is dependent.

4   Referring to the case study at the end of the chapter, explain how the product ranges at Toys 'Я' Us and Imagine reflect the needs of their respective customers.

5   Explain the reasons for the domination of the non-specialist retailer in the UK retail industry (as shown in Table 1.1).

6   Boots the Chemist is a retailer that began as a specialist, but over the years has broadened its product assortment. Explain why you think Boots the Chemist has evolved in this way.

7   Analyse the contribution that product ranges make to the positioning of retailers within their product sector, using retailers of your choice and Figure 1.2 in your discussion.

REFERENCES AND FURTHER READING

Alexander, N. (1997) *International Retailing*, Blackwell, Oxford.

Brassington, F. and Pettitt, S. (2002) *Principles of Marketing*, Pearson Education, Harlow.

Burt, S. L. and Sparks, L. (2003) *Competitive Analysis of the Retail Sector in the UK*, report submitted to the Department of Trade and Industry, Institute for Retail Studies, University of Stirling.

Cook, D. and Walters, D. (1991) *Retail Marketing: Theory and Practice*, Prentice Hall, Englewood Cliffs, NJ.

Davies, G. (1992a) 'The Two Ways in Which Retailers Can Be Brands', *International Journal of Retail and Distribution Management*, 20(2): 24–34.

Davies, G. (1992b) 'Positioning, Image and the Marketing of Multiple Retailers', *International Review of Retail Distribution and Consumer Research*, 2(1): 13–33.

Dennis, C., Fenech, T. and Merrilees, B. (2004) *e-Retailing*, Routledge, London.

Howe, W.S. (1998) 'Vertical Market Relations in the Grocery Trade: Analysis and Government Policy', *International Journal of Retail and Distribution Management*, 26(6): pp. 212–224.

McGoldrick, P.J. (2002) *Retail Marketing*, McGraw-Hill, Maidenhead.

Mitchell, A. (2003) 'Embrace the Experience So Marketing Can Benefit', *Marketing Week*, 6 March.

Morrell, L. (2004) 'Cooking Up a Storm', *Retail Week*, 26 March.

Oxford Dictionary (1996) *The Oxford Compact English Dictionary*, Oxford University Press, Oxford.

Parry, C. (2003) 'Factfile: Supermarkets Sweeping Clean', *Marketing Week*, 4 December.

Samli, A.C. (1998) *Strategic Marketing for Success in Retailing*, Quorum Books, Westport, CT.

Tat Key, H. and Park, S.Y. (1998) 'An Expanded Perspective on Power in Distribution Channels: Strategies and Implications', *International Review of Retail, Distribution and Consumer Research*, 8(1): 101–115.

WARC (World Advertising Research Centre) (2004) *The Retail Pocket Book*, WARC, Henley-on-Thames.

Wills, J. (1999) *Merchandising and Buying Strategies: New Roles for a Global Operation*, Financial Times Retail and Consumer, London.

Web sites

ONS (2003) National Statistics Online: http://www.statistics.gov.uk/notices/RSIReview 241003.asp

www.statistics.gov.uk

http://www.toysrus.co.uk

Chapter 2

The role of retail product managers

LEARNING OBJECTIVES

The purpose of this chapter is to:

■ Develop an overall understanding of the retail product management process, using traditional organisational buying process models and consumer-led models as learning aids.

■ Appreciate the complexity of the retail product management process, and understand how this complexity can vary according to different types of buying situations or tasks.

■ Understand the central role that the buying organisation plays within a retail business, and how that organisation is structured in order to carry out the retail product management process.

■ Become familiar with the central roles that people play within a buying organisation, including those of the retail buyer, the merchandiser, and the category manager.

■ Understand the interaction that retail product managers have with other departments within the retail organisation, and the influences that these people might have on product management decisions.

■ Build an understanding of the personal skills required for retail product management and how a career path in this area of retailing might develop.

INTRODUCTION

Given that the management of a product assortment is both strategically and operationally central to a retailer's success, considerable attention must be paid to the organisation of the sections of the retailer that carry out these functions. The main aim of this chapter is to provide an insight into how retailers organise their product management activity, explaining what and where product management activities are carried out and the type of people who are involved in the process.

RETAIL BUYING ORGANISATIONS

A retail buying organisation could be defined as the entity within a retail business that carries out the essential task of bringing goods into the retail business from the supply base, to be sold on to consumers. Although small retailers may need to carry out buying operations alongside other managerial tasks, in most sizeable retail organisations, product management is a centralised operation, where a team of dedicated personnel plan product ranges and place orders for products with their supply base. These operations are often carried out either at, or near, company headquarters, where product management personnel usually account for the greatest number of people within any centralised retail operations area. Within these 'buying offices' huge sums of money are committed to producers around the world in order to secure deliveries of goods to satisfy customers' demand.

The buying organisation is the section within a retail business that is most directly concerned with the product offer, planning product ranges to arrive for customers when they want to buy them, making sure the product quality and price are at the levels customers expect, and ensuring enough products are delivered to guarantee availability in all retail outlets. The people who essentially 'control' the product offer are referred to, either in title or as a collective team, as retail buyers. The buying organisation is not, however, the only 'department' or section within a retail business that is involved with product management. For example, whereas buyers plan and buy the product ranges, it is up to the logistics department to handle the physical delivery of millions of products through the supply chain via distribution centres and into the stores, or on to customers' homes. Once the products are in a store, visual merchandising teams need to display them as attractively as possible in order to entice the customer to buy. The interaction between central and support operations within the buying organisations will be considered in more depth later in this chapter.

THE RETAIL PRODUCT MANAGEMENT PROCESS: A TRADITIONAL VIEW

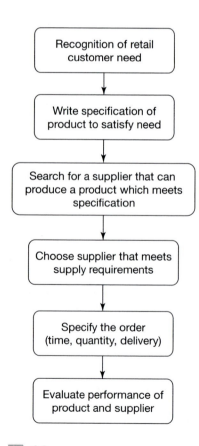

Retail buying is of one of a number of instances where an individual is purchasing products on behalf of a business organisation. The activity can therefore be classified as organisational buying, and so the traditional theory of organisational buying behaviour can be called upon in order to provide an understanding of the process that retailers use when buying products for their outlets to sell, and to provide some indication of the likely behaviour of retail buyers in their role as organisational purchasing personnel.

In their extensive study of organisational buying behaviour, Webster and Wind (1972) devised a general model of the organisational buying process. An adaptation of this model is shown in Figure 2.1.

Recognition of retail customer needs

Product management contributes to the strategic success of a retail business. As discussed in Chapter 1, the product range needs to be managed so that the changing needs of customers can be satisfied. The recognition of new product requirements is the starting point for a series of buying decisions. Tracking customer requirements is

Figure 2.1 *A traditional view of the organisational buying process adapted to retailing*

part of the product manager's responsibility in many retailers, in terms of 'keeping an ear to the ground'. The following information sources may be used to provide this knowledge:

- internal sales data;
- trade publications;
- consumer publications, such as special interest magazines;
- suppliers;
- market research (internal or external);
- competitor analysis.

This aspect of product management will be discussed in more detail in Chapter 4.

Write specification of product to satisfy need

The identified or recognised consumer requirement then has to be turned into a product opportunity for the retailer. This stage of the buying process involves the consideration of a set of product features, which blend together in the most appropriate way to benefit the target customer. Once this process has been carried out a record of the product features will be specified, either on paper in the form of a technical specification, and/or in the physical format as an approved product prototype (see Chapter 4 for further detail). In reality, this second stage often starts the buying process, with a product suggestion (often from a supplier), followed by an evaluation of market opportunity for that product by the retailer. However, refinement of product features is likely to be required even if the product was a supplier's suggestion, particularly if the product is to be marketed under a retailer's own label or brand.

Search for a supplier

Even though one particular supplier may have made a product suggestion, this does not necessarily mean that they will be the supplier who ultimately receives an order for that product. It may not have the capacity to produce the product in the quantities required, or the price may not be as competitive as another supplier offering similar products. The search for suppliers and the assessment of the potential of suppliers suggests that there are many alternatives for a retailer to choose from. This is often not the case (see Chapter 5), but a supplier's ability to meet the requirements of the retailer in the supply of an individual product line is certainly a decision that has to be made in most buying situations.

Specify order

Once the product and supplier combination has been decided, the supply requirements have to be formalised, in terms of how, when and where the product is delivered. It will also be necessary at this stage to determine the quantities needed. Chapters 6 and 7 are concerned with those aspects of product management that ensure a product is available when and where a customer wants to buy it.

Evaluate performance of product and supplier

Evaluation of outcomes of the buying process is essential if product management objectives are going to be met. Monitoring performance involves both quantitative measures such as sales information and supplier performance indicators, and qualitative measures such as customer research and feedback via retail sales personnel. From a long-term view of product management, learning from buying errors is as important as achieving sales success.

COMPLEXITY OF BUYING TASKS

One of the drawbacks of the traditional buying process model is that it assumes that for every organisational buying situation, a buyer goes through the whole process, shown in Table 2.1. Obviously, the cereals product manager at Tesco plc would not need to do this when placing an order for a familiar product like Kellogg's cornflakes, for example. In certain contexts some of the stages shown in the traditional retail buying process will be omitted, and this is acknowledged by another traditional buying process framework, referred to as the 'buy-class'.

In the new task buying situation, all of the stages outlined above will be carried out, even if, as frequently happens, they do not follow this sequence. An example of the new-task buy would be where a retailer had identified a new own-label product opportunity. It would be necessary for the retailer to consider the positioning of the product in line with customer requirements and other competitive products in the market. The retail product manager then establishes the product and supplier criteria, selects a supplier, draws up the order detail, and then monitors the performance of the new product.

The modified re-buy is a situation where there is a necessity to change some, but not all, of the product and supplier variables. A situation that could be classed as a modified re-buy is where a supplier has not performed to the retailer's satisfaction, and a new supplier is introduced. Similarly, there may be a problem with a minor product feature, such as the packaging, therefore some of the stages of the buying process have to be revisited, but the whole process does not have to be started from scratch.

In the straight re-buy situation, the retail buying process is routine. The only stage that is involved is specifying the order. For example, when re-stocking an existing product, the only decision would be product quantities and delivery details. All the other variables would stay the same.

Table 2.1 *Different buying situations and the effect on the buying process*

Buy class Stages	New task	Modified re-buy	Straight re-buy
Recognition of retail customer need	Yes	No	No
Write specification of product to satisfy need	Yes	Maybe	No
Search for supplier to produce specified product	Yes	Maybe	No
Select supplier	Yes	Maybe	No
Specify order	Yes	Yes	Yes
Evaluate performance of product and supplier	Yes	Yes	Yes

Source: Adapted from Davies 1993: 66

LIMITATIONS OF THE TRADITIONAL BUYING PROCESS MODELS

The two models shown in Figure 2.1 and Table 2.1 were grounded in the field of industrial business-to-business buying rather than retail buying, and they are generalisations of the processes carried out within this context. The result is that the complexity of the retail buying process is significantly underplayed.

The first limitation is the use of the term 'buying' to describe the processes and tasks. Arguably, buying could be considered in a narrower context as one part, albeit a very central and important part, of the retail product management process. As retail organisations have grown, 'buying operations' have become more complex and sophisticated, carried out by teams of people rather than individuals, and relying on the support of customised information systems. The term product management perhaps more realistically reflects that buying is a part of a broader set of activities that take place in modern retailers, as discussed in Chapter 1.

The second limitation is that product and market specifics often bear a considerable influence on the way in which the buying process is carried out. Managing staple products like washing powder is very different from the tasks involved with the planning and selection of a range of coats or dresses, because of the variables that fashion and seasonality introduce.

Another consideration is that the relationship between the retailer and the supplier will have a significant bearing on the way in which the buying process is carried out and this is not acknowledged in the traditional models. For example, the length of time they have been doing business together and how substantial the monetary and product exchanges are between them will alter product management procedures and processes (see Chapter 5 for more detail).

A final criticism of the traditional buying process models is that they concentrate on operational tasks, and neglect the strategic elements of a retail product manager's job, such as range planning, supplier development and profitability management. The buying operation itself is described in isolation, without consideration for its relationship with other operational areas of product management, such as space allocation or promotional planning (see Figure 1.4). Nonetheless, proposing product areas to be carried, selecting products and suppliers, and specifying order details are the key responsibilities of retail product managers and so these traditional models do provide a preliminary introduction to the retail product management process.

Since the 1990s a 'new' approach to product management has emerged, and has been adopted by many of the larger retail businesses, especially those in the grocery and fast moving consumer goods sector. This approach, which will be broadly termed 'consumer-led retail product management' acknowledges the limitations of traditional business to business buying process models, and more closely reflects how retail product management activity is carried out in many large retail organisations today.

CONSUMER-LED APPROACHES TO RETAIL PRODUCT MANAGEMENT

One of the problems associated with a large and complex retail organisation is that there is a danger that those people responsible for carrying out the buying for a retailer may get detached from the realities of retailing. Buyers are sometimes criticised by store personnel for 'sitting up there in the ivory tower of head office', and whilst a buyer cannot be expected to be in stores every day, there has been a move to alter product management structures in retailers to more closely link head office buying with store-level activity and to gear all product management activities towards the consumer. Reacting and responding to the purchasing requirements of customers, and anticipating their future needs and wants, based on market research and analysis, rather than 'gut feeling' is at the crux of consumer-led product management. The buying office organisation described in this chapter is changing in the light of this new approach to buying, as we will see later in this chapter. A consumer-led approach makes a direct link between the manufacture and supply of product, and the demand patterns found in consumer markets, and therefore relies on close collaboration between product managers in both retailer and supplier organisations. The diagrams in Figure 2.2 show the essential differences between a traditional retail buying organisation and a consumer-led buying organisation.

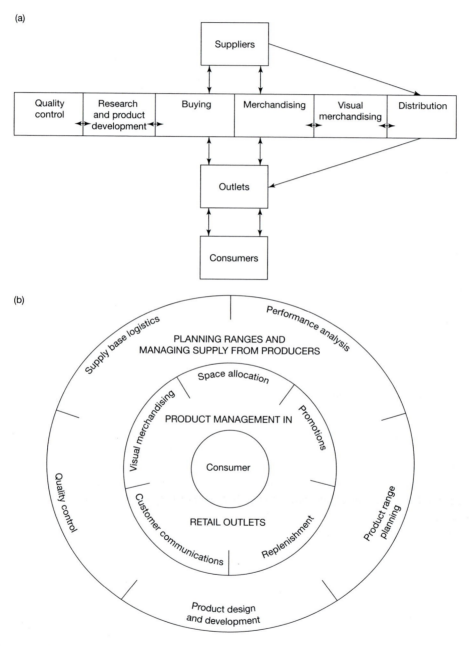

Figure 2.2 *A traditional buying organisation (a) compared with a consumer-led buying organisation (b)*

In the traditional buying organisation, there is a more function-orientated structure. The boundaries of responsibility are clear and each department works discretely as part of a larger process. The advantage of this type of structure is that expertise is built within these various functions, but the main disadvantage is that department boundaries can become barriers, the experts become inward looking within these departments and an overview of the whole product management process is less easily achieved. Suppliers, the retail head office and the outlets tend to operate as separate layers within the product management process.

In the consumer-led buying organisation, satisfaction of the retailer's customers is the central objective for all. It is a collective responsibility to achieve this, but activities are co-ordinated by a product manager who maximises the performance of a particular group of products, referred to as a category. The product management effort is integrated through retail operations with suppliers, logistic service providers, product category managers and outlet managers all supporting a flow of products that satisfies consumer demand.

BOX 2.1 DEBENHAMS (RETAIL) PLC

Debenhams is the UK's largest department store retailer. Founded in 1850, the group now operates 102 stores with a geographical spread from Exeter to Inverness. In the period 1985 to 1997, Debenhams was owned by the Burton group, but the department store chain was de-merged from the specialist clothing retailers (now trading under the name of the Arcadia Group) to enable it to develop its own strategic direction. The company entered the home shopping sector in 1998 with Debenhams Direct, followed by the launch of their transactional web site. With 13 per cent market share in the UK Debenhams are building an international presence with stores in 13 different countries.

The central buying office for the stores is located behind their flagship store on Oxford Street in central London. The diversity and the volume of products sold in Debenhams makes it one of the largest buying offices in the UK with around 750 people.

Most of the buying departments conform to the structure shown in Figure 2.3, which outlines typical career development paths within the Buying, Merchandising and Distribution section.

The role of the buying team is to develop profitable product ranges that reflect current trends, which offer the Debenhams customer product choice at all times. The role involves supplier sourcing, negotiating costs, quality and quantities, and monitoring delivery schedules. The merchandise teams decide how many units of every single stock keeping unit will be sold throughout the branch network, and work closely with the buyers to ensure that need is satisfied by the supply base. The distribution team have the responsibility of ensuring that each store has the goods to satisfy the expected demand and generate profit. Success in a highly pressurised environment, where new challenges emerge on a daily basis, relies on departmental teamwork.

Source: Adapted from company careers literature and web site information

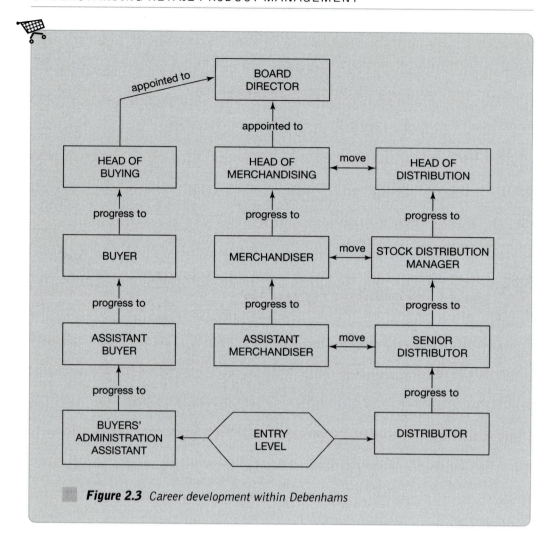

Figure 2.3 *Career development within Debenhams*

CENTRALISED RETAIL BUYING ORGANISATIONS

Product management in most sizeable retail organisations is a centralised operation, and buying offices are usually housed at, or near the company headquarters. In employment terms, buying personnel usually account for the greatest number of people in any centralised retail operational area. Figure 2.4 shows where a buying organisation might fit within a multinational, multi-channel retail organisation, assuming that a centralised product management approach is adopted.

Centralised decision-making for product management offers a retail organisation many advantages. McGoldrick (2002: 284) provides a summary of these, which includes the following key points:

- Increased buying power allows buyers to negotiate better terms with suppliers.
- Specialist buyers can devote more time to product/market analysis.
- Sales data can be aggregated to improve forecasting.

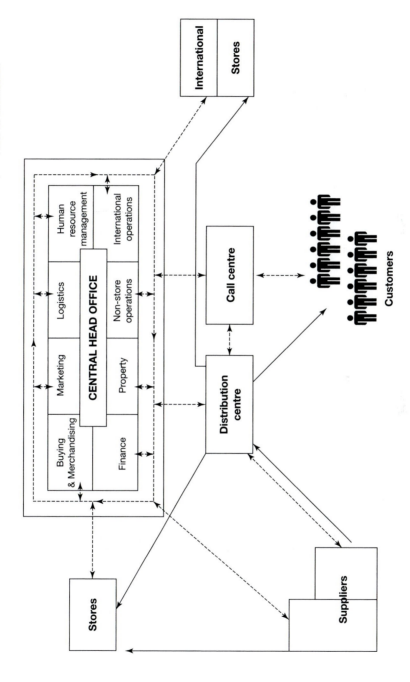

Figure 2.4 The multinational, multi-channel retailer: organisational structure

Legend:
→ = Flow of products
---→ = Flow of information

- Economies of scale are achieved, resulting in lower sourcing and selection costs per product; buyers' salaries are comparatively high within a retail business.
- The quality level of the product offer is better controlled, for example by having a team of technologists and quality controllers who work centrally alongside buyers, and quality controllers who halt the progress of faulty products in a centralised warehousing operation.
- A more consistent product assortment is presented in order to reinforce the retail brand identity and support national promotions. Retailer branded product development is cost-effective and consistency in cross-category sub-branding can be more easily achieved.
- The quality of buying and stock control decisions is consistent across outlets.
- Store personnel are freed from buying responsibilities, allowing them to concentrate on creating a high quality shopping experience for customers in the retail outlet.

Wills (1999) suggests that buying office structures are determined by sectoral differences. In clothing, the structure incorporates the technologist's role because of the importance of styling and fit; in the electrical sector there is more emphasis on the role of the 'trader' because of the dominance of manufacturers' brands and the emphasis on product/price promotions; whilst in food, buyers concentrate on new product development, with a trader or merchandiser focusing on price and quantity negotiations and a logistics manager becoming a key part of the buying team because of the leading role it takes in food retailing and distribution. These roles are discussed in more detail later in the chapter.

One of the problems encountered in a centralised retail organisation is the split between head offices and stores. Although they are working for the same company, and have the same goals, conflict between store personnel and head office personnel is common in many retail businesses. This conflict frequently arises when store personnel feel that the wrong products have been 'sent by head office' for them to sell. In the case of seasonal goods, products have to be 'pushed' into stores, so that they are ready in sufficient quantities for the seasonal uplift in sales. Likewise, fashion trends may seem extreme, until the rest of the high street is offering similar skirt lengths, trouser widths, or colour combinations, and so the initial reaction in a retailer's outlet to new styles may be negative.

An open channel of communication between the central buying organisation and branch stores is key to the product management process. Feedback from customers via store personnel, store management and retail operations area management on the more and less successful aspects of the product range is vital if steps are going to be taken to rectify mistakes, or prevent the repetition of errors. Sales information from the most sophisticated electronic point of sale system only tells product managers what has sold, and who has bought it. These systems do not give information on why something has not sold, so some mechanism for capturing qualitative data on the product range should be part of the product management process.

DECENTRALISED BUYING

Retailers, who have a product range that is dominated by products with a relatively stable demand, have more opportunity to allow the retail outlets to have an element of control over the buying for their stores. Store, or even department managers may place orders, according to the sales pattern occurring within their outlet, within the parameters of a centrally determined product assortment. This allows the outlets to respond to local variations in demand whilst maintaining a consistent corporate product offer. In some cases, however, the product itself requires a decentralised approach. Highly regional products, such as local newspapers or heritage gifts, must be sourced locally. Additionally, fresh produce may be bought on a local or regional basis because of the (relatively) fragmented supply market, and the need to minimise transportation and storage times.

Allowing the retail outlet to respond effectively and efficiently to local product preference is a way of improving customer service and the productivity of the outlet. In this respect, store retailers have an advantage over non-store retailers like the large mail order companies, who, by the nature of their business, rely on a centralised approach to buying and distribution. Internet retailing on the other hand offers the potential for retailers to provide a wealth of tailored solutions to individuals in response to information that they build about the shopper and their purchasing habits. However, translating this potential into a profitable venture for retailers is a challenge many e-retailers are currently grappling with.

BUYING ORGANISATION MANAGERIAL ROLES

This section describes some of the managerial roles that might be found at each level within a multiple retail buying organisation. The discussion begins with the core personnel within a product management department, and then goes on to consider the auxiliary teams that may be included within the buying office structure, or play an influencing role in the buying decision process.

Buying director

There may be more than one buying director in a retail organisation, but it is not likely to have more than one represented at main board level. The multinational grocer J. Sainsbury plc for example, has a 'Trading Director' sitting on their 12-person-strong board of directors (Sainsbury's web site, 2004), and Tesco have a 'Commercial and Trading Director' (Tesco, 2004). Buying directors represent all aspects of the buying organisation within the retail company. Their position corresponds with that of a general merchandise manager within a US buying organisation, although a main board director would be equivalent to a vice-president. Buying directors oversee a large number, if not all, of the product areas, and are responsible for setting the overall aims of the product management teams within the company. They must lead these teams in the pursuit of achieving strategic objectives through product management and be involved in planning decisions that have long-term effects on the retailer's ability to perform. A buying director is likely to be involved in the following type of decision-making:

- changing major suppliers;
- introduction of new product ranges or new product categories (but not new items);
- deletion of product ranges or categories;
- concessions arrangements (see Chapter 4);
- major promotional campaigns;
- strategic aspects of range planning, such as multi-channel retailing;
- adoption of systems and management approaches, within the product management area.

As well as, or instead of, a buying director, there may be a merchandise/merchandising director. This will be a similar role, primarily concerned with strategic product planning.

Merchandise managers

Merchandise managers are senior buying and merchandising personnel who oversee a division, or a number of interrelated buying departments. This level of management is most likely to be found in variety stores, department stores or in mail order, where it is important to show some degree of co-ordination and consistency in terms of styling, colour range and quality level across buying departments. One merchandise manager may oversee all of the ladieswear offer, including clothing accessories and footwear, whilst another might oversee all home furnishings, including furniture, floor coverings, soft furnishing, lighting, household accessories and gifts. This level of manager is sometimes given director status in large retail organisations, such as Marks & Spencer plc.

Buying controllers

Buying controllers are situated in the buying and merchandising management hierarchy between buyers and merchandise managers. They usually oversee the buying and merchandising operations of a small number of departments. It may be useful to have a buying controller to help manage large buying departments, or to co-ordinate activities of concessions departments; however, in the pursuit of organisational efficiencies and improved communications, many retailers have attempted to create flatter organisational structures and in such instances, this level of management has been removed. In the case of the smaller retailer, buyers might report directly to the merchandise director, removing both the controller and the merchandise manager from the hierarchy.

Buyers

The buyer has traditionally been seen as the figurehead of the department that carries out the buying process on behalf of the retailer. Buyers may have operational control of the department, with the rest of the buying team reporting to them; however, in some organisations the responsibility for running the department is shared between a buyer (or selector) and a merchandiser (or stock controller). Buyers tend to be more concerned with the qualitative side of buying; they have to be aware of all the features of the product that bear upon its ability to give customer satisfaction and they must have an extensive knowledge of what is available within the product market for which they have responsibility. Price negotiation is usually a task for the buyer, but in some organisations this is clearly a merchandiser's responsibility. Buyers need to be knowledgeable about consumer demand and trends related to their product area, and they often work closely with marketing teams on promotions.

Merchandisers

Merchandisers tend to be concerned with the quantitative aspects of buying, and are usually responsible for estimating sales, planning deliveries and distribution of the goods to stores. This role is sometimes referred to as stock/inventory controller, or stock/inventory planner. Most merchandisers also have responsibility for the financial management of the department including sales analysis and forecasting, budget planning and allocation, profit margin analysis, and markdown implementation (reducing selling prices). Occasionally, a merchandiser also has product selection responsibilities, depending on the use of the title within the organisation, and in some retailers merchandisers plan space allocations. As the merchandise systems used in a buying department have grown in sophistication, so too has the role of the merchandiser; it is now seen as more strategic, with greater emphasis on issues like availability and customer focus. This can have the effect of pushing the buying role further into the area of design, product development and selection, with less control over range planning and direction. Some organisations, such as Gap and Zara do not have buyers at all – relying on designers to develop products and merchandisers to edit the range (Wills, 1999). Next plc, the highly successful UK clothing retailer considers itself as a product-led organisation (Next plc, 2004a). Working as a team, buyers, designers, technologists and merchandisers ensure that product ranges are well styled, good quality and good value for money. The merchandiser's role within this team includes: analysing and evaluating the previous season's sales and trends; working with buyers and designers to build and develop the range; proposing departmental budgets; developing and managing excellent working relationships with suppliers; and maximising turnover and profitability (Next, 2004b).

The term merchandising in some retail organisations is interpreted slightly differently and relates to a role that is more concerned with displaying products than range planning. Career Choices UK for example describes a merchandising role as follows:

> you will work closely with buyers and marketing to decide which products to sell and where and how to display them in the shop. You are responsible for creating attractive displays and placing products so customers can see them easily and are more inclined to buy them. You then produce a picture or map called a planogram, and send it to all stores for them to put into place.
>
> (www.careerchoices.org.uk)

This is often the use of the term merchandising in the grocery or CTN (confectionery, tobacco and news) sectors, where visual display is a more quantitative process, involving complex space allocation calculations (see Chapter 8). In clothing and home furnishing sectors, where visual display is more creative, the role of visual merchandiser comes into its own (see Chapter 10).

Category managers

In many sectors of the retail industry the merchandiser's role is expanding to reflect the growing reliance on information systems to guide the product planning process, and the need to make fast, analytical judgements on how products are performing. In some retailers this augmented merchandiser role has emerged as that of a category manager's role, which is seen to be the most appropriate way for a consumer-led approach to be organised (see later). Here, the buyer–merchandiser dyad is abandoned in favour of a broader, cross-functional organisation, with more emphasis on teams than individual roles. In this approach to product management, areas of product responsibility are likely to be narrower than in a traditional buying department, but the category manager is involved in the performance of a range of products from idea conception right through production, supply, store distribution, to final consumer sales, and if necessary, after sales. In effect they are a central retail manager for a small part of the total retail offer. The success of that part comes from reacting fast to the changing sales patterns of a particular product area and managing the product most effectively and profitably.

Assistant buyers

In large retail organisations, buyers, merchandisers and category managers are likely to have one or more assistants. It is important to distinguish between an assistant buyer/merchandiser/category manager and a buying assistant. An assistant buyer, for example, plays a key role in the buying process, and may be solely responsible for some buying decisions. Assistants will have a full understanding of the workings of the department and will provide support to their team leader on the operational aspects of the department. In many cases an assistant is in training for a full buyership. Assistant merchandisers play a similar role on the quantitative side of the buying process.

Buying (administration) assistants

A buying assistant, sometimes called a buying administration assistant or buyer's clerk, is a junior member of the team, providing administrative support and carrying out routine duties within the department (frequently performing a combination of buying and merchandising duties). Experience within a buying office is a valued asset in retailing, and so a buyer's assistant who shows potential could easily progress to assistant buyer or assistant merchandiser, and, as such, is a suitable entry level for a graduate.

Allocator/stock distributor

The allocator is another junior role within product management. Allocators carry out the process of ensuring the right stock is made available at the right time in each of the retailer's outlets. The role is generally one that is linked to a retailer's stock information system. Although some of the tasks involved with stock allocation are repetitive, central office allocators are often recruited as graduates, so that analytical skills and knowledge of the retailer's business will develop simultaneously and allow quick progression upwards to an assistant merchandiser position.

ADDITIONAL BUYING DECISION-MAKERS

As well as the people working within each product management or buying department, other people or sections within a centralised retail buying organisation may play an important role in buying decision-making, including technologists, product development teams, corporate design teams and logistics teams.

Technologists and quality controllers

Although most buying decisions are centred on the ability of a product to satisfy a customer need, at a price the customer is willing to pay, a retailer has to ensure that it meets its legal obligations with regard to the products it sells. It also has to consider its long-term image in the eyes of the public. It is, therefore, necessary to ensure that a product conforms to legal standards, and provides value for money. A buyer is usually a marketing orientated person, who may need some advice when it comes to assessing certain product features and criteria. This is where a technologist can be a useful member of the product management team. The technologist will be up to date on product standards, manufacturing process innovations, raw material properties and so on. They are not primarily concerned with sales and profitability of individual items, but by ensuring product standards are met and maintained, they play a key role in the long-term success of retail product management. The quality of products such as Heinz baked beans or Philips lightbulbs is assured by the brand, and in such cases the manufacturer takes the responsibility for maintaining the trust in product quality of the customer. However, from the retailer's point of view, it is especially important that their own-labelled products do not violate any product law or tarnish the retailer's reputable name. A technologist, together with a team of quality controllers in a large retail organisation will monitor products against the retailer's specifications and check that production and supply facilities are up to the standards expected.

The product development team

Where a retailer is involved in putting together a product offer which is unique to its own company, and where suppliers are not able to provide the required level of input into product innovation, it may be necessary for the retailer to set up a development team for a particular product area. For example, Tesco plc have an experimental kitchen whose staff work on new food products. Many fashion retailers have a team of designers, pattern cutters and sample machinists who make garment prototypes for their suppliers to copy.

BOX 2.2 MARKS & SPENCER'S SANDWICH DEVELOPER

Lucy Sprugnell works as a product developer in the food division of UK retailer Marks & Spencer. Her area of responsibility covers the retailer's well-known sandwich offer and sushi, the increasingly popular Japanese 'fast food'. The role of the product developer is to maintain a flow of fresh ideas, which can be anything from a whole new range, to simple changes to existing products. Replacing plain lettuce with rocket and balsamic dressing as a salad ingredient is one small change that can add newness to a product.

A large part of a product developer's role is research. This involves consulting relevant publications, and talking to suppliers and industry specialists. For Lucy, reading food magazines and cook books, attending cookery demonstrations and sampling food in a wide variety of eateries allow her to identify relevant product trends. Visiting 40 tapas bars in 5 days was the daunting prospect on a recent trip to research new sandwich filling ideas. Often she will be developing products for filling gaps in the market and meeting changing customer needs. Once an idea has been accepted as fitting the product criteria identified by the food development programme, Lucy then gets involved with sourcing, so that the best supplier is used to produce the product in the quantities that Marks & Spencer require. Product testing and presentation are other important aspects of the product developer's role, to ensure that the final product tastes and looks good.

Packaging can have a major effect on sales. An example from Marks & Spencer's sandwich category is wraps, which were not selling at the levels expected, although they were a popular product. Reworking the packaging using brighter colours increased sales. According to Lucy, the best bit of her job is seeing a product launch go well and getting positive customer feedback.

Source: Mason, 2004

Product development is a time consuming and costly process, for example it takes approximately nine months for Tesco plc to develop a new product (Wills, 1999). However, in a business environment where customers react favourably to new product ideas product development is essential if a retailer wishes to offer a wide variety of contemporary products to the customer. In the case of small electronic goods, products can have a lifecycle as short as 6–9 months, therefore the speed at which product innovations are brought to market is crucial to the success of both retailer and supplier.

Corporate design

If a retailer is own-label active, then establishing a department to manage the corporate brand is essential. This is particularly important in packaged goods retailing, where the graphical representation on the outside of the product is what sells the item. The use of logos, corporate style and colours are all of concern here, and a retailer may issue a corporate design manual or guidelines to ensure that all own-label suppliers conform to the same graphical standard. People who work on new packaging designs, whether outside design agencies or internal design studios, will also use these instructions. Computer-aided design, internationally standardised colour systems and internet communications have helped retailers to achieve consistency in corporate design, preventing the need for reworking of original artwork, whilst offering fast and flexible design options for consideration.

Logistics

In grocery and fast moving consumer goods the logistics department play a key role in any buying decision. Factors that have led to the incorporation of logistics into product management include: the need for special transportation and warehousing operations; short shelf lives in some product areas; the need to be very efficient in logistical operations to achieve profitability on low margin products (see Chapter 3); and the growing importance of product availability as part of a high customer service provision.

A logistics manager would be able to highlight implications of placing orders that might not be apparent to the buyer. For example, a buyer might be offered a price reduction on a product, providing a large quantity is ordered. The logistics manager would be able to advise on any additional storage, handling or transportation costs incurred by accepting a larger than normal delivery. Such costs could outweigh any price reduction given by the supplier.

BUYING COMMITTEES

The extent to which buyers or category managers have authority to place orders on behalf of their organisations varies from one retailer to another. In some retail businesses, buyers must have orders over a certain value sanctioned by their operational superior. In others, buyers have the autonomy to run the department as they see fit, which allows a more entrepreneurial approach to be taken; however, buyers or product managers ultimately stand or fall according to the performance of their department or category in terms of sales and profits (see Chapter 12). A balanced approach can be maintained through the use of a buying committee, where both the product itself and the buying plans proposed for that product are scrutinised by a panel of experts within the organisation. The main advantages and disadvantages of using a buying committee are given in Table 2.2.

The different buy classes shown in Figure 2.2 illustrate how retail buying decisions vary in their complexity. They can also have a direct bearing on the involvement of buying committee members in the process. In a new-task situation, many product management personnel will be involved either directly or indirectly, whereas straight re-buys may well be carried out by one member of the team (the assistant buyer, for example).

The retail decision-making unit

When various members of the buying committee gather to consider a purchase for the retail organisation, they will be acting as a decision-making unit (DMU). The theory of the roles that people play within the DMU in organisational buying has been explored by the traditional organisational buying behaviour theorists (Webster and Wind, 1972) and these can be applied to the retail buying committees when they are used for product management decision-making.

Table 2.2 *Buying committees: advantages and disadvantages*

Advantages	Buying is sanctioned by the highest authority, so the decision is not that of the individual, but of the whole organisation
	The cumulative experience of many senior people within the retailer is brought to the decision-making process
	Experts can be called upon to make a contribution on specific aspects of the decision
Disadvantages	Gathering the committee takes time, so buying opportunities may be missed
	Senior individuals may use their status to force their personal opinions through the committee process
	Different members of the committee will have different areas of expertise and different knowledge gaps, which may make consensus difficult and lead to conflict

Sometimes referred to as the 'initiator', the *user* is the person who directly uses the product item. In retail buying, the user is a retailer's customer, or potential customer. It is difficult to involve customers directly in retail buying decisions, so a decision-making unit must consult market research sources and retail sales personnel to obtain an accurate representation of the customer's viewpoint. Larger retail concerns may use consumer panels as part of their marketing research operations, to provide qualitative feedback on new initiatives.

People who play the role of the *influencer* in the decision process can come from various sources. Technologists, designers, product developers and engineers provide expert opinion on specific product attributes, whilst merchandisers or logistics managers may exert a commercial influence, based on the knowledge of previous sales patterns and supply problems of similar products.

The *buyer* is the person who organises the day-to-day running of the buying process. Buyers themselves, or their assistants, usually carry out this role, which is different to the role of the *decider*, who makes final decisions regarding the purchase of products. The *decider* is normally in a position of higher authority in the buying office, such as a buying director or merchandise manager, and essentially sanctions and approves proposed buying plans; but in a straight re-buy situation, buyers, or even their assistants, may act in both the *buyer* and the *decider* roles.

The *gatekeeper's* role is to control the flow of information into the decision-making unit. The role may be taken by a junior member of the buying team who makes the initial assessment of products and suppliers, and therefore checks the flow of irrelevant information into the group. On the other hand, a buying controller or a merchandise manager, who controls information because of their seniority or experience in product markets, may perform the role.

In order to illustrate these roles, the example of a purchase of a new kitchen appliance by a multiple hardware/homeware retailer is outlined in Box 2.3.

BOX 2.3 COLLECTIVE DECISION-MAKING

In response to the growing trend towards specialist kitchen appliances, the kitchenware buyer for a medium-sized homeware retailer has been considering the purchase of a new product item: a home pasta-making machine.

In order to evaluate the likely demand for this product, the buyer analysed a number of secondary sources, including market research reports and supplier's catalogues. He also canvassed the views of a number of store managers, who turned out to be predominantly in favour of the product idea. In collaboration with the merchandiser, a sales estimate for the pasta-maker was drawn up.

The buyer asked his assistant to call in a selection of sample pasta-makers, and obtain prices from a number of suppliers. When they arrived he showed the samples to the other people working in the buying department, the assistant buyer, the merchandiser and the buying assistant, and between them the buying department chose the sample, which, in their opinion, had the best design and offered the most variety of pasta shapes to the customer. They then considered which products represented the best value for money and they also considered whether one or a range of alternative brands of pasta-makers should be stocked. The merchandiser felt at this stage one product variation should be trialled; a higher order quantity placed with one supplier would give more scope for price negotiation than small quantities placed with a few suppliers.

The three samples that had been considered the best in the department's informal product evaluation were then passed to the product technologist for an initial assessment of the product's ability to perform and meet safety standards. A brief report was prepared for the buyer. Having read the technical report the buyer rejected one of the samples on the basis of difficulty of operation; he then presented the two remaining samples to his merchandise manager. The merchandise manager liked the idea, and told the buyer that he had seen a pasta-making machine on a stand at a trade fair that he had attended in Germany the previous week. He retrieved a catalogue from his briefcase and gave it to the buyer who immediately contacted the unfamiliar company to obtain a sample and price. The product was comparable to the other two samples in the selection and so the buyer presented all three samples at a departmental range review two days later.

The buyers, merchandisers, technologist and senior management all discussed the product features and benefits, as well as prices and in the end the sample from a local distributor was selected as best value for money. The merchandise director, who stated that it was important for the retailer to be innovative providing the stock investment was not too high, sanctioned a trial order.

Group dynamics

The roles fulfilled by buying personnel in their operational day-to-day activities can be generalised to a certain degree. However, each person who contributes to the process is an individual, with his or her own set of characteristics, background and personality. Buyers have often played the role of opinion leader and change agent in the retail organisation, and as such may have a form of authority over those with 'higher' status within the organisation. Group dynamics, therefore, can often influence the way in which individual retail decision-making units operate. In addition, the culture of the organisation in which the DMU operates will also have a bearing on the buying process. For example, some retailers have a highly structured hierarchy in their buying offices, through which product plans have to be dragged in a series of presentations and reviews, whilst others have a flatter, more entrepreneurial, culture, where new ideas are quickly trialled and either supported, or eliminated. Similarly, the external business environment may impact on the way in which the group works together; for example, in a growing economy, more risks may be allowed, whereas in adverse trading conditions buying organisation personnel may be less confident to implement new ideas without a consensus of opinion. Any person entering the field of the retail buying office, whether as an employee or as a potential supplier, should familiarise themselves with the workings of the various individuals within the buying organisation and how the organisation works as a whole (Gregory, 2003).

DESIRABLE ATTRIBUTES IN RETAIL PRODUCT MANAGERS

The description in this chapter of the organisations and processes that are involved in retail product management has perhaps given the reader a sense of the complexity of this area of retail management. Achieving high levels of success in retail product management, however, depends on the combined efforts of individuals who make contributions to the process. Diamond and Pintel (1997) found that the following qualities are important for a successful career in a retail buying organisation.

Analytical skills

Decision-making is at the heart of any job within a buying organisation. Collating data from many different sources, extracting and assimilating important information, reading situations, making evaluations, prediction and judgements are all things that buyers, merchandisers and category managers do on an ongoing basis and all require some level of analysis. As retailing becomes faster moving and more competitive, the need for analytical powers increases. The merchandising side of the product management function requires a high level of numeracy, coupled with the commercial acumen to interpret figures as retailing realities.

Communication skills

Working at the hub of a centralised retail structure, a buying office must have lines of communication with all other sections of the retailer. Frequent communication with marketing, logistics, finance, and human resources and, in particular, with stores, is vital if the buying organisation is to play its part in the product management process effectively. In addition, buying departments constantly liaise with suppliers, therefore communications are both internal and external. Communications that are formal (for example, memos, presentations or reports) or informal (answering general queries by telephone or email for example) have to be transmitted in written or verbal format. Related skills such as negotiation, persuasion, assertiveness and diplomacy, often have to accompany the basic ability to communicate, and as high profile representatives of the retail organisation, retail product managers should present themselves in a way that is consistent with the corporate image.

Objectivity

Retail buying personnel operate on behalf of the commercial organisation that employs them. Decisions are made for the benefit of the organisation rather than the individual, therefore the ability to divorce personal taste or preference from the business role is an essential qualification. A retailing adage states: 'a retailer must buy what it sells [to consumers], not sell what it [the retailer] buys'. Being objective requires a buyer to be flexible, so that they can adapt their powers of analysis and objectivity to an ever-changing retail environment, whether it is changing customer requirements or competitor actions.

Product knowledge

Buying personnel may join a retailer with some formal product training; otherwise it is likely that some on-the-job training will be required to ensure that specific technical product features are fully understood by the retail product manager. Without this knowledge, buying personnel are less able to make appropriate buying decisions. Accumulation of product knowledge is part of the training process of an assistant buyer. The difficulties of buyers making decisions without technical product knowledge are highlighted in Box 2.4.

BOX 2.4   COLOURED BY LACK OF EXPERIENCE

A young buyer working at a women's wear multiple retailer demanded that a supplier reprinted a piece of fabric to obtain an exact colour match with their corporate colour palette. Under duress, the supplier reprinted the fabric three times for the unhappy buyer. Eventually the supplier managed to get the buyer to understand that no matter how many times the fabric was reprinted, the colour would never match exactly because the base fabric had a 'nap', (a directional surface, as in satin or velvet), which reflected light in a different way to the standard shade.

Source: Miller, 1997

Formal qualifications

Although it is possible for a junior associate in a retail organisation to make their way into a product management position, a more likely route today is to enter the buying and merchandising part of a retail business as a graduate. Many of the large retailers will consider graduates from any degree discipline, but it is acknowledged that some business training is very useful for this area of retailing. Increasingly specialised retail courses are being offered at universities around the world, and a graduate with a good degree in retailing is likely to be extremely attractive to a retail organisation wishing to recruit trainee buying and merchandising team members. For some buying positions, such as clothing or food, a degree with a relevant technology base, such as textiles or food science, may be more important than a business background; however, product management is a commercial role, and therefore strong business acumen must be developed alongside technical product knowledge.

In addition to the qualities outlined above, it may be necessary or desirable for a buyer to be proficient in a second language, so that they are better equipped to negotiate with overseas suppliers. Above all, buying personnel need to have the flexibility to promptly address all the challenges that retailing presents to them.

BUYING GROUPS

The buying aspect of retail product management is a time consuming process, and requires considerable expertise, which are resources that some retailers, especially small, independent concerns, do not have access to internally. One solution that might be viable for retailers of this type is to become a member of a buying group. Buying groups effectively act as a buying organisation, but instead of acting on behalf of stores that are owned by the same business, they are acting on behalf of stores that are owned by many different business operators.

Buying groups can be found in most sectors of the retail industry. Many small convenience stores rely on the services of 'symbol' groups, such as Spar or Londis to give access to product management services and buying economies on a wide range of products through the collation of ordering quantities and the use of wholesaling operations. The extent to which the stores have to conform to a standardised store fascia and mode of operation varies from group to group.

Buying groups are also part of the international retail scene. Some buying organisations have a network of buying offices across the globe, sourcing on behalf of a group of retailers with similar operating methods. Associated Merchandising Corporation, for example, operates on behalf of some of the largest US department store chains, and has buying offices in the Far East, Asia and Europe. The groups are formed by key players from a number of geographically separated retail markets getting together to share expertise in buying and other operational areas. The main product-related operational benefits that members of this type of affiliation gain are buying economies and power, and buying expertise gained in a wide supply market; however, other advantages include the transfer of expertise in areas such as trading formats, technology and systems, brand formulation and marketing (see AIS case at the end of the chapter).

The use of combined buying power can offer the small, independent retailer many of the advantages of the multiple's centralised buying organisation, whilst retaining a degree of entrepreneurial independence for the retail operator. It can also allow larger and more powerful retailers to spread their influence on a wider scale in a global retail environment.

Buying alliances

In the competitive world of retailing, the major players have become adept at exploring a whole gamut of strategies to achieve some kind of advantage over their rivals. Buying expertise is a rare and highly valued commodity in retailing and a number of large retailers have explored ways of tapping into each other's area of expertise in the pursuit of their own corporate objectives. One method is to form a buying alliance with a fellow retailer. Supermarket group Sainsbury's have used alliances with other retailers as a first step into new non-food categories: for example, toys from Early Learning Centre and children's clothing from Adams. Similarly, US department store retailer Kohl's launched an exclusive range of Laura Ashley furnishings to boost its existing offer with a high quality retail brand (*Retail Bulletin*, 2004). Another form of buying alliance is the internet exchange; a systems-based facility for retail collaboration in purchasing, discussed in more detail in chapter 5.

SUMMARY

In this chapter the way that retailers have traditionally organised the product management process has been outlined. Multiple retailers, by definition, have a central buying operation which liaises with the retailer's supply sources and makes decisions about product variety and assortment on behalf of the network of outlets. Centralisation not only brings the economical advantages of large-scale buying, but it also allows a retailer to control the implementation of retail brand strategies through the product range.

The importance of the people who carry out this vital and multi-faceted task can be overlooked in the effort to systemise retail operations but without their expertise and experience there is a danger that consumer trends and product innovations would be interpreted inappropriately or ignored. Retail product management personnel need to possess a unique combination of high-calibre skills and personal attributes to succeed in a highly responsive and deadline orientated working environment. An organisational structure that supports this role is essential if product management goals are to be achieved.

CASE STUDY ASSOCIATED INDEPENDENT STORES

Associated Independent Stores (AIS) is a non-food voluntary buying group that operates on behalf of around 260 independent retailers. Together the members have around 590 outlets and a combined turnover of £1.3 million. Although department store retailers account for less than half of the membership, they dominate the organisation in terms of volume bought through the organisation.

Although the aim of AIS is to improve its members' profit performance, AIS itself is a non-profit making concern. Member retailers pay an annual subscription to the organisation, which varies according to their individual turnovers. By collating their orders through the AIS organisation, the individual members are able to gain access to a much wider range of merchandise than they would be able to otherwise. The small retailer is often faced with a restricted supply base because of their inability to reach minimum quantities imposed by manufacturers. The buying group's ability to negotiate competitive prices for its members gives the independent an opportunity to compete against the multiple retailers, as well as improve profit margins.

Based in Solihull, near Birmingham, geographically central to the UK, the AIS office consists of a series of showrooms, offering the independent buyer the opportunity to view merchandise in four main product classifications: fashion, housewares, furniture and floor coverings. In addition, AIS holds around 40 sample shows a year in specific fashion and furniture product categories, and provide a clothing buying service to members with limited internal resources. An important, and growing part of the service to members is the development of AIS own-branded merchandise by its team of product managers. These ranges are shown alongside supplier branded products at the sample shows, and include 'First Avenue' fashions for both women and men, 'Classmates' schoolwear, 'First Impressions' linens and cookware, and 'Guildcrest' furniture. The ranges are developed with suppliers from a global market. By acting as an administrative intermediary, AIS make payments to suppliers, for the total group shipment, and then the individual stores are invoiced for their individual purchases.

The structure of the AIS organisation is similar to that found in the buying office of a multiple retailer. Product managers look after specific categories of merchandise and liaise with suppliers on behalf of the member stores, however, representatives from the retail members are involved in all aspects of the organisation, including the board of directors. Representatives are involved at all stages of the merchandise sourcing and development process; before AIS selectors source merchandise they hold a strategy meeting with members from a cross-section of stores to discuss the direction for the forthcoming season. In terms of the supply base, AIS are moving towards partnerships and supply chain management in order to monitor and control merchandise standards, improve service and build a more customer focused and profitable supply network.

As well as the benefits available in buying operations, members also receive a weekly summary of the AIS group sales, and regular detailed sales analysis reports on specific product areas, allowing members to compare their own performance with similar retail businesses. They can also access a wide range of marketing support services in areas such as marketing intelligence, visual merchandising, point of sale schemes, promotional material, and advertising. Regular newsletter and email communications keep members informed with up-to-date industry facts and trends and networking opportunities are organised with the view to reducing the isolation that independent retailers can feel. A training service is also offered on aspects of retail management such as selling skills and visual merchandising.

Source: Mintel, 1998; AIS web site, 2004

QUESTIONS

1 When recruiting graduates for buying and merchandising careers, what qualities would be deemed essential and desirable for (a) buyers and (b) merchandisers?

2 Discuss the key responsibilities of merchandise directors, buyers and merchandisers.

3 Describe the role of the influencer within a retail decision-making unit.

4 Explain the difference between a category manager and a buyer.

5 Referring to the case study on Associated Independent Stores, discuss the benefits that membership of a buying group can bring to small retail businesses.

6 In multiple retailers, buying decisions are rarely made by one person alone. Discuss the reasons why this is so.

7 Make a comparison between the tradition approach to product management and the consumer-led approach to product management, within the context of one retail sector.

8 Outline the traditional buying process for a chosen product item. Discuss instances that allow some of the stages of the process to be omitted.

REFERENCES AND FURTHER READING

Cash, R., Wingate, J. and Friedlander, J. (1995) *Management of Retail Buying*, Wiley, New York.

Diamond, J. and Pintel, G. (1997) *Retail Buying* 5th edn, Prentice Hall, Englewood Cliffs, NJ.

Gregory, H. (2003) 'The Buying Game', *Grocer*, 26 April.

Mason, S. (2004) 'M&S Food Developer Sets Sandwich Course', *Retail Week*, 11 April.

McGoldrick, P.J. (2002) *Retail Marketing*, McGraw Hill, Maidenhead.

Miller, L. (1997) 'The Changing Role of Buyers', *Drapers Record Focus*, October.

Mintel (1998) *Department Stores: Retail Report* (March), Mintel International Group, London.

Swindley, D. (1992) 'The Role of the Buyer in UK Multiple Retailing', *International Journal of Retail Distribution Management*, 20(2): 3–15.

Webster, F.E. and Wind, Y. (1972) *Organisational Buyer Behaviour*, Prentice Hall, Englewood Cliffs, NJ.

Wills, J. (1999) *Buying and Merchandising Strategies: New Roles for a Global Operation*, Financial Times Retail and Consumer Reports, London.

Web sites

Associated Independent Stores: http://www.cranford.hounslow.sch.uk/ks/Post16study/3. BUSSTUD, accessed 09/05/05

www.careerchoices.org.uk, accessed 28/06/2004

www.careerchoices.org.uk/scripts/opportunitiesdisplay.asp

http://www.debenhams.com/site_services/illustrated_summary.jsp?FOLDER%3C%3, accessed 28/10/2004

www.londis.co.uk

Next (2004a) Next plc Results for Half Year Ended July 2003: http://order.next.co.uk/press/finReport/ jul2004.asp?press=C, accessed 27/10/2004

Next (2004b) Next Careers: Graduate Information: http://order.next.co.uk/graduate/merchandiserrole. asp, accessed 27/10/2004

http://order.next.co.uk/careers/graduate/merchandiser_role.asp, accessed 27/10/2004

http://www.j-sainsbury.co.uk/index.asp?pageid=389, accessed 09/05/05

http://www.tesco.com/corporateinfo, accessed 09/05/05

Chapter 3

Category management

LEARNING OBJECTIVES

The purpose of this chapter is to:

- Introduce the concept of a category as a classification for groups of merchandise that is linked to the way customers shop for products.
- Develop an overview of the stages of the category management process, including category definition, category planning and implementation.
- Understand the contribution that supply partnerships make to the category management process.
- Appreciate the scope of category management within a retailer with reference to the buying organisation structures that reflect the category management process.
- Explore the concept of a category lifecycle, and the influence it has on category planning.
- Become familiar with management systems that have developed from the fundamental concept of consumer-led product management which are complementary, to a category management approach to buying, namely efficient consumer response (ECR), quick response (QR).
- Identify the limitations of category management and its applicability amongst different types of retailers.

INTRODUCTION

The preceding chapter concerning buying organisations described a set-up that is common in multiple retailers, where product management activities are essentially shared between buyers and merchandisers working in tandem within a product-orientated department. The chapter concluded with a discussion of the emerging approach to product management that allows for a closer relationship between the supply of products and the customer, referred to as the consumer-led approach. The main aim of this chapter is to introduce category management as an evolving approach to retail product management and to consider its implications for the retail organisation and its supply chain.

CATEGORY MANAGEMENT

Category management has been defined as 'the strategic management of product groups through trade partnerships, which aims to maximize sales and profits by satisfying consumer needs' (IGD, 1999: appendix). Within this definition, key words point to the difference between category management and other buying approaches.

- *A category is a strategically managed product group*: Rather than products being grouped by departments, into which they are placed according to operational convenience, products are put into groups that are carefully defined according to consumer shopping behaviour. All products within a category can be managed using a strategy that is specifically formulated for that group of products.
- *Category management relies on trade partnerships*: In category management, suppliers play a very active role in the management of the product group. Suppliers become partners of the retailer that is using category management, and the two parties work together in pursuit of mutual goals.
- *Category management aims to maximise sales and profits*: The definition highlights the importance of the performance of the product group (sales and profits), but by linking this performance to consumer satisfaction, the definition indicates that long-term performance objectives can only be reached if consumer needs, both for products and in the shopping process, are met. Additionally, the definition indicates that performance refers to that of the product group, as opposed to that of each single product item. A category may include a number of leading manufacturers' brands, retailers' own brands and some speciality products, all of which have their own specific sales values and profit margins. However, from the point of view of the retailer, what is important is the performance of the whole category and its contribution to the company's overall profitability.
- *Category management satisfies consumer needs*: The definition for category management highlights that it is a consumer-led process, and that only by having a deep understanding of consumer needs and providing a product assortment that fully satisfies each shopper as they interact with a product category, can performance be maximised in the long term. Category management relies on having an understanding of a consumer's relationship with a product type, for example, the level of interest they have in a product category, how they prefer to shop, and how different shopping occasions may influence the decisions they make about buying products within a category.

According to Harris (cited in GEA, 1994) category management is a philosophy, a process and an organisational concept. These aspects of the category management approach to product management will be used to frame a further discussion of category management.

CATEGORY MANAGEMENT AS A PHILOSOPHY

As an approach to thinking about how products are managed within a retail business, category management requires a broader vision than its preceding management orientation, which typically would be buying and merchandising led. Rather than being chiefly concerned about products from a features and procurement viewpoint, and then forecasting sales for those products, category managers have first and foremost to consider the performance of the category in relation to consumer demand and then strive for the most profitable way to supply that demand. Consideration of features and procurement therefore become a part of, but not the focus of, the category manager's remit, while forecasting is replaced by responding.

Fundamental to the adoption of a category management philosophy is the way in which suppliers are viewed. Whether they are termed partners or allies, the key to the philosophy is supplier integration. Traditional lines defining functions that a supplier performs are broken down, as competencies are shared as well as information. If a supplier is able to perform an aspect of product management more efficiently (for example, product development), then it should contribute that part of the process. If a retailer is more efficient, then it should perform the function. The resulting efficiency gains result in a lower-cost product, and the cost savings can be negotiated between the parties.

CATEGORY CHAMPIONS

Many of the projects that have helped to develop the category management philosophy have involved large multiple retailers and leading product/market suppliers (see Box 3.1). The suppliers who take on a major role in the category management process are often referred to as *category champions* or *category captains*; whilst they are expected to be able to accept the presence of other suppliers and their contribution to the overall success of the category from the consumer (and retailer's) point of view, they have a major interest in the category and its performance as a whole because their own success is dependent upon it. For example, many category champions produce assortment plans or planograms for retailers that include all products within a category, whether they are their own, another supplier's brand or the retailer's own-branded products. A supplier that is in a very dominant position within a category may even manage the inventory for a retailer (see 'Supplier-managed inventory', Chapter 7).

THE CATEGORY MANAGEMENT PROCESS

Category management is generally viewed as a step-by-step planning and implementation process that helps retailers and suppliers achieve both performance-based objectives and longer-term strategic aims. This process is outlined in Table 3.1.

Definition of a category

The way in which a category of merchandise should be defined has yet to be fully established but there is general agreement that it should be established by the way consumers buy the product in question (Wills, 1999). Generally, products within a category should be reasonable substitutes for one another (differences being forged by criteria such as brand, flavour or colour variation, product quality and price level), although products within some categories might have an element of being complementary to one another. For example, some grocers might consider 'exotic foods' as a category, into which products such as refried beans, taco shells and salsa sauce might all fall; these are complementary rather than substitute products, but in the purchase of such products it is more logical for consumers if they are displayed together. The definition of a category is likely to change between retailers, according to the size and degree of specialisation in the format used. Some categories may have recognisable sub-categories, which may become categories in their own right within a specialist retailer; for example, a 'hair-care' category might be broken down into sub-categories of shampoo, conditioner, two-in-one conditioners, and styling products. As discussed in Chapter 1, product management is increasingly about providing 'solutions' to lifestyles or personal process domains, and so complementary goods that work together to provide those solutions are more likely to define a retail category. Mitchell (2001) uses the term super-category to describe product ranges that provide a high level of customer focus. This would include premium product ranges like Tesco's Finest or Sainsbury's Blue Parrot

Table 3.1 *The category management process*

Category definition	Define the category	Determine the products that make up the category from a consumer's perspective. Consider the role of sub-categories or individual SKU's taken in the category
	⇓	
	Establish the strategic role of the category within the total product assortment of the retailer	Develop a strategic plan for the category, considering long-term trends
	⇓	
Category planning	Establish the measures upon which category performance will be assessed	Determine the way in which the performance of a category will be evaluated. Consider various costing and profitability approaches and include both quantitative and qualitative assessments
	⇓	
	Formulate a strategy for the category	Develop a marketing and supply development plan to achieve both short-term and long-term category objectives
	⇓	
	Establish the category marketing mix	Determine the various tactics to be used within the marketing and supply plan, e.g. space allocation, promotions
	⇓	
Category management implementation	Establish category management roles	Assign responsibilities for category management implementation within both retailer and supply partner organisations
	⇓	
	Category review	Measure, monitor and modify the category

Source: Adapted from Fernie and Sparks (1998: 33), Basury *et al.* (2001)

which are geared to the specific needs of certain customer groups (affluent quality seekers and health conscious parents respectively). In fact, these product ranges currently transcend the usual notion of a product category, requiring a new tier of retail marketing and brand management beyond traditional category management. However these groups of products are defined and managed they certainly play an important retail brand-reinforcing role (see Table 3.2).

The role of the SKU within the product category

When a retail product manager is reviewing the choice within a product category, the individual roles that are played by the different brands or product variations will be acknowledged (McGrath, 1997). Some products within a category are 'traffic builders', generating high sales and have a

Table 3.2 *The role of the product category*

Retail brand reinforcer	New categories High fashion and symbolic categories High technology product categories Includes strong (retailer or manufacturer) brands Create excitement and theatre in store
Cash-flow contributor	Established categories Non-symbolic categories Consistent value provision
Profit generator	Growing categories Fashion categories Symbolic categories High profit margins
Service provider	Stagnant or declining categories Staple product categories Well established market leading brands Competitive with other category providers – low profit margins
Destination	Growing or well established category Contains leading brands Deep and wide assortment Considered the best retail offer by target customer

large market share: they draw customers into the store, and their absence would risk customer loss. Other products, such as own-label goods, have roles that are clearly concerned with achieving sales or profit objectives. Some stock keeping units (SKUs) create excitement or play a key role in the reinforcement of the retail brand image and some products play roles that are directly confrontational with other members of the category, for example an own-branded product that fights for market share with a brand leader, or a low price own-label variant of a frequently purchased item, that defends retail market share and promotes store loyalty. Each (SKU) member of the category should be making an individual contribution to the performance of the category. If a brand or variation does not have a clear role, then a product management decision may need to be taken. For example, could one brand be deleted and the sales successfully transferred to another, more profitable brand. Does the category include enough excitement generators? If the category falls within a growing market, can interest be increased and sales within the whole category further improved by offering more variations of excitement generating products? Do we need three different pack sizes of one product item; would sales be harmed if we only offered the smallest and largest?

The strategic role of the category

Product categories themselves have different characteristics, which mean that they have to be managed in different ways in order to achieve optimum profitability. Some categories may be dominated by premium brands, whilst others might be more value driven, for example. Table 3.2 shows five different roles that categories might play within a total product assortment. If a category is composed largely of premium brands, then most of the brands in the category are, or should be, quite profitable. If, on the other hand, the category is comprised mostly of value and own-label brands, then the opportunity to obtain higher profit margins will be lower, for both the retailer and the supplier. There may be opportunities for retailers and suppliers to work together to improve the profitability of certain product categories, via product innovation and/or brand repositioning. For example, the ice-cream product category has been upgraded in the UK market by the introduction of premium luxury ice-cream, ice-cream confectionery, high profile marketing campaigns by companies such as Häagen Dazs and the development of premium own-label products. Beer and athletic footwear (trainers) are examples of other categories that have shifted from value to premium (Vishwanath and Mark, 1999).

PRODUCT CATEGORY LIFECYCLES

When selecting products, retail buyers need to be aware of the cyclical sales pattern that both individual products and product categories tend to follow. The product lifecycle theory has been a great source of debate over the years, but is generally accepted as having some value when it comes to understanding the sales and profit implications of products over time (Brassington and Pettitt, 2003; Baker, 2000). Although the product lifecycle, which relates to a specific product item, or brand, may be of some value to the buyer of branded fast moving consumer goods, the category lifecycle is perhaps a more useful concept for many buying decisions, and has implications for the way a category is managed (see Figure 3.1). The position of a product or category within its lifecycle can guide a buyer when making decisions about the depth of their product assortment, as shown below.

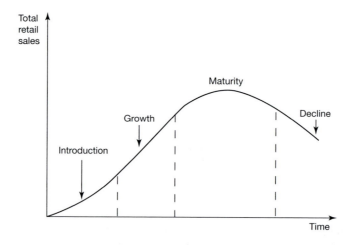

Figure 3.1 *The category lifecycle*

Introduction

If a category is in the introduction stage, a retailer will offer limited assortment; for example, one product variation or one brand. It will be keen to minimise risk and investment in terms of space allocated and monetary value, but a new product can create excitement and could be the start of an important product category. New categories may start as sub-sets of larger categories. When mobile phones were first introduced there was little brand choice, the product was functional, and may well have been part of a larger category, perhaps called 'small communication appliances'.

Growth

When a category is in the growth stage a retailer has the opportunity to increase assortment, introducing more brand alternatives, and more product variations. As more consumers become interested, product variations to fulfil the needs of different target groups become viable. In this stage, a retailer may decide to introduce their own-branded products and promote a category to maximise sales and profit opportunities. As the mobile phone market grew, the brand choice proliferated, alternative designs became available, and the choice of associated service packages increased, tailored to different types of user. Specialist retailers devoted to this product category alone emerged, and space devoted to the category in more general retail outlets was greatly increased.

Maturity

A large assortment is offered in the maturity phase, including many brands and many product variations (including own-label in most product categories). The category becomes established and more competitive between retailers. As the mobile phone market matured, price became a key selling feature and distribution became extensive. Additional product features such as texting, cameras and internet access were introduced to extend the lifecycle. An increasing array of mobile phone accessories is offered including chargers, hands-free sets, special graphics and ring tones. Mobile network provider O2 launched their own-branded phones in this stage of the cycle.

Decline

Here, the product category loses appeal, to be replaced by another growth category. Retailers should cut the assortment back to leading brands, and the best-selling variations. In the case of mobile phones, the product comes close to saturation, when replacement and upgrading become the main opportunities for new sales, whilst health concerns may cause the product to eventually lose appeal. The advertising of mobile phone retailers started to focus on the 'shame' of having an older and less stylish mobile phone (Thurtle and Wilkinson, 2002). Price competition is rife among producers and retailers, and so little investment is made in terms of space allocation or promotional activity. Some specialist mobile phone retailers were squeezed out of the market as sales in the category began to slump.

Although the general concept of the lifecycle pattern can be useful as a basis for the understanding of consumer purchasing patterns, many products have a lifecycle that is completely different to the standard. Some products have a highly seasonal cycle, which may or may not occur within an overriding category lifecycle (see Figure 3.2). Seasonality brings great sales opportunities to retailers, both in terms of the opportunity to offer new ranges of products and the opportunity to maximise sales volumes. It also presents the risk of overstocking, as outlined in Chapter 6.

Some products have a very steeply curved lifecycle at the growth stage and at the decline stage, with a very short period of maturity. These products can be described as fads, and are particularly prevalent in the toy and teenage fashion accessories market. Again, fads offer the retailer the opportunity to generate high sales over a short period of time, but the risk of having a stockpile of an outdated fad are very high. Other products, which can be described as staple products do not conform to the lifecycle pattern because the demand is more or less continuous, for example those for sugar or orange juice.

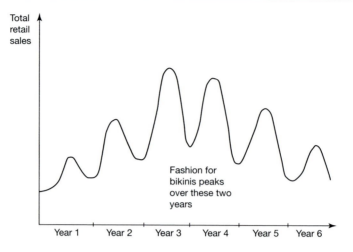

Figure 3.2 *The category lifecycle for bikinis*

THE ROLE OF THE CATEGORY WITHIN THE RETAILER'S TOTAL ASSORTMENT

Category management not only looks at the detail of the product SKU 'members' within the category, but is also concerned with the role of the whole product category within the retail outlet, and the contribution the category makes to the strategic positioning of the retail brand identity. Retailers are using category management in the pursuit of product differentiation to gain a competitive advantage over their rivals; they need suppliers who understand their retail market positioning and who can help them to improve the performance of their strategic product categories, not only from the point of view of short to medium term profitability, but also to enhance an image of creativity, innovation and excitement (Din, 2000). Category orientated point of sale display materials can reinforce a strategic product category positioning, as illustrated by the case at the end of this chapter. Table 3.2 explores the various roles that categories might play within the retailer's total product assortment.

ESTABLISH THE PERFORMANCE MEASURES FOR THE CATEGORY

An integral part of a management approach that looks towards efficiency in demand management as well as supply management, category management has profitability as its key performance indicator. Chapter 12 discusses the different ways in which profit performance can be measured, from the very basic gross margin calculation, through to more sophisticated measures that take a whole gamut of costed activity into account. Fernie (1998: 31) recommends activity-based costing for evaluating category performance because it not only considers the costs of supply (logistics and selling) but it also takes account of the costs associated with demand management, such as the costs of product introductions and the costs of promotional activity. More recent approaches to performance measurement have included the concept of the scorecard, which allows success to be measured across a number of indicators, according to their relevance to the retailer concerned (Fernie and Sparks, 2004).

FORMULATE A STRATEGY FOR THE CATEGORY

Having defined the category and its role within the retail business, and established optimum profitability as the success indicator, the next step in the category management process is to draw up a strategy for that particular group of products. It is at this stage that issues such as promotional activity, product assortment planning, own-brand strategy and proprietary brand support need to be blended together in order to maximise category profit performance. The position of the category within its own lifecycle will impact upon the viability of the strategy (see above).

THE CATEGORY MIX

The set of tactics used to achieve the optimum range assortment and obtain efficiency in promotions, product innovation and replenishment, will be determined by the strategy formulated for the category. In essence the category receives its own marketing mix, within the parameters of the retail branded identity. For example, by conducting efficient promotions, a retailer does not waste resources by promoting brands whose performance does not pay. Taking a more analytical approach to promotional activity can vastly improve the profitability of a product category, by removing costs associated with promotional activities that are not in the best interests of the retailer's product range performance. Many promotions require time and effort to set up, data input amendments, production of special communications and packaging, and may result in deflecting sales to a product with a lower product profit (away from an own-label product, for example). Unless promotional activity is going to result in overall better performance of the category, or bring some other long-term benefit to the retailer (such as loyalty to a store because of its offers), then it may be better to resist the promotion.

Point of sale displays can also be viewed with the same analytical judgement; for example, changes to shelf allocations, or the use of point of sale materials should only be undertaken if they have the potential to improve the performance of the whole category for the retailer. Prices may also be manipulated in order to maximise category performance. The use of 'known-value' items is important in value-driven categories such as packaged bread, where there is considerable price competition, whereas in premium-product driven categories, such as wine, retailers have more opportunity to increase margins and benefit from impulse based promotional offers.

The way a retailer implements category management is best considered in the final part of the category management description, that of an organisational concept.

CATEGORY MANAGEMENT AS AN ORGANISATIONAL CONCEPT

From the point of view of the category definition, category management requires an understanding of how customers shop; this has traditionally been the concern of marketers rather than buyers within a retail business. Category management, therefore, brings a much stronger marketing orientation to the product management process. Category management has the effect of reducing the role of the buyer, and augmenting the role of the merchandiser, but essentially a category management role is a cross-functional one. According to Wileman and Jary (1997: 132) 'the intersection of buying and merchandising and marketing is the heart of retail brand management, and its focus is category management'. Promotional activity in store is geared towards improving category performance and becomes included in a category manager's remit.

The implementation of category management relies on collaborative and co-operative supply partnerships (see Chapter 5). Category management requires a focus team organisation that spans across both supplier and retailer's organisational boundaries. Essentially, retailers and suppliers

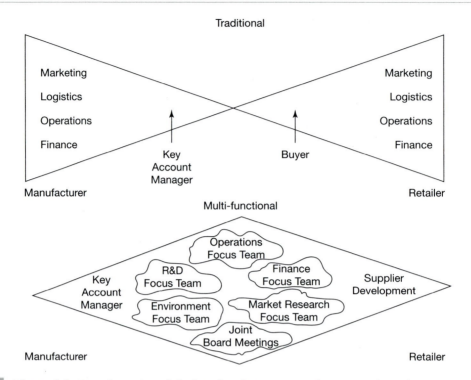

Figure 3.3 *Transformation of the interface between manufacturer and retailer*

Source: Adapted from Fernie and Sparks, 1998: 33, Kogan Page Publishers and Basbury et al., 2001

pool their resources to manage various aspects of their partnership with the view to improving category performance (see Figure 3.3).

CATEGORY MANAGEMENT AND EFFICIENT CONSUMER RESPONSE (ECR)

Category management, as we have seen, is a way of organising buying and merchandising activities to make product ranges work hard for both the retailer and the customer. Central to the philosophy behind category management is that the product range should be responsive to customer demand. Being truly responsive to the consumer, however, requires not only the retailer's buying organisation to become responsive, but also the whole of the retailer's supply chain. After all, rapid response to consumer buying patterns relies on all activities that are involved in getting produce from factories to customers. Category managers may be alert to the performances of their product ranges, but if they are not able to rely on suppliers of goods within those categories to respond quickly, then the contributions of the category to organisational success will diminish.

Category management therefore is usually part of a broader consumer-led approach within a retailer's supply chain, which encompasses buying activities, promotional activities and product development; replenishment systems; logistics operations; suppliers and their manufacturing facilities. Efficient consumer response (ECR) is a term that describes this type of all-encompassing supply chain management system. It is a managerial approach that starts with consumer demand, and then gears the whole of the supply chain to responding to that demand. It is a customer driven, demand-pull product management system; 'a seamless interface from consumer purchase to manufacturing schedules' (Lowson *et al.*, 1999: 40); it is different to a supply-push, or buying-led approach, based on the principles of sales forecasting, with products supplied in preparation for estimated demand. ECR, however, encompasses much more than a stock control system; it involves not only all the operational areas of retail management, but also involves the way in which retailers, suppliers and third-party service suppliers (such as logistics companies) work together to achieve two fundamental objectives simultaneously – maximising customer satisfaction and minimising total costs.

ECR as a concept emerged in the US in the late 1980s as retailers, particularly in the grocery sector, faced increasing price competition from discounters. In order to avoid a downward-spiralling price orientated battle between suppliers and retailers, all vying for an increased share of diminishing profit margins, a new philosophy emerged which promoted the idea of retailers and their suppliers establishing mutually beneficial, co-operative, cost-cutting working practices, with the critical success factor of final customer satisfaction as the driver of all initiatives. The establishment of a group of products as a category, which essentially have similar demand patterns, are reasonable substitutes for one another and can be viewed from a marketing viewpoint as a sensible strategic business unit on which to base a marketing plan, has been an important contribution to the successful implementation of ECR programmes. The diagram in Figure 3.4 illustrates the underlying reasoning of ECR.

Efficient consumer response found acceptance in the European retail industry in the early 1990s. In the shaping of efficient consumer response a number of high profile retailer and supplier partnerships trialled new management initiatives and systems under the guidance of some well-known management consultancies, who had seen how successful the just-in-time philosophy had been in gaining efficiency in the supply chain for manufacturing companies. Just-in-time manages the supply of components according to their usage in a production unit, whereas ECR manages the supply of goods through the retail supply chain according to their demand by consumers. ECR is not a small undertaking, as its various facets, shown in Figure 3.5 illustrate.

Figure 3.5 shows the scope of ECR as a holistic system, encompassing a broad range of activities where improvements in efficiency might be made. These activities might previously have been boxed into 'supply chain', 'retail management' and 'marketing' activities. Within an ECR system,

BOX 3.1 ECR INITIATIVES

The following selected retailers and suppliers have been involved in ECR initiatives:

Suppliers
Colemans of Norwich (Robinsons Britvic), Kraft Jacobs Suchard, Birds Eye Walls, Procter & Gamble, Nestlé, Coca-Cola

Retailers
Tesco, Safeway, Somerfield, Sainsbury's, Coop Italia, Dansk, Promodes Caprabo, Delhaize Le Lion, A. Heijn

In addition, the following consultancies have played a major part in progressing the ECR concept: Coopers and Lybrand, Kurt Salmon Associates

Source: Lowson *et al.*, 1999; Fernie and Sparks, 1998; Fernie, 1999; GEA, 1994

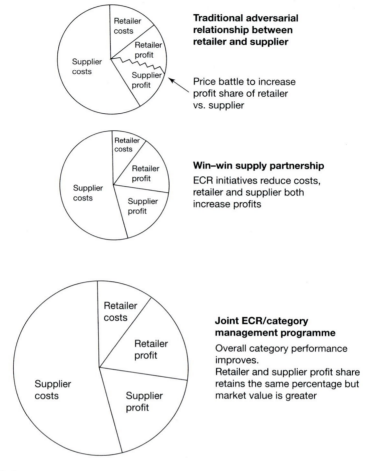

Traditional adversarial relationship between retailer and supplier

Price battle to increase profit share of retailer vs. supplier

Win–win supply partnership
ECR initiatives reduce costs, retailer and supplier both increase profits

Joint ECR/category management programme
Overall category performance improves.
Retailer and supplier profit share retains the same percentage but market value is greater

Figure 3.4 *The principles of efficient consumer response*

such boundaries become meaningless because all parties work as 'allies' with consumer purchasing power and patterns as the focus for all activities. The level of efficiency gained in the satisfaction of customers is the measure of success of the system, and the rewards are obtainable by all contributing allies in the system. The first level of activities (efficient store assortment, product introductions, promotions and replenishment) is chiefly concerned with the management of consumer demand and the initial response to it and is typically category management activities. The second level (automated and continuous replenishment, synchronised manufacturing, integrated supply networks, nil defect logistics and strategic development) are concerned with the management of product supply.

Information flow and data technology

A key feature of ECR, which was omitted from Figure 3.5 for the sake of clarity, is the information flow (see Figure 3.6). ECR relies on efficient information flows above all else, and as such the development of ECR systems has relied on the increasing sophistication of 'enabling technologies' such as electronic data interchange (EDI) and the internet. In addition, many of the improvements that needed to be made within an ECR system depended on high levels of data analysis. This would

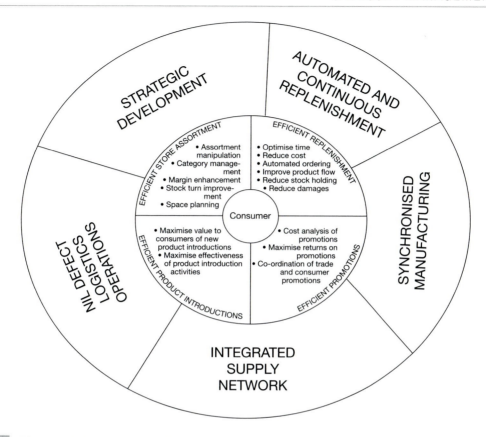

Figure 3.5 *The scope of efficient consumer response*

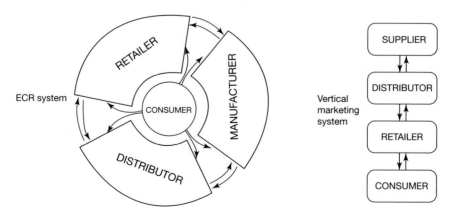

Figure 3.6 *Information flow in an ECR system compared with a vertical marketing system*

not be possible if data management technologies had not been available to provide the information upon which improvement action could be taken (Fernie and Sparks, 1998). The contributing allies within an ECR system cannot be efficiently geared to the consumer unless data is managed and shared between all parties. Information flows within the ECR system are complex but, like the operational activities, are centred on the consumer from all angles, rather than solely from the retail perspective, as in a more traditional vertical marketing system.

ECR, as a management philosophy and an operational system, works well where demand for products is relatively consistent. However, if demand fluctuates considerably, due to the influences of seasonality or fashion change an ECR system is unable to cope. Products have to be grown or made; if demand is outstripping supply, retailers can ask their suppliers to increase production. However, this means more raw materials, more workforce and so on, things that cannot be changed overnight. Alternatively, if demand slows down, it is difficult to halt production immediately. Although manufacturing has become much more flexible over the years, in order to achieve the economies of scale to supply goods at low costs, most factories still need large orders of similar product, therefore in some areas of retailing ECR in its pure form is not applicable. A 'relative' of ECR is quick response (QR), which is similar in that it is a managerial approach to supply chain activity that is geared to responding to consumer demand. However, QR encompasses a variety of supply chain practices that prepare for responses to changing demand as a result of seasonal or fashion trends. ECR and QR are discussed further in Chapter 7.

BOX 3.2 INFORMATION OVERLOAD?

Information overload can seriously dent the confidence of any buyer who has used intuition and flair to tap into the kind of trends that no amount of data analysis would support. Merchandise management systems may have a positive restraining effect, but they can also stifle entrepreneurship and creativity, words that are increasingly being used in a positive sense in business management.

There is no doubt that integrated information systems have improved the availability of products in stores, and have given a product manager a much more detailed view of their business. Has the product itself, however, become drowned by information overload? Responding to consumers fast and efficiently will certainly reduce shopping frustration levels: shoppers can have what they want, when they want and where they want, as new marketing channels and retail formats open up a multitude of ways in which goods can be acquired. Does all this rapid response produce more wonderful, exceptional, inspirational 'must have' products?

Many consumers still seem less than satisfied with the product ranges on offer, criticising retailers for offering too much of the same thing, and for blandness. Information technology has taken most of the laborious number crunching out of a merchandiser's job, allowing them to manage the product range more closely and strategically; but for buyers, information overload concerning past sales can prevent them looking forward with enthusiasm for new ideas. The enabler has become the controller. However, the answer to this problem may lie in the use of information technology itself (of course!).

Data mining is a process where captured customer data is manipulated to find linkages between people and the products that they buy, and this technique may prevent product range rationalisation going too far. One supermarket chain found that although feta cheese was a slow-selling item, a target for elimination in a category management drive perhaps, this type of cheese was predominantly being purchased by customers who formed the highest spending group. The slow seller was therefore allowed to maintain its presence within the category because of its 'high class' clientele. Like the EPOS information that went before it, data-mined information only tells a retailer about current customers and their purchases, rather than why someone is not a customer of a store, or a purchaser of a product, but it does give a deeper understanding about the role that individual products play in the individual customer's shopping basket, and supports the need for 'exceptional' products.

Source: Tredre, 1995; Wills, 1999

CATEGORY MANAGEMENT LIMITATIONS

Category management as a central tenet of the ECR movement has provided benefits to participating retail–supplier collaborations. As an example, the case study at the end of this chapter documents the experience of a leading frozen food producer and an Italian retailer. On a less positive note, however, Wills (1999) suggests that ECR has remained an impenetrable concept, relying too much on theory and jargon, with the costs of achieving efficiencies outweighing the resulting benefits. In addition, many of the initiatives have reflected what many well-run retailers were already doing. However, the far-reaching facets of ECR and the new philosophy of category management certainly support the more analytical approach to product management, discussed in Chapter 2. The full-scale adoption of category management requires a considerable amount of reorganisation within the retailer and has met with a number of inhibiting factors such as: skills shortages (for example, in enabling information technology management); the difficulties associated with accepting suppliers as allies or partners with whom information should be shared; the reluctance to change inappropriate organizational structures; and the lack of clear strategic plans for product ranges (Wills, 1999).

Another concern with the implementation of category management is the resulting lack of variety being offered to customers. Concentrating on efficiency in logistics and merchandising may result in highly efficient retailing; however, there is a risk that the consumer experience is being given lower priority. This could be a dangerous strategy when store-based retailing is becoming increasingly threatened by much more efficient (from the customer viewpoint) home-based retailing formats. Category-managed product ranges are safe and offer the majority of customers in the majority of purchase decisions, 'efficient' selections of market-leading products; however, these selections may start to appear boring and over-managed. Even though there is a suggestion that information technology may help to prevent retailers drifting too far in this direction (see Box 3.2), the view that retail product assortments can become boring under category management is reinforced by Webb (1999), who asserts that retailers who put an emphasis on the profitability of the category rather than considering the holistic appeal of the store are contributing to the 'banalisation of retailing', where product ranges are 'uninspiring and ubiquitous'.

A further drawback of category management is the threat to smaller suppliers. The practice of establishing category captains to improve the performance of the entire product category runs the risk of putting larger suppliers in a position where they can abuse their power by improving their own market share at the expense of the other suppliers within the category. It has been suggested that retailers benefit from leading suppliers fighting to contribute the most to the category management process, whilst the second and third tier brands are squeezed off the shelf.

59

In some countries, retailers are required by law to allocate a percentage of shelf space to smaller suppliers, for example in France approximately 10 per cent of shelf space has to be given to local suppliers (McCawley, 2000). Forcing smaller suppliers out of the category adds to the banalisation of retailing, resulting in the multiple retailers and major suppliers managing a category for their own purposes, whilst shoppers are driven away in the process. It is significant that retailers such as Selfridge's department store have retained a buying-led organisational structure rather than a category management structure in the pursuit of a clearly defined product differentiation strategy (Wills, 1999).

Category management has been most successfully adopted in large product categories that include dominant and organised suppliers. Smaller retailers often do not have the structure or resources to implement category management and a fragmented supply base is generally not suitable either. The integrated ECR systems that are available today are generally complex and expensive to implement, incorporating a wide range of business activities. Aer Rianta for example installed an £800,000 system in 2001, which will handle merchandising, assortment planning, merchandise management, forecasting, replenishment, vendor and purchasing management, POS and distribution centre management (Porter, 2001). Category management may fail to bring anticipated rewards if retailers and suppliers are too focused on their own problems and fail to properly assess customer needs.

Category management nevertheless is becoming more widely adapted as a business philosophy at least, and is starting to be explored in the context of new product sectors, such as clothing, health and beauty and DIY (Dewsnap and Hart, 2004; Porter, 2001). The Institute of Grocery Distribution (IGD) continues to bring industry expertise and advice to support retailers who are interested in implementing category management, and is able to cite many success stories for retailers (IGD, 2003).

SUMMARY

Category management is a way of organising retail product management so that suppliers, central operations and outlet level activities are integrated into the process, which is geared to responding effectively to consumer demand. The category manager has overall responsibility for a group of products defined by customer shopping orientations. The category management process, however, relies on the contribution of cross-functional teams and supply partners.

Category management is a buying approach that ties in with the concept of consumer responsive supply chain management and aims to optimise efficiency while maintaining agility. It is, however, not always applicable; smaller, more specialised retailers would find the full-scale implementation of category management restrictive and not cost-effective, and so more traditional buying organisations and processes retain their status in today's industry.

CASE STUDY SAGIT–UNILEVER

Sagit is part of the multinational conglomerate Unilever, and is the leading frozen food supplier in Italy where frozen food is a growing market; traditionally it has had a low market penetration because of the availability of fresh alternatives, and a lack of consumer interest. However, as the quality of frozen foods has improved, Italian consumers have started to favour their convenience from the points of view of storage, meal preparation and waste avoidance.

Sagit has been involved in a number of category management projects with its retail trading partners. As in other projects, Sagit, as the supply partner, has been able to bring a wealth of information to the category management discussion on the way consumers behave. This information, derived from a number of marketing research projects, is summarised below:

- impulse purchasing for frozen foods is low;
- many customers in general grocery shopping trips do not buy frozen food at all;
- customers who buy frozen foods buy very few products (for example only two or three products are selected from a product assortment of over 250);
- frozen food buyers are store loyal rather than brand loyal;
- store promotions were found to be the most effective form of product promotion, due to the lack of brand loyalty.

The objective of Sagit's category management project with Italian retailer GS was to improve the performance of the whole category, thereby offering mutual benefits to both retail and supply partners.

The starting point was to establish which products were to be grouped as a category. To perform this task adequately, the way in which consumers approached frozen products with a view to selection was investigated. This resulted in products being grouped according to their primary ingredient (for example, meat, fish or vegetable) and then according to their function (for example, ready prepared meals, pre-prepared meal components, fancy sweet dishes and fancy savoury dishes).

The second stage of the project involved a review of the product assortment. This resulted in some changes to the product range:

- a more prominent selection from leading brands, including key product items;
- elimination of non-profitable items and those with a very marginal contribution to sales or profits;
- introduction of 16 new products and the removal of 57 existing products.

The third stage involved space management – regarding the layout, fixturing, display and allocation of shelf space to products:

- displaying the product according to the categories of merchandise described earlier in the category definition stage, by natural product and then by use;
- a vertical presentation of products, as opposed to their lying flat;
- clearer product information;
- alternative placement of high turnover and low turnover goods to encourage shoppers to consider all products within the assortment;
- placing products with a high propensity to be impulse purchased in more visible and busy display areas;
- placing products that are more inclined to be pre-planned purchases in areas that require customers to cover a larger proportion of the display;
- other space allocation decisions were determined by sales and profit objectives, the size of the SKU, stock-turn and lead times.

The final stage involved in-store communications:

- point of purchase material helped to define the category as a pleasant environment, for example a welcome garland was placed at the start of the department;
- clear price marking was applied throughout;

■ the sub-categories were clearly marked in the section of the display;

■ specific product orientated point of purchase material was used to reinforce the brand leadership of Sagit's (Findus) products.

The results of the project were very encouraging; in particular for Sagit and their retail partner SG. Annual sales for the whole category improved by 5 per cent (compared to a market growth for frozen foods of 2 per cent). Sales of Sagit products increased by around one-third, and sales of SG's own-branded products increased by nearly 40 per cent. Other brands within the section experienced stable or decreased sales volumes.

There were additional benefits that were identified by qualitative research after implementation of the category management initiatives. Generally the visibility of the category had been greatly improved: 98 per cent of customers noticed the new displays and in-store communications, and were very positive about the ease and pleasantness of the shopping experience within the department. They also considered the general organisation of the department to be improved, along with the clarity of the displays, the visibility of items, prices and promotions.

Source: This case study is based on a paper published in the Proceedings of the 10th International Conference on Research in the Distributive Trades, Institute for Retail Studies, University of Stirling, 1999, and has been adapted with the kind permission of the authors Gennaro Cuomo and Alberto Pastore

QUESTIONS

1   Assess how category management contributes to the efficient consumer response approach to product management.

2   Outline the main objectives of category management.

3   How does the role of the category manager differ from that of a buyer and a merchandiser?

4   Outline the category management process, referring to the Sagit–Unilever case study to illustrate your discussion.

5   What are the main drawbacks of category management? What steps can a retailer take to overcome these?

6   Compare and contrast the traditional buying process (Chapter 2) and the category management process (Chapter 3).

7   Analyse a product category of your choice in a large supermarket according to the roles played by the various product items.

REFERENCES AND FURTHER READING

Baker, M.J. (2000) *Marketing Strategy and Management*, Macmillan, London.

Brassington, F. and Pettit, S. (2003) *Principles of Marketing*, 3rd edn, Pearson Education, Harlow.

Dewsnap, B. and Hart, C. (2004) 'Category Management: A New Approach for Fashion Marketing?', *European Journal of Marketing*, 38(7): 809–834.

Din, R. (2000) *New Retail*, Conran Octopus, London.

Dussart, C. (1998) 'Category Management: Strengths, Limits and Developments', *European Management Journal*, 16(1): 50–62.

Fernie, J. (1998) 'Relationships in the Supply Chain', in J. Fernie and L. Sparks (eds), *Logistics and Retail Management*, Kogan Page, London, ch. 2.

Fernie, J. (ed.) (1999) *The Future of UK Retailing*, Financial Times Retail and Consumer Reports, London.

Fernie, J. and Sparks, L. (eds) (1998) *Logistics and Retail Management*, Kogan Page, London.

Gattorna, J.L. and Walters, D.W. (1996) *Managing the Supply Chain*, Macmillan, London.

GEA Consultenti Associati Gestione Aziendale (1994) *Supplier–Retailer Collaboration in Supply Chain Management*, Report published by the Coca-Cola Retailing Research Group, Europe.

IGD (Institute of Grocery Distribution) (1999) *Category Management in Action*, IGD, Watford.

IGD (2003) *IGD Category Management 2003 Report*, Institute of Grocery Distribution.

Lowson, B., King, R. and Hunter, A. (1999) *Quick Response: Managing the supply chain to meet consumer demand*, John Wiley, Chichester.

McCawley, I. (2000) 'Small Suppliers Seek Broader Shelf Access', *Marketing Week*, 17 February.

McGrath, M. (1997) *A Guide to Category Management*, IGD, Letchmore Heath.

Mitchell, A. (2001) 'Assessing the Scope of Grocery Super-categories', *Marketing Week*, 25 October.

Porter, J. (2001) 'All the Categories Come Together as CM Finds Its Feet', *Retail Week*, 25 May.

Tredre, R. (1995) 'Thread Barons', *Observer*, 19 November.

Thurtle, G. and Wilkinson, A. (2002) 'Chipping Away at the Hi-tech Sector', *Marketing Week*, 7 February.

Vishwanath, V. and Mark, J. (1999) 'Your Brand's Best Strategy', *Harvard Business Review on Brand Management*, Harvard Business School Press, Watertown, MA, 169–187.

Webb, B. (1999) in J. Fernie (ed.) *The Future of UK Retailing*, Financial Times Retail and Consumer Reports, London.

Wileman, A. and Jary, M. (1997) *Retail Power Plays*, Macmillan, London.

Wills, J. (1999) *Merchandising and Buying Strategies: New Roles for a Global Operation*, Financial Times Retail and Consumer Reports, London.

Part II

The retail product management process

From conception to delivery

Chapter 4

Product range planning and selection

LEARNING OBJECTIVES

The purpose of this chapter is to:

■ Identify the dimensions of a retailer's assortment plan and understand the various internal (retailer-related) and external (business environment related) factors that will influence the way the assortment plan is drawn up.

■ Gain an appreciation of the attention to detail that product managers must apply when selecting products to include in the assortment, in order to achieve maximum satisfaction to the user.

■ Build knowledge of the criteria upon which products are judged when they are considered for inclusion within a product range.

■ Understand the relationship between products and consumers and understand how this relationship affects product selection.

■ Explore the way product assortments are reviewed, as part of the process of monitoring product performance.

INTRODUCTION

Planning product ranges and selecting products are central tenets of retail product management. Variety, depth, price level and availability are variables that need to be combined in order for a retailer to achieve a balanced product assortment. The aim of this chapter is to explore how a retailer creates a product offer that consists of the products that reflect the needs, wants and aspirations of the target customer. This exploration covers the various stages that retail product managers go through before finalising the product range. Retail product managers, and in particular retail buyers must translate customer needs and wants into actual products, focusing on product features that are going to provide value to the customer in use.

THE PRODUCT RANGE

A product range is the total product offering expressed in terms of width and depth. The width of a product range depends on the variety, or number of different types, of product category. Depth, on the other hand refers to the amount of choice offered in terms of product and brand variation within a product category. Increased depth will allow a retailer to cover a number of different price levels, should this be part of their overall product strategy. A product range within a large retailer may include many thousands of single product items, and so in order to manage them effectively, the total range is subdivided. Most product ranges are subdivided and managed according to product feature and sales pattern similarity, and those characteristics are used to determine how particular products are grouped into categories, departments or sections (depending on retailer terminology). The term 'product range' can be used either to refer to the total product offering of a retail outlet, or to a sub-set of products, and the term 'product assortment' is generally synonymous with 'product range'.

Although a common way of managing product groups, product similarity, however, is not the only basis upon which total product offers can be divided. Alternative ways of sub-dividing product ranges include:

- *End use*: Rather than grouping products that are substitutes for one another and therefore are in competition, products may be grouped on the basis of being complementary with each other for end use. B&Q, the international DIY retailer for example, groups products according to 'projects' such as installing a new bathroom suite, or tiling the floor. Supermarket retailers sometimes group products around meal 'themes', as a way of encouraging related sales. As discussed in Chapter 1, consumers who are time poor and convenience driven, are likely to value retailers who provide products that are grouped according to lifestyle solutions.
- *Price*: Retailers may organise product ranges according to the price level at which groups of products are pitched. For example, variety store retailers might have a 'budget range' that is bought separately from other ranges. Alternatively, a premium range of luxury foods in a supermarket may be managed in its entirety by a team operating separately from the other food categories.
- *Brand*: A brand of a product can be the most important product feature for some customers, and some brands have authority across a number of different product categories. It may therefore be more appropriate to manage ranges by brand rather than by product category. Department stores, like Debenhams, which have over fifty of their own house brands, often manage products by brand in order to create and maintain a strong, consistent and co-ordinated identity (sometimes referred to as the brand's 'hand writing'), from the development stage through to display within the store.
- *Core and non-core*: For many retailers, products can be divided into core and non-core ranges. Core items are those that have consistent demand, which the retailer matches with continuous availability. These products are generally what are termed 'staple items' and they tend not to undergo change. Non-core lines may be seasonal, only being stocked for a short time period within the year, or they may be subject to fashion trends and will be replaced by different fashionable items once their appeal dies. Core lines for a home improvement retailer would include white and magnolia paint, white kitchen and bathroom tiles, terracotta quarry floor tiles and plaster mix. Non-core ranges would include fashion ranges in paint colours, speciality floor tiles and Christmas decorations.

It is important to note that these approaches are not mutually exclusive; indeed, they may all be used within one large retail organisation.

THE ASSORTMENT PLAN (MODEL STOCK LIST)

The assortment plan is a valuable aid, not only for the management of products from a buying perspective, but also as a very useful document for store management, because it denotes what, in physical product terms, should be on display within the store at any particular time period. The assortment plan gives an indication of the width and depth within each category and sub-category of the product range that should be available within a retailer's outlet. It is essentially a list of product types that are planned to be stocked at a particular time (hence the term 'model stock list'). In some retail businesses the assortment plan will not change throughout the year, but in others a new model stock list may need to be drawn up for each major selling season. It may also be necessary for retailers to issue a number of different assortment plans if they have a major variation in size of store.

The assortment plan will usually sub-divide the merchandise within a product category according to variables that are relevant to consumer choice, but it will not normally be carried out at SKU (stock keeping unit) level, unless the merchandise is extremely specialised and/or of high value. The kind of variable shown on the assortment plan will be:

- price level (not exact prices);
- styling design themes;
- colours;
- flavours;
- pack size;
- fabrication/type.

The assortment plan for the red wine category in a convenience store might look something like Table 4.1. By specifying particular attributes on the assortment plan, the buyer ensures that the product range offers the customer a good variety from which to choose. However, the plan also allows flexibility so that buying opportunities can be maximised and responses made to fashion trends. For example, a wine from a new producing region such as Argentina can be incorporated into the range (other regions, medium price).

The product assortment plan is fundamental to the range planning of fashion merchandise, and is built up gradually and in more detail as the planning for the season progresses. Fashion buyers need to make sure that they cover all the key colours, silhouettes and design themes that they identify as being important for the coming season.

Some assortment plans include the size distribution that will be available for each type of merchandise; whether or not this is included on the plan, it is a product manager's responsibility to make a sizing decision when placing an initial order. Whether the order concerned is for nightdresses or for cornflakes, the size variation offered to the customer must still be considered. For many products size distribution is not an issue, but for others product variations have to be accounted for:

- *Sizing*: body size for clothing, bed size for linens, cubic capacity for refrigerators.
- *Body sizing variations*: ladies 8, 10, 12 etc., trouser inside leg length, waist size; men's: chest size, waist size, trouser inside leg length; children's: by age, height.
- *Pack sizing variation*: weight, volume, multi-pack variation.

Table 4.1 *Assortment plan for red wine*

	Price level	Type	SKUs
French	High	Beaujolais, Claret, Cabernet Sauvignon	7
	Medium	Cabernet Sauvignon, Cotes Du Rhone	5
	Low	Vin de table	1
Spanish	High	Rioja, other	3
	Medium	Tempranillo, other	2
	Low	'Spanish'	1
Italian	High	Chianti, other	3
	Medium	Valpolicella, other	2
Other regions	High	Australian	4
	Medium	Chilean	2
Litre bottles		French	2
		Spanish	1
Boxes		French	1
		Italian	1

CONSIDERATIONS FOR THE ASSORTMENT PLAN

There are a number of considerations that retail product managers have to account for when drawing up their assortment plan. Some of these are practical in nature, but they will all influence the performance of the product range.

Store size, characteristics and fixturing availability

The product manager must have an idea of how much space should be devoted to each category (the expansion or contraction of categories will be evident on the different seasons' assortment plans). It goes without saying that larger stores can carry a higher number of categories; however, allocating store space for product planning is not simply a case of dividing it into boxed areas. Walkways, architectural features (pillars, windows, stairs and so on) have to be accounted for. The amount of space given to a product category is usually related to sales (see Chapter 8 on space allocation); however, in the case of a small but high value category such as jewellery, for example, a higher than average sales-to-space ratio may be achieved.

The display fixtures available also have to be considered. If no suitable fixtures are available and investment into new fixtures is not appropriate due to financial or physical constraints, then it may be better not to buy that category of merchandise, (see Chapter 10 for a discussion on the flexibility of display fixtures). For example, a buyer might feel strongly about a trend for full-length evening dresses for the Christmas party season. However, the number of fixtures available for full-length garments may be limited, because the store usually concentrates on separates (trousers, skirts and tops). The space for products that require chilling or freezing is determined by fixture size and availability.

Complementary merchandise

In creating an assortment plan the buyer must consider the balance of merchandise, so that transaction values can be raised as high as possible. An obvious example would be the balance between suits and shirts or blouses, but it could also be applicable to foliage and flowers in a florists, or pasta and pasta sauces in a grocery store.

Profitability of merchandise

Whilst the anticipated profit margins may be a valid consideration for the retailer when drawing up the assortment plan, the customer is not interested in a retailer's profitability, and so profit expectations should be considered alongside all the other requirements of a balanced offer and not be allowed to dictate the plan.

Corporate objectives

For some retailers it may be top priority to be able to guarantee a very high stock service level for the customer. With other retailers, customers understand that the offer is more diverse, that they as individuals may not be guaranteed the exact product item required, and that a number of very similar substitutes will be available. In fact, in such a situation, the customer may well be heartened if they do not see a rack of the same items if their purchase item needs to show a high level of individuality, such as a gift. Some retailers will take a product line off sale if they cannot offer a full range of sizes to the customer. Such shortages may occur because the product is selling so quickly that the manufacturers are unable, temporarily, to keep up with demand; however, the retailer makes the decision not to compromise their service promise to the customer, even though possible short-term gains could be associated with selling broken size ranges of 'hot' items. Upmarket retailers like Jaeger on the other hand, deliberately do not display all the available sizes, so that stores retain an uncluttered and spacious feel (Buttle, 1993).

Fine-tuning the assortment plan will utilise all of a retail product manager's knowledge and experience gained from a variety of external sources. One of the most valuable sources of information is the stores and their personnel; and in the majority of successful retailers, buyers have a specified amount of time dedicated to store visits. Store visits enable the buyer to hear at first-hand from the sales associates what the customers like and do not like about the product range and perhaps what they expect to find in the range on offer: this will highlight the strengths and weaknesses in the total product offer. Feedback systems may be formalised, for example by using surveys, or 'want slips' that are completed by the sales team, but these methods have the risk of bias and low response, therefore building a rapport between the product management teams at head office and the store managers and sales teams is an ongoing and necessary challenge. Many enlightened retailers admit that this two-way communication is one of the key challenges of retailing and are prepared to devote time and resources to maintaining a satisfactory information flow. Zara, the international fashion retailer for example, encourages its store personnel to talk directly to its design teams about garment styles that work well with customers (Clements, 2000a).

For many retail businesses a highly disciplined approach to merchandise planning has been the underpinning of their success. However, for a number of retailers, part or all of the product range is acquired on the basis of opportunity. For example, the buyers at T. J. Hughes, the discount department store, allocate around one-third of their budget to opportunity purchases (Wills, 1999), which might include second goods, end of lines, or excess factory stock.

PRODUCTS AND CONSUMERS

Traditional marketing theory suggests that 'customer needs' should be the trigger for a retail buying decision. However, in reality consumers in developed countries are motivated by wants and aspirations rather than physical need (Maslow, 1970) and so shopping motivations include many psychologically based individual and social needs other than the basic necessity of product retrieval (Tauber, 1972). A shopping trip may present the opportunity for a day out with family members, a relief from boredom, or an opportunity to find out about new trends with a group of friends (Griffith, 2003). Selecting the right product requires an understanding of the complexity of the modern shopper, and an ability to blend product detail in a way that satisfies both the physical and emotional needs of that shopper. This must be carried out within the context of the retailer's positioning strategy, referred to in Chapter 1. A childrenswear retailer like Adams, for example, might combine the needs of parents (practical, well fitting and safe clothing) with the wants generated from children (comfortable, fun and 'cool' clothing) within a value for money, medium price market positioning.

THE INFLUENCE OF CONSUMER TRENDS ON THE RETAIL OFFER

In Chapter 3 the concept of the category lifecycle was introduced. The influences on the lifecycle of a product category are many and varied. If buyers are to use the lifecycle as a predictive tool when planning product assortments, they must appreciate the underlying consumer trends that affect the rate of growth of the associated product market. Consumer trends include demographic trends, consumer economic trends, technological trends and societal trends, including lifestyle and fashion trends. A full discussion of consumer trends is outside the scope of this text (readers are referred, for example, to Miles *et al.*, 2002); however, an overview with implications for product management is given to highlight the importance of tracking consumer trends.

Demographics

As consumers pass through the various stages of their own personal lifecycle, the products that are relevant to their needs change, beginning with diapers and milk products, passing through the world of toys and home entertainment, fashion accessory fads and music orientated products in the teenage years, home furnishings and aspirational products in their twenties and thirties, followed by bulk supermarket purchases, holidays, and healthcare as they reach their own maturity and decline. Thus the demographic profile of market populations, given by the unavoidable influence of birth rates and death rates, affects the potential for growth in age-relevant product markets. Demographic changes are slow moving and general, and are only really relevant to a buyer in terms of the overall potential of a product category, but the extent to which retailers and producers invest in or support a particular product category may be determined by demographic trends. For example, in the late 1980s and early 1990s a number of womenswear retailers launched childrenswear ranges in response to the increased birth rate at this time, for example, Gap in 1986 (1990 in the UK), Next in 1988 and Principles in 1995 (Mintel, 1999).

Demographics are not only related to age profiles: they also include the way the population changes in terms of working patterns, geographic shifts, ethnicity, family size and so on. An example of a retailer responding to ethnic diversity is Tesco, which in 2003 launched 175 new

Asian product lines into selected stores, to complement the existing branded offer. These include Indian spiced tea and mixes to make masala dosa (a South Indian pancake) and gulab jaman (a traditional ball-shaped sweet). Ready-to-use Asian vegetables such as okra are another development (Tesco internal communications, 2003).

Consumer economics

The amount of personal disposable income that consumers have available to spend in retail outlets is influenced by a number of general economic factors including:

- unemployment levels;
- regional employment patterns;
- interest rate levels;
- inflation levels;
- earnings levels.

In spite of the effect of cyclical variations in economic growth, the general trend in the level of consumer expenditure in developed countries has been upwards for the last century, and so an increasing proportion of our expenditure is on discretionary purchases, as opposed to the necessities of life such as food and housing. As we progress into the twenty-first century, growth in many of the traditional retail sectors (such as food and clothing) is relatively stagnant, whilst spending levels on travel and leisure services are continuing to rise.

Like demographic trends, the effects on product choices of consumer economic health are relatively long term and general, yet it is vital for retail buyers to be sensitive to consumer confidence in the light of real and perceived economic change. In the fairly rapid onset of the economic recession of the late 1980s and early 1990s, many UK retailers reacted too slowly to a downturn in consumer expenditure level, resulting in the need for heavy discounting to shift large quantities of discretionary purchase items, such as clothing, jewellery, household furnishings and appliances, which impacted upon the financial results of leading retailers of the time, notably Ratners, MFI and the Burton Group. Meanwhile, in the UK grocery sector, traditional super-market retailers like Tesco, Sainsbury's and Safeway launched Value, Economy and Saver ranges (respectively) in response to the constrained consumer purse and opportunistic market entry by European discount retailers such as Netto and Aldi. These own-label products, with basic packaging and rock bottom prices became prevalent in many food product categories in the early 1990s, yet by the end of the decade were restricted to a small number of staple items. Conversely, periods of economic prosperity offer retailers the chance to encourage their customers to trade up to higher quality, luxury or indulgence products and push up transaction values.

Social trends

Alongside demographic and economic trends, the ever-changing nature of the society which we inhabit impacts strongly on the products we choose to live amongst and consume. 'The products that we buy are a reflection of ourselves' and 'we are what we eat' are statements that reflect the relationship between people as social beings and how they spend money. As this edition went to press, two of the strongest general product trends in mature retail markets would appear to be transportable personal technology-based products and products that have minimum negative environmental, social and health effects (Craven, 2003). In order to illustrate how product managers have exploited opportunities given by societal change, a small number of product examples are cited (see Table 4.2).

Table 4.2 *Examples of products that reflect social change*

Product example	Societal trends
Washing powder in ready measured 'tablets' or sachets	Increased numbers of working women; the time-constrained consumer
'Red-letter day' gifts	Need to escape from everyday life; interest in experiences rather than tangible products
Organic foods	Health consciousness and fears; environmental and ethical concerns
Mobile phones	Multiple occupations, time-constrained lifestyles; increased use of communication technology; safety concerns
Laminate wood flooring	Interest in easy maintenance home furnishings; working family members; fashion; more frequent interior decoration changes
Ready-to-eat Japanese food	International travel and diversity; fashionable lifestyles; health consciousness
Men's grooming products	Fashion trends in hair and facial hair styling; interest in celebrities and their endorsement of styling and product usage

BOX 4.1   READY-TO-COOK MEALS CONTINUE TO BOOM

The growth in pre-prepared foods since the 1990s illustrates the extent to which social trends have influenced the grocery market. Products such as pre-washed salads, vacuum-packed soup, frozen pizza, ready-to-eat chicken tikka masala, salad bars, and even ready-prepared bangers and mash are all available in supermarkets. The following social trends have all played their part in moving this industry forward: longer working days; part-time (sometimes multiple part-time) occupations; increasing numbers of working women; less free time for the majority; ability and willingness to 'buy time'; increasing single-person households; fragmentation of the family nucleus; increasing participation in leisure activities; an ageing population and more elderly people living independently. The ready-to-cook food market was worth an estimated £567 million in 2004 (Mintel, 2004). In particular, pizzas and ethnic food, which compete head to head with take-away food outlets, have continued to show strong growth recently. Grocery retailers are very enthusiastic about this trend, as it allows them to develop premium product ranges, such as Tesco's Finest, Asda's Curry Pot and Stir Fry Bar, Sainsbury's Bombay Brasserie and Marks & Spencer's Cook! range. Distinctive packaging is used to identify product variations, for example Marks & Spencer's Italian range uses the red, green and white colours of the Italian national flag. Producers and retailers of ready meals and pre-prepared meal components, who have enjoyed the growth in convenience food shopping, are now addressing the growing social concerns about health and environmental issues by launching reduced fat, vegetarian, organic and gluten-free ranges.

Source: Mintel, 2000; Clements, 2000b; Singh, 2003; Mintel, 2004

The influence of technology

Changes in technology can have a very serious effect on the lifecycle of a product. Retailers like the Dixons Group plc who have considerable interest in the electrical and electronics product markets are faced with rapid product innovations and updates. In such a market the timing of product launches and product deletions can be crucial to maximising sales volume and profitability. For example, a new product innovation that improves the quality of a computer printer would ideally be introduced at a time when the stock of the previous printer model is low. Once the new product is launched, the price of the previous model drops and there is a real danger of obsolescence. If the timing of the launch is delayed, however, the retailer runs the risk of losing first-to-market sales to a competitor.

Technological developments are not only important for the electronics sector; they can play an important part in the continuous improvement of product features, from the raw material, the production processes, the packaging – even to the method of retailing the product itself. The home entertainment retail industry has been fundamentally changed by the technical advances that allow consumers to download music and moving imagery via a personal computer, rather than buying CDs and videos or DVDs in shops. This disintermediation trend is fundamentally altering the way consumers buy music. The whole process can become home based, and customised, with a continuous 'try-before-you-buy' facility.

The legal requirement

Product managers have to ensure that as well as offering consumers products that are appealing and interesting to the changing body of consumers, they are also acting within the law. The law (for example the Sales of Goods Act 1995 in the UK) states that a product which is sold has to be of satisfactory quality, fit for all intended purposes and as described, and so a retail buyer must have detailed knowledge of the product legislation that is associated with the ranges they sell. The product may need to comply with a relevant quality standard, with respect, for example, to compatibility of technology or consumer safety. There may be a requirement for detailed product information, particularly with respect to claims made by product descriptions or brands, for example in 'healthy eating' or 'low fat' products. Standards and legal requirements may also apply to processing and packaging, and the methods used for storage, display and handling of goods may be subject to health and safety regulations (meat products for example). Compliance with the law with respect to the product range may be necessary at both domestic and international levels, depending on the geographical spread of the retailer's outlets. Keeping track of product legislation may require the attention of a dedicated person (or team) such as a technologist. In 2001 the UK's Food Standards Agency launched a review of meaningless product descriptions, including words such as 'pure' and 'natural' that were used in both packaging and advertisements (*Marketing Week*, 2001).

NEW PRODUCT DEVELOPMENT

Product innovation is becoming increasingly necessary for retailers to keep customers interested in their product range. In a retail market that is saturated and competitive it is especially important to provide customers with the interest and excitement that newness engenders (Bruce and Biemans, 1995). New product development, however, is resource hungry and, with failure rates as high as 80 per cent (in the grocery sector), retailers need to manage the formulation, screening and launch of new products to the best of their ability (Stagg, Saunders and Wong, 2002). Some of the larger retailers have built a facility for product innovation in house. For fashion retailers it may be a design studio that produces sample garments using new fabrics and styling ideas. In a food retailer it may be a development kitchen that blends new combinations of ingredients for pre-prepared food products, while new packaging ideas are created in a graphic design department. For other products research, design and technology departments produce prototypes using the latest materials and technologies. Clearly, this type of operation carries considerable overhead costs, but without the facility, retailers are reliant on suppliers for new product development. Some suppliers see their competitive advantage lying in their innovative approach, but others are much less proactive and tend to follow product trends, saving costs. As the need grows to bring new products on to the market quickly, retail buyers have less time to devote to new product development, and so suppliers who are innovative will become increasingly sought after (see Chapter 5).

THE PRODUCT SELECTION PROCESS

Getting the right product, in terms of type and quality, might seem an easy task to the outsider, and for some products the powers of the individual may not be stretched too far in order to do so. For example, a product such as Kellogg's cornflakes has been around for a number of decades, it has a steady demand from a loyal customer base, the recipe does not change significantly, and so the decision to buy more of this product is much more concerned with the quantity required and the time of delivery than what the actual product itself is. On the other hand, it only takes a short walk around a European shopping centre in the last week of January to see examples of products that are the result of poor decision-making regarding type and quality, sitting in large quantities on shelves for the world to pick up and put down; products that will not shift, no matter how much the price has been reduced.

Making decisions about exactly what the product range should include, down to the minutest detail has always been the crux of a buyer's job. Whether the range is selected from a manu-facturer's range or developed in house, the final version that arrives in store is the responsibility of the buyer or selector. This chapter examines the procedures buyers go through in order to minimise those late January pile-ups. As mentioned in Chapter 2, many retail organisations break the buying task down so that one team of people is predominantly concerned with the qualitative aspects of a purchase (the selectors) and another team is predominantly concerned with the quantitative aspects (the merchandisers, or stock controllers). In other retailers, a category manager assumes the role of product selector. Vazquez and Bruce (2002) for example found that in food retailing, where packaging is an integral part of the product, design managers some-times work alongside buyers within the 'category team' in order to improve integration and the speed of the product development and selection process, whilst retaining design consistency. However, the term buyer will be used in this discussion because it is the most commonly used title for this operational task.

PRODUCT SELECTION CRITERIA

When making decisions about introducing a new product or brand or making changes to an existing product, to update it perhaps, a buyer has to consider a product in fine detail. Each individual criterion that bears upon the product's ability to satisfy a consumer has to be considered, as well as the totality of the features.

Physical properties

These are the tangible aspects of the product, represented by size, weight, and volume, and by the components or ingredients. They are likely to be critical in the appeal of the product (although not always in the immediate shelf appeal, in the case of packaged goods) and will have a direct bearing on the consumer's evaluation of the product. Some products need special properties in order to perform their required function, for example a quilt has to have the property of warmth, or 'tog value', in order to be of any use, and a raincoat has to be waterproof, whilst ice-cream needs to taste sweet and delicious. Getting the physical property correct may require the help of a product technologist, employed by the retailer or a supplier. The inclusion of physical properties that give increased customer value can be a way to encourage customers to use product benefit rather than price to guide their purchasing, for example, ultra-violet (UV) protection in children's clothing. Some physical properties may need to be avoided or minimised in order to provide an attractive product proposition. For example, in a response to growing health concerns food retailers and manufacturers are reducing salt content in processed food products (*Times* editorial, 26 February 2004; *Retail Bulletin*, 26 March 2004).

Packaging

For many products, it is the packaging that initially attracts a potential customer, and so the design of the package in which a product is enclosed is as important as the formulation of the product within. Packaging performs a variety of functions, including aesthetic appeal to customers, protection of the product, added value for the customer (for example, a container that can be used when empty), an aid to product use (such as a spray container), a contributor to brand identity and a vehicle for promotional messages.

Increasingly, packaging must also conform to company environmental policy and/or consumer expectations in the light of their personal environmental concerns. In addition, the design of a pack can be influenced by logistical requirements for space efficiency. For example, the boxes in which fruit juices are packaged have become increasingly tall and slim, so that more 'facings' of product can be squeezed onto supermarket shelves.

BOX 4.2 POSITIONING VIA PACKAGING

Innovative packaging can give a product a distinctive look, can win awards, giving unpaid-for communications advantage to a company, and can help to position in the premium price end of a product market. However, unusual or different packaging can cause a significant investment in new production techniques, headaches in the supply chain due to different handling requirements or crate sizing and runs the risk of adverse customer reaction. All of these things mean that the packaging of established products rarely changes radically.

Nevertheless, packaging can be an effective way of positioning a product. For example, different 'get-ups' are used by supermarkets to signify the differences between their budget lines, regular own-label and premium own-branded products (see Figure 4.3 Sainsbury's biscuits). When Cadbury decided to reposition confectionery brand Boost as an energy source for clubbers, not only did they add new ingredients glucose and guarana, but also the packaging was brightened using vivid citric shades and sparkles.

Source: *Grocer*, 31 August 2002; Wilson, 2002

Style

Product styling has always been relevant to clothes, accessories, and home furnishings, but increasingly style is finding its way into many product categories (see Box 4.3). Although difficult to define, the style of a product is generally dependent on the blend of shapes, colours and materials and has more to do with aesthetics than functionality in the product's design. For example, Apple broke the mould in computer styling when they launched the iMac; using colour and transparent materials, the product looked stylish and fun, whilst retaining top technical performance. Apple has continued to use a combination of design, ease of use and performance to differentiate their product offers (Dwek, 2002). Style is related to fashion and 'taste'; a fashion is a following of a trend in the style elements that are incorporated into a design, and the taste level is connected to the extent to which the design elements do or do not conform to established fashions. In addition, style may be manifested in the features that stimulate our sensory channels, for example the texture, smell, taste and sound of a product. The style of a product includes what Loosschilder and Schoormans (1995) refer to as 'abstract attributes', which are subject to substantial differences with respect to their recognition and perception by consumers and are therefore difficult to quantify.

Utility

A product's utility is concerned with how it performs in use. This will depend on how it is designed and produced. The following variables all bear upon the utility of a product: function; maintenance; durability; versatility; health and safety and environmental issues.

The number of functions and their operations will be important criteria, especially for labour saving appliances and other technical goods. For example, in the purchase of a food processor, the number of functions available may make one competitor's product superior to another. The extent to which a product needs to be maintained also influences its utility. The ease of cleaning and the need for servicing are both issues that consumers will be concerned about. Leather furniture, for example, needs to be accompanied by maintenance instructions, and after-sales service provision may be a key feature for technical goods like computers.

Durability, or how long a product lasts in use is another facet of utility. Toys, for example, need to be able to withstand considerable wear and tear, without collapsing in a heap of dangerous components. The number of uses that a product offers also contributes to utility; for example, a plain dark suit is a much more versatile garment than a vibrantly coloured dress; on the other hand, the dress may have more utility for special occasions. Health and safety considerations also impact on utility: if a product proves to be dangerous to customers in normal use, then it has no utility; and the extent to which a product supports environmental concerns may bear strongly upon utility for some customers. For example, a washing machine that uses less water and power may be the differentiating factor between one appliance and another for the environmentally concerned customer, rather than the number of functions that can be performed. Utility therefore is based on the physical properties and the design of the product, and has a close relationship to quality. Something that is made with high quality materials, and is manufactured to a high standard is more likely to be durable and to perform its functions well. However, utility, like style, is often subject to the motivations and interpretations of individuals. The ability to customise products according to individual requirements is an increasingly important trend in product design (see Box 4.3). The ubiquitous toy doll 'Barbie' can now have her skin shade, hair and eye colour customised according to the wishes of her owner.

BOX 4.3 WHITE GOODS?

The term 'white goods', which was once used for refrigerators, cookers, washing machines and smaller kitchen appliances has become something of a nonsense, since kitchen products are becoming widely available in chrome, and a variety of colours, including fashionable fluorescents. The boom in lifestyle and home improvement media interest has encouraged producers and retailers to add fashion and aspirational elements to their products, instead of focusing purely on the functional aspects. Zanussi, for example, offers over 4,500 different combinations of cooking system, tailoring oven size, hob layout, fuel type and colour finish to the requirements of individual customers. Functional elements are not being ignored, however; Samsung has developed a model of microwave that can read the bar code on a frozen meal and linking into the manufacturer's database, carries out the cooking instructions automatically.

Source: Porter, 2000

Product quality

Product quality is determined to a certain extent by its physical properties. However, the components or ingredients used may themselves be subject to physical variation that determines the level of quality. For example, a jumper may be made of 100 per cent wool, but the quality of the wool used may determine how soft and smooth the garment feels. The quality may also determine how long the garment lasts, which is an aspect of the product's utility, as discussed above. The raw materials and the production processes used therefore will have a direct influence on the overall quality level of the finished article. For some products, it is important to comply with a European, or international product standard in order to attain a specified level of performance or safety in use. These product standards have a numerical reference that denotes the particular performance level or safety level. Carrying the standard denotes compliance with this quality level.

Product quality is not just about performance. Customers are increasingly concerned from a social and ethical stance about what goes into a product and how it is made. For example, increasing numbers of consumers want reassurance that the ingredients in food products are grown without genetic modification or by organic farming methods. Likewise, there is increasing concern about the use of child labour and sweatshop conditions for production workers in manufacturing units around the world. As consumer requirements become increasingly sophisticated attention to this type of product criterion detail will increase and retailers will need to provide reassuring information about the product for the customers (see Box 13.1).

Product quality assurance

Achieving consistency in the level of quality in the product range is very important to retailers, in order to maintain customer trust and satisfaction. Although retailers do not usually have a direct influence on the quality of a product, because their role is normally buying and selling rather than manufacturing the product, it is such an important part of their own retail marketing strategy that they may feel it necessary to invest in a system of quality assurance to make sure that goods of inferior quality do not reach the customer. After all, a retailer can take all kinds of steps to gain redress from a manufacturer over faulty goods, but losing a customer, and damaging the retailer's image may be an irrevocable consequence. Quality assurance systems aim to maintain a consistent level of quality in the flow of goods, and quality control systems aim to halt the progress of faulty products in the supply chain.

A definition of quality is 'the whole set of features and characteristics of a product or service that are relevant to meeting requirements' (Baily *et al.*, 1998). The important notion regarding product quality, therefore, is having satisfactory outcomes; it is not an enduring battle to raise standards. In fact, the pursuit of a quality level that is higher than is necessary to satisfy customers has as many drawbacks as setting a quality level too low.

Some likely consequences of setting the quality level too low are:

- not all faulty products are detected;
- customers are faced with faulty products in store;
- customers may be lost for good;
- high level of complaint;.
- high level of returned merchandise;
- have to reduce price of merchandise to shift stock, or have to remove product from sale.

Likely consequences of setting the quality level too high are:

- production costs increase, resulting in higher prices to customers;
- too many products are rejected, resulting in low stock levels;
- only a limited number of suppliers may be capable of reaching the quality level, thereby reducing choice of potential suppliers for the retailer;
- high quality level may not be apparent or relevant to customers; another product feature may be more important to customers, for example, the fashion element.

One way that suppliers can reassure their retail customers regarding quality standards is by becoming registered for the Quality Management Standard (denoted by EN 29000 or ISO 9000). This standard assures retail customers that the supplier is implementing the necessary procedures within the organisation to be able to ensure that a consistent, agreed level of quality is produced. If this quality level is not maintained, then the buying organisation can sue the producing company. Theoretically, if a supplier is ISO 9000 registered the retailer does not need to implement any quality control measures themselves.

Quality control

Retailers using a supplier who does not have a quality assurance scheme may need to set up procedures of their own to prevent any faulty products reaching the customer. Quality control can take place at any point in the supply chain, and it may involve retailers' quality control personnel working closely with supplier's production technologists to resolve any problems. The usual places for quality control to occur are as follows.

- *Factory*: Goods may be inspected during production and / or when finished, at the production site. This has the advantage that any problems can be investigated immediately and (hopefully) resolved quickly.
- *Distribution centre*: Goods may be inspected on a random basis as they enter the warehouse. This is the final point at which faulty products can be detected in non-store retail formats.
- *Store*: Store personnel can be trained to watch out for faulty merchandise, especially if delivery is direct from supplier to store.

BOX 4.4 PRODUCT RECALLS

Product recalls are bad news for a retail product manager. Not only are they harmful from a customer relationship viewpoint, they also mean loss of sale for the category or department. Product recalls usually concern product safety, especially children's products, where a retailer can take no risks. Very often, products are recalled as a precaution rather than as a result of an unfortunate incident.

In October 2002 Ikea issued a national press release giving details of the product recall for 'Snuttig', a soft toy identified as a safety hazard for children. According to the press release Ikea know of no accident concerning the toy 'but the mere suspicion that it might occur is a good enough reason for us to recall Snuttig'. The problem revolved around a tendency for seams to split in the outer casing of the toy, exposing inner bags, which were of inferior quality and could have caused beads enclosed to spill out. The risk of a child inhaling a bead and choking made the product unsafe. Ikea had sold over one million Snuttig toys worldwide. While the product had been tested for safety initially, a quality problem was highlighted when a customer returned a broken toy and this prompted further testing. Ikea estimated that the problem would only be present in 2 per cent of the total quantity sold, but all products were recalled and customers were offered a different toy or a refund.

Ever the creative thinkers, an Ikea designer was once able to turn a quality problem into a product opportunity. A line of toys were halted in production when it became apparent that the eyes were in danger of falling off. Ikea were presented with a factory full of workers standing idle and piles of raw materials for the toys. An Ikea designer quickly developed a new product idea: 'Famnig' a cushion with arms. So an eyeless toy was transformed into a lovable soft cushion, proving popular with customers and the employees in the factory. In fact, Famnig sold so well that the factory had to take on more workers to keep pace with customer demand.

Source: Ikea web site

THE PRODUCT SPECIFICATION

A product specification is an important document in the quality control process as it provides the link between the end result of a buyer's negotiations with a supplier and the delivery of bulk purchases. It ensures that the goods that arrive in the retailer's outlet exactly match the buyer's requirements. The product specification is a detailed description of the product, and will include:

- relevant product coding information;
- labelling and packaging instructions;
- component materials;
- production method details;
- dimensions (with full size specification for alternative sizes);
- sketch or blueprint (a technical representation of the item).

In theory, a supplier should be able to make a product having read the specification, but of course a sample of the product to copy is preferable. If the product does not meet the specification, then a quality control problem arises, and needs to be resolved through action or negotiation (or both). Product specifications are particularly useful when a product has been developed exclusively for a retailer. Prior to delivery, negotiations may have revolved around a set of prototype samples. The specification will be a written summary of the final approval sample, which itself might be 'sealed' to indicate that approval. The sealed sample and the specification therefore become the 'standard' for quality control purposes.

Having an appreciation of the acceptable level of quality for a particular retail outlet is part of the understanding that a retailer's supply partners need to have of their customer's positioning (see Chapter 5 for further discussion on supplier relationships). As the level of understanding increases, the retail buyer will be able to depend on the supplier to use its own initiative when it comes to quality matters, and rely less on the role of documents and procedures to maintain quality levels. Many large retailers have a zero defect policy, which means that there is no tolerance of faulty goods within the supply chain. If a supplier is unable to maintain this commitment, it runs the risk of incurring financial penalty or being de-listed.

BRAND

Although the 'brand' is an intangible product feature, for some consumer purchase decisions it might be the only attribute that counts. For example, if a convenience store does not stock Nescafé instant coffee, one consumer may substitute tea or another beverage until s/he can shop for the brand elsewhere, whilst another consumer may happily switch brands to Kenco. The brand therefore can represent a product in its totality and it becomes a guarantee of the quality level expected as well as a recognition cue (Stagg, Saunders and Wong, 2002). In the case of manufacturer brands, the value (or equity) is built up by the supplying organisation rather than the retailer, whereas in own-label or retailer's own brands, the brand value is a complex blend of the product, and the consumer's relationship with the retailer, referred to by Davies (1993: 125) as the 'process brand'.

Other indications of quality level or guarantee of consumer satisfaction that might be applicable to products would include: a trademark, an industry certification (for example, a guild of craftsmen), approval by an association (for example, the soil association for organic produce) and a designer name. Celebrity-endorsed products are another way of communicating product quality. For example, Boots has developed Christmas gift products endorsed by TV chef Jamie Oliver and TV gardener Alan Titchmarsh, while homewares and gift multi-channel retailer Past Times has signed up Laurence Llewelyn-Bowen, the flamboyant presenter of TV home styling programme *Changing Rooms* to promote a special range called the 'Laurence Collection' (*RetailWeek*, 2003 and 2004, 10 September editorial). An interesting development is the use of restaurant brands in food products, which is again a type of endorsement of quality. Examples include Pizza Express, Bombay Brasserie and Mumtaz (see Figure 4.1).

RETAILER BRANDING

Retailer branding has grown in line with the increasing dominance of the multiple retailer and it has been one of the manifestations of the shift in power from the manufacturer to the retailer. By taking control of the product from idea conception (even if it is the idea to copy!) through product development to order specification, retailers have been able to sell keenly priced own-label (private label) versions of products, whilst retaining similar or improved profit margins. Once viewed by consumers with scepticism regarding quality, own-label products are now happily accepted as reasonable substitutes in many product categories (McGoldrick, 2002). Retail brands have been credited with the ability to build footfall and loyalty to retailers, whilst helping

Figure 4.1 *Restaurant branded products. The Bombay Brasserie Naan Bread represents the use of authentic products (each naan is made in the traditional hand method) and is available in Sainsbury's, Waitrose and Morrison's*

Source: Courtesy of PizzaExpress and Bombay Brasserie

to insulate against price competition (Dick *et al.*, 1996; Vazquez and Bruce, 2001), even though success in different categories can vary (Semeijn, Van Riel and Ambrosini, 2004).

Own-label products have penetrated deeper into some sectors of the retail market than others. In Europe, they are particularly prevalent in food and clothing sectors, and less important in the DIY and electrical sectors (Euromonitor, 1999). As a whole, the UK is the most retailer-branded dominated country, with around one-third of retail sales, whilst in the US own-label sales account for only around a fifth overall.

Managing a retailer's brand portfolio

Managing the brand portfolio is at the heart of many retailers' product strategy. Between the extremes of 100 per cent retailer branded (for example Gap or Marks & Spencer) and all supplier branded (which might be found in an independent electrical retailer for example) a retailer might use one or more of the following approaches to branding:

- *Exclusive brands*: Made exclusively for a retailer by a manufacturer, these products bear a brand that identifies neither party. Aldi, for example, uses this approach.
- *Own brands / house brands*: brands in their own right whose association with a retailer is clear, but not in high profile; for example, Sainsbury's Perform and Protect clothes-wash products, Boots No.7 cosmetics, or House of Fraser's Linea women's clothing range. Supermarket clothing ranges like Tesco's Cherokee and Asda's George would be included in the own-brand classification.
- *Own label*: Products that simply bear the retailer's name. They may have their own identity (Waitrose, for example, use a very individual own-label brand identity) or they may have an identity that mimics a brand leader.
- *Retailer sub-brand*: These carry the retailer's name, together with a sub-brand. The products

have a unique positioning, often indicated by distinctive packaging designs. For example Tesco's 'Finest' range of gourmet convenience foods have silver packaging and a flowing typeface, whereas their 'Value' sub-brand includes distinctive blue and white stripes, with a bold red typeface.

Extending the retail brand

A commitment to the retail brand in product management has a number of advantages in addition to the financial implications alluded to earlier. Retailers are able to control the brand's identity and image, innovate and target products to maximise market opportunities, and extend and contract the branded ranges as they see fit. They are also able to easily stretch a brand across product categories and sometimes even out of the traditional retail format. For example fashion retailer French Connection launched an FCUK (French Connection UK) branded flavoured vodka drink for sales in pubs, clubs and off-licence retailers (Hedberg, 2001) An example of cross-category branding is Sainsbury's Blue Parrot Café range which targets parents who wish to buy healthy and nutritious convenience foods for their children. The range covers many product categories including fresh and dried fruit, cereal bars, and fruit drinks. Similarly, Tesco's finest range has been stretched from its base in food items to cover wines and toiletries. Manufacturers' brands, however, bring prestige and strong positive consumer associations to the retailer's outlet and have the benefit of product development and marketing support that the retailer does not need to contribute towards. It makes sense therefore for a retail product manager to carefully consider the retailer-manufacturer brand balance within the product assortment, considering the product brand strategy and the overall corporate brand values.

CONCESSIONS

Concessions are a way of allowing a retailer to extend the product range offered within the outlet, without experiencing some of the risks associated with buying merchandise. The basis of a concession, which may be referred to as a 'shop-in-shop' is that a retailer allows a supplier of a particular brand of merchandise a designated amount of space within an outlet from which those goods are sold. The actual terms of the agreement will vary from retailer to retailer. In some agreements the supplier will provide staff to sell the merchandise, in others it is simply a matter of using dedicated fixturing. In some deals the retail product manager has to buy a minimum quantity of merchandise in order to secure the in-store promotional support (fixtures and point of sale material), whereas other concessions operate on a sale or return basis, which carries a lower risk for the retailer. The rewards that a retailer gains from using concessions also vary; for example, they might receive a flat rate 'rent' for the selling space, or they might receive a percentage of the sales income. If the agreement is based on the retailer actually purchasing the stock, then they will gain the full amount of sales income, but the profit margins may be lower than those on other merchandise. Usually the branded supplier will want to dictate the selling prices to the retailer in order to establish consistency with their other stockists (they may have their own retail outlets, for example).

Running concessions is a good way of supporting a strong brand, which may encourage customer traffic and therefore sales of other merchandise, but a retailer must ensure that the agreement that they have with the concessionaire is flexible enough to prevent valuable selling space being devoted to inappropriate merchandise. The brand must have an image that is consistent with the retailer's image and the other merchandise on offer. Concessions that work well have the potential to offer the retailer benefits of healthy supply partnerships, such as receiving priority treatment for re-orders and special orders, as well as joint marketing campaigns.

PRICE/VALUE AS A PRODUCT FEATURE

Although the price is a tangible feature of a product, the extent to which the price attached to a product represents value is, like the style and the brand, subject to different perceptions and interpretations by different customers. In the setting of a price, a retailer has to consider both the value perceptions of the consumer and the financial objectives of the business. Pricing is such an important part of product management that much of Chapter 12 is devoted to pricing decisions within the context of assessing product management performance.

MONITORING THE PRODUCT RANGE

Within the general appreciation of the long-term trends that affect the product classification that a buyer has responsibility for, the product range must be regularly reviewed in order to ensure that the range continues to offer the customer products of interest. The sales performances of the products within a range are usually monitored on a continual basis via an EPOS (electronic point of sale) system. Most sophisticated EPOS systems can now be integrated with a stock management system, which updates the stock position against sales. However, from the point of view of monitoring product performances EPOS systems need to be able to report on the sales of product groups at various levels in order to satisfy the needs of different managers within the retail organisation. Store managers or department managers will need reports that give category comparisons over time and between similar outlets. Product managers in the buying office will be interested in reports that show individual product item performances over time of the products in the ranges they are responsible for so that trends can be spotted. They will be less interested in store performances, but may be interested in reports that combine sales of product lines in similar outlets. In this way they may be able to make better decisions on the ranges according to outlet profile. EPOS systems that are incorporated into a fully integrated information management system within a retail organisation will be able to report not only on the sales performance of products, but also the profitability of the product and how, for example, those performances relate to the amount of space allocated to the product.

THE PRODUCT RANGE REVIEW

As well as the continual monitoring of product performance outlined above, most retailers carry out formal, in-depth range reviews on a regular basis to fully evaluate the performance of products and decide upon any necessary remedial action. This may result in some products being deleted, or the identification of the need for a product amendment. Gaps in the range may also be established, providing opportunities for new products. The range review will consider both quantitative and qualitative aspects of a product's performance. Figure 4.2 illustrates the likely inputs into a range review and the kind of decisions that are made during the review.

The range review is an all-encompassing, detailed discussion of the performance of a range of products; therefore, issues such as supplier performance, promotions and in-store merchandising have to be considered alongside issues which are directly to do with the physical product (such as sales reports, returns figures and quality reports). The range review is an opportunity for those who are concerned with managing a product's performance to combine their expertise. The formal gathering of such a committee ensures that all viewpoints are covered and the outcomes are supported collectively. Range reviews may be carried out on a monthly or biannual basis, although more frequent reviews may take place if, for example, a product range is new, or has fluctuating sales patterns. Reviews may also vary in terms of the width of product range considered, from a sub-category to the complete assortment.

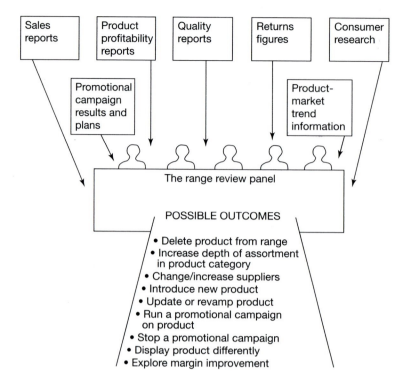

Figure 4.2 *The range review*

TRACKING PRODUCT/MARKET TRENDS

In order to ensure that product/market trends do not go undetected, or their effect on the product management process ignored, a retailer may instigate some form of auditing or tracking process. In many instances the information gathering process is ongoing and informal. In other instances information may be formally gathered and used as an input into the range review. The following stages should be included in this process whether or not the process is formalised.

Stage 1   Consumer trend analysis

This involves the identification of changes over time that allow predictions to be made about future product preferences. It will include analysis of demographic, economic, societal, technological, lifestyle and fashion trends. Information will be used from a variety of sources, including both internal records and external agencies.

Stage 2   Product sector analysis

In this stage of the analysis, the changes identified above should be interpreted into specific predictions with regard to the product category in question. The action of competitors should also be taken into account: for example, is a competitor likely to be proactive or reactive in response to a product market opportunity or threat? Information gained from suppliers, with regard to new product innovations in particular, may be useful in this process.

Stage 3   Catchment area analysis

The previous stages may reveal changes that will happen at different times in the markets that the retailer serves, or their effect may be restricted to specific geographic locations. At this stage therefore, the consumer trends and the product sector changes must be interpreted at the local level, taking catchment area, store size and store format into consideration. Information can be gleaned from marketing database agencies and existing store comparisons.

Stage 4   Product range analysis

Here, the current product range is reviewed in the light of the preceding set of analyses, and decisions regarding new product category additions, category extensions and product deletions are made. Internal performance data will be scanned to show evidence of emerging sales trends. Retailers who have the benefit of both EPOS data and customer data (generated by a loyalty card programme) can make this type of decision at store, rather than company level, using geodemographic profiles of store customers and store sales patterns (McElhatton, 2003).

SUMMARY

In a crowded retail marketplace, having the best product range for your target customer is still one of the most effective ways of achieving competitive advantage. Developing and selecting the right products involves keeping a track on customers' preferences, anticipating demand for new products and ensuring that each product lives up to customers' expectations in all its various features and attributes. Reviewing the product range on a regular basis will ensure that the offer continues to interest and satisfy the experienced and discerning shopper.

EXERCISE   RETAILER BRANDING

J Sainsbury's is one of the UK's leading supermarket retailers with stores spread across the country. With a long history in grocery retailing, Sainsbury's is known for its range of high quality products. At the same time, Sainsbury's has a diverse customer base, and so the company needs to remain competitive on price with other supermarkets in this increasingly aggressive retail market sector. Sainsbury's own brand is the most important part of the product offer; throughout the company's history, the Sainsbury brand has been synonymous with good quality, well-presented products, with between 50 and 60 per cent of the range being sold under the various versions of Sainsbury's brand. The photographs in Figure 4.3 show the extent of retailer branding within the boundaries of Sainsbury's biscuit category.

Exercise questions

1   Describe the type(s) of retailer branding that Sainsbury's is using within its biscuit category.
2   What is the purpose of using a variety of retailer brands within a product assortment?
3   Analyse the packaging of the products shown in Figure 4.3 and explain how and what the packaging is communicating to potential customers.
4   Consider where the biscuit category is in its lifecycle and bearing the photographed products in mind, discuss the implications of the lifecycle stage for product management.

5   For each of the products shown in the photographs, provide a list of product criteria that will have
     been considered in the development and selection process for the biscuits. Present your list in order
     of priority for each product item.

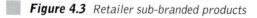

Figure 4.3 *Retailer sub-branded products*

QUESTIONS

1   Outline the various approaches to retailer-controlled branding. Why is there so much variation in retailer-branding strategies?

2   Describe how branded goods provide a quality assurance to retail buyers. What steps can a retailer take to assure quality in their own-branded products?

3   Examine the role of the range review within the product management process.

4   Choose a product item, and discuss the consumer trends that have influenced the demand for that product. Also, consider whether consumer trends have influenced any part of the product's presentation, for example packaging, product formulation, marketing communications about the product, or method of selling.

5   Find four products that you consider to be in the different stages of their category lifecycle. Justify your findings.

6   For a product of your choice, examine the product selection criteria that would be important in its selection process.

7   Discuss the following terms in relation to products: utility, style, fashion, customisation, ethical.

REFERENCES AND FURTHER READING

Amine, A. and Sandrine, C. (2003) 'Efficient Retailer Assortment: A Consumer Choice Evaluation Perspective', *International Journal of Retail and Distribution Management*, 31(10): 486–497.

Baily, P., Farmer, D., Jessop, D. and Jones, D. (1998) *Purchasing Principles and Management*, 8th edn, Pearson Education, Harlow.

Baker, M.J. (2000) *Marketing Strategy and Management*, Macmillan, London.

Brassington, F. and Pettitt, S. (2000) *Principles of Marketing*, Pearson Education, Harlow.

Bruce, M. and Biemans, W.G. (1995) *Product Development: Meeting the Challenge of the Design–Marketing Interface*, Wiley, Chichester.

Buttle, F. (1993) 'Jaeger Ladies', in P.J. McGoldrick (ed.), *Cases in Retailing Management*, Pitman, London.

Clements, A. (2000a) 'Zara Leads Conquering Armada', *Retail Week*, 14 April.

Clements, A. (2000b) 'Can't Cook? Don't Bother', *Retail Week*, 21 April.

Craven, N. (2003) 'Retailers Must Innovate to Keep Customer Happy', *Retail Week*, 1 August.

Davies, G. (1993) *Trade Marketing Strategy*, Paul Chapman, London.

Dick, A., Jain, A. and Richardson, P. (1996) 'How Consumers Evaluate Store Brands', *Journal of Product and Brand Management*, 5(2): 19–28.

Dwek, R. (2002) 'Apple Pushes Design to the Core of Marketing', *Marketing Week*, 24 January.

Euromonitor (1999) *Private Label in Europe Report*, March.

Gilmore, J.H. and Pine, B.J. (1997) 'Four Faces of Mass Customization', *Harvard Business Review*, 75(1): 91–102.

Griffith, D. (2003) 'Intimacy, Rites of Passage and Social Support: Symbolic Meaning from Lifetime Shopping Experiences', *The International Review of Retail, Distribution and Consumer Research*, 13(3): 263–278.

Grocer (2002) 'Boost for Flagging Clubbers', 31 August.

Hedberg, A. (2001) 'FCUK Plans Brand Extension Foray into Alcoholic Drinks', *Marketing Week*, 4 October.

Hiscock, J. (2003) 'Most Trusted Brands 2003', *Marketing*, 1 May.

Loosschilder, G.H. and Schoormans, J.P.L. (1995) 'A Means–End Chain Approach to Concept Testing', in Bruce and Biemans (eds).

Marketing Week (2001) 2 August.

Maslow, A.H. (1970) *Motivation and Personality*, Harper & Row, New York.

McGoldrick, P.J. (2002) *Retail Marketing*, McGraw Hill, Maidenhead.

McElhatton, N. (2003) 'Next Generation EPOS', *Marketing*, 11 September.

Miles, S., Anderson, A. and Meethan, K. (2002) *The Changing Consumer*, Routledge, London.

Mintel (1999) *Children's Clothing Retailing Report*, Mintel International Group, London.

Mintel (2000) *British Lifestyles Report*, Mintel International Group, London.

Mintel (2004) *Ready to Cook Foods, UK Report*, Mintel International Group, London.

Pellegrini, L. (1993) 'Retailer Brands: A State of the Art Review', *Conference Proceedings of the 7th International Conference on Research in the Distributive Trades*, Institute for Retail Studies, University of Stirling, September, pp. 348–363.

Porter, J. (2000) 'White Heat', *Retail Week*, 25 February.

Rafiq, M. and Collins, R. (1996) 'Lookalikes and Customer Confusion in the Grocery Sector: An Exploratory Survey', *International Review of Retail, Distribution and Consumer Research*, 6(4): 329–350.

Semeijn, J., van Riel, A.C.R. and Ambrosini, A.B. (2004) 'Consumer Evaluations of Store Brands: Effects of Store Image and Product Attributes', *Journal of Retailing and Consumer Services*, 11(4): 247–258.

Singh, S. (2003) 'It's Healthy – If You're Wealthy', *Marketing Week*, 6 March.

Stagg, C., Saunders, J. and Wong, V. (2002) 'Go/No-Go Criteria during Grocery Brand Development', *Journal of Product and Brand Management*, 11(7): 459–482.

Tauber, E.M. (1972) 'Why Do People Shop?', *Journal of Marketing*, 36(4): 46–49.

Vazquez, D. and Bruce, M. (2001) 'Design Management: The Unexplained Retail Marketing Competence', *International Journal of Retail and Distribution Management*, 30(6): 323–330.

Wills, J. (1999) *Merchandising and Buying Strategies: New Roles for a Global Operation*, Financial Times Retail and Consumer Report, London.

Wilson, R. (2002) 'Perfect Packaging' *Marketing Week*, 13 June.

Web sites

Ikea: http://www.ikea.co.uk

Ikea: http://www.ikea.co.uk/about_ikea/press-room/press-release-mat.asp?pr_id=717, accessed 28/01/03.

International Organisation for Standardization: www.iso.org.en

Retail Bulletin (2004) http://www.theretailbulletin.co.uk, accessed 26/2/04

Chapter 5

Managing the supply base

LEARNING OBJECTIVES

The purpose of this chapter is to:

- Introduce the different types of suppliers that retailers might use to source products and understand the ways these suppliers can be accessed.
- Explore the various factors that are assessed by retailers when selecting, evaluating and monitoring suppliers.
- Develop an overview of the way relationships between suppliers and retailers tend to develop over time, and understand how this can affect the way retailers and suppliers work together.
- Understand the notion of a supply partnership and what this entails for retailers and their suppliers.
- To understand how the supply base can help a retailer to achieve its product management objectives.

INTRODUCTION

Most retail businesses do not manufacture the goods that are sold through their outlets. Outside supply sources, as the producers of the product range, are the mainstay of most retailers' success. The main aim of this chapter is to consider how a retailer's supply base is managed. Access to a wide supply base that delivers products at an acceptable level of quality, on time and in the right quantities goes a long way towards achieving a retailer's product management objectives, and stocking products from sources of supply which have particular relevance and interest for the final consumer in terms of brand recognition or product expertise, can be a source of competitive advantage.

TYPES OF SUPPLIER

There are a number of different alternatives that retailers might consider to be suitable sources of supply. The choice will depend on factors that are principally associated with the size of the purchasing retail company. For example, a large multiple retailer such as Sainsbury's will require huge quantities of mainstream products such as Heinz tomato ketchup to be delivered on a regular basis and so suppliers must have sufficient production capacity to satisfy the order level required by the retailer. Heinz, on the other hand, would not be interested in supplying a local convenience store with their weekly order of one dozen bottles of ketchup directly, so these products have to be obtained by small retailers via a wholesaler. The challenge for both retailers and producers is to find a suitable match between supply source and distribution channel.

Power

Many studies of the relationships between retailer and suppliers have been based around the concept of distribution channel power and control (Stern and El Ansary, 1988). The assumption is that the greater the market share of an intermediary or producer, the greater the power of that channel member and therefore the more control they have over the exchanges that take place within that distribution channel. The rise of retail power through the process of market concentration and increased own-label product development has been well documented in both trade and academic sources (for example, Harris and Ogbonna, 2001; Thomas, 2003). This power, combined with the more recent phenomenon of the category champions (see Chapter 3), is polarising consumer goods markets into a combination of power retailer–supplier partnership emporiums and regional specialists, with the medium sized business finding it more and more difficult to offer meaningful retail experiences in between.

Market share, however, is not the only determinant of power in the distribution channel. Strong brands are also able to exert considerable influence over retailers' supply selection strategies irrespective of the retailer's market ranking. The strength of a brand's appeal to consumers may override other product selection criteria, such as quality or price, and so the retailer effectively has no choice in terms of supply source other than to deal with the branded goods manufacturer or a distributor for that brand. In mail order catalogues, for example, a brand such as Levi's might be allocated one whole page for their denim products, but the final product selection is left to the supplier rather than the retailer.

Manufacturers

Large retailers frequently deal directly with a product manufacturer. That manufacturer may own one or more production units, which in turn could be geographically spread on a national or international basis. Manufacturers will normally have a sales office or a showroom, either attached to a production unit, or in a location that is convenient for the retail customers. From the sales base the liaison between retail buying and merchandising teams and the supplier's sales and product development teams can take place. Even in today's world of e-commerce, close physical proximity can help a supplier to achieve a higher sales service level, which can be a source of competitive advantage.

Retailers who deal directly with manufacturers are likely to be placing orders that are so large that they could be considered to be booking production space as opposed to ordering items; therefore, most direct buying is restricted to multiple and mail order retailers. A small retail concern may be able to buy directly from a small manufacturing concern, but is likely to use indirect sources of supply, such as an agent, or wholesaler when ordering goods from large producers. The growth of the multiple retailers has largely contributed to the contraction of the wholesaling industry throughout Europe, especially in the food and clothing sectors.

Agents

An agent acts as a selling intermediary for a product manufacturer. By collating orders from smaller retail organisations through a network of agents, a manufacturing concern is able to efficiently supply a large number of smaller customers. Together, their orders make up quantities that are economical to produce. Agents are likely to work from a sales office/showroom that is located as conveniently as possible to the retail customers. They usually work on a commission basis and may represent more than one producer. Agents are particularly useful for retailers in the early stages of global sourcing.

Wholesalers and distributors

Wholesalers and distributors work in a similar way to agents, in that they will accept small orders from retail customers. The difference is that wholesalers actually take ownership of the goods between the producer and the retailer. They therefore supply the retailer from their stock as opposed to the producer's stock, as in the case of the agent. They will apply a profit margin to the products they sell to the retailer, usually determined by themselves, rather than the producer. There are advantages and disadvantages associated with the use of intermediaries such as wholesalers or distributors. A key advantage is that the retailer can buy goods in small quantities, thereby reducing the financial investment in stock. Additionally, by purchasing small quantities frequently, the retailer uses less space for storage, allowing them conversion of as much of their premises as possible to selling space. Intermediaries allow small retailers access to leading brands and an increased selection of suppliers. Small retailers would not have the resources to search out these suppliers, nor would their individual orders be worthwhile for the larger manufacturer to supply. The main disadvantage is that the retailer has to pay the wholesaler's profit margin on top of the cost price for the product. Cutting out intermediaries allow large retailers to sell at lower prices whilst generating the same profit margins for themselves. Another disadvantage is that intermediaries are not normally able to guarantee exclusivity, apart from perhaps on a very small geographic scale.

BOX 5.1 THE EROSION OF THE WHOLESALE MARKET: A MAJOR THREAT TO THE SMALL INDEPENDENT RETAILER

Holmetown Post Office is a small independent retail concern, selling convenience and basic grocery products to a small catchment area. Their product offer includes a selection of fresh fruit and vegetables. Five years ago, James, the proprietor of Holmetown Post Office had a choice of three wholesale fruit and vegetable suppliers in the nearby city. Now there is only one wholesaler trading. Up until last year, this wholesaler delivered fresh produce on a daily basis, but now they consider it uneconomical to deliver daily and have cut the round to three times per week. James is pleased that the best wholesaler has remained in business, but he feels they can now dictate terms, as they have no competition, which is not in his interest. He also has to take more risks in terms of ordering quantities, and has to find the space for the extra produce to cover an additional day's supply. This is not easy when the total selling area amounts to 180 square metres.

The demise of wholesale markets is generally attributed to the growth of the large supermarket groups. These retailers deal directly with producers, who then become dependent on them for their livelihood. The small and medium sized retailers who cannot compete on price with the larger retail concerns go out of business, making the role of the wholesaler redundant.

'Grey market' sourcing

This term refers to the practice undertaken by retailers to obtain branded merchandise from traders who do not have a 'licence' awarded by a manufacturer to sell their goods. The legal issues associated with this type of sourcing are complex, but 'grey' goods have been sold in reputable retailers like Tesco and Asda, who effectively have challenged the legality of having to have a 'licence' to sell consumer goods like clothing and toiletries. One of the problems with dealing in grey goods however is guaranteeing the authenticity of the product.

Alliances and concessions

It is quite common for more general retailers, such as department stores or supermarkets, to use the expertise of a specialist retailer or manufacturer to add value to a product selection (as indicated in Chapter 2). The arrangement for this offer might be on the basis of a concession (shop within a shop), an alliance or products supplied on a sale or return basis. A concession is best described as a business within a business, or a shop-within-shop. A set area, or a pre-determined amount of space is devoted to a specific range of products, the supply of which is controlled by an entity other than the host retailer. The concessionaire pays the host on the basis of a fixed rental rate, or as a percentage of sales, and may provide their own staff to sell the products. Whatever the financial arrangement is, the marketing aim is to boost the appeal of the host retailer's product range with products supplied by another brand. Examples of retailer–retailer product range alliances include Sainsbury's links with Early Learning Centre (toys) and Adams (children's clothing). Alliances like these can enable a host retailer to enter a new product market, by devoting store space to a product specialist retailer, while they build up their own product expertise. For the specialist retailer, the alliance gives them a new channel to reach large numbers of new customers.

THE SUPPLIER SEARCH

How does a retail organisation find suitable suppliers? The likely answer to this question from many retail buyers would be 'not very easily', but the problem is not so much about the lack of suppliers in the market, but about finding the right kind of supplier. The search for good suppliers is therefore an important and ongoing task for retail product managers and is likely to fall within the remit of the buyers or sourcing managers, who have the best product and market knowledge.

In reality, retail buyers find that it is the suppliers that seek them out most of the time. Suppliers consider retail buyers notoriously difficult to reach, but it is generally acknowledged that taking a complacent approach to the supply base is dangerous. If retail buyers are not up to date and expertly informed about the supply possibilities in their product field, then they are not performing their role as organisational buyer adequately. An innovative supply source rejected by a busy retail buyer could become the next source of competitive advantage for the competition. It is frequently the task of an assistant buyer to make the initial assessment of a supplier's suitability for a retail business. Many multiple retailers source on a global basis; therefore, the supplier search can involve extensive travel to producing areas of the world. Dealing through agents or buying groups is a way of accessing a wider supply market (see Chapter 2 for a discussion on buying groups).

Global sourcing

Direct sourcing of products from around the world requires considerable expertise and resource expenditure, so it is only worthwhile if large volumes of product can be bought at much lower prices than would be available from local suppliers. However, there may be reasons other than costing constraints that prompt retailers to source from the global market. Some products are indigenous to certain countries, and therefore have been sourced abroad for centuries. Coffee, bananas and spices are examples of this type of product. Unique products may only be available in some countries, such as handcrafted items, which use a combination of raw materials and skills that are only available commercially from low production cost countries. Finally, certain branded items may only be available from an overseas source. Global sourcing usually requires retail buyers to make a trade-off between more variety in the supply base and longer lead times. Domestic suppliers may not be able to offer the lower costs and product diversity of a global supply base, but they should be able to respond more quickly to changes in consumer demand.

Of course, items from a variety of international sources are available through agents and wholesalers, but if a retailer is hoping to develop their own exclusive products from an overseas source, there may be little alternative to getting onto a plane with a bankers draft. Anita Roddick, founder of the Body Shop, has been famous for her trips around remote parts of the globe in the search for unique body care product ingredients. Her travels have resulted in a highly differentiated product range, in-store promotional product information opportunities, and extensive press coverage of her endeavours to establish trading links with developing countries.

BOX 5.2 NATIONAL RETAILERS RETURN TO LOCAL PRODUCE

One of the criticisms of the centralised buying of the large multiple retailers is that they tend to be national rather than local when it comes to making product selections. Can a buyer in a retailer's UK head office know the beer or cheese preference of customers in stores dispersed as widely as Cornwall in the south-west and Inverness in the north? It is much simpler to look at national product market reports and plan the product ranges according to those brand shares. Centralised decisions and distribution provide a retailer with opportunities to cut costs and build powerful relationships with market-leading suppliers.

Customers, however, become very attached to brands, and can have strong allegiances to those that can only be found in a restricted region of the country. Consumers increasingly are looking for variety and uniqueness, product features often found in products made by small, local companies. Regional products, therefore, are being viewed less as an inconvenience to centralised assortment planning and more as an opportunity for a differentiated and value-added product selection for the consumer.

Initiatives like Tesco's 'Locally Grown' label indicate not only the country of origin, but the region and sometimes even the farm where the produce is grown. Asda has a similar 'Local Choice' label, which is based on a network supply chain scheme, where orders are placed to local suppliers through a main regional supplier who consolidates deliveries and transports them to Asda stores. Asda define a local product as 'those that are made locally, grown locally and reared locally; are a local taste or delicacy and recognized by customers as local; and for which there is significant customer demand' (ASDA.co.uk 2004).

An example of a successful local product range being sold in major supermarkets is 'Cegin Cymreig' ('Welsh Kitchen') ready meals. These products comprise Welsh ingredients and packaging sources and reflect local tastes. Variations include Chicken Cymru (Welsh chicken) and Cawl Mamgu (Granny's broth).

One of the problems for smaller local suppliers is coping with the demands of large sophisticated retail organisations with their strict procedures and standards. However, the supermarkets themselves, in conjunction with government agencies are providing supplier development programmes which help to gear suppliers to the 'supermarket challenge'. Abdy (2001) summarised arguments for and obstacles to local sourcing. Arguments for local sourcing:

- fresher food, has not been in the supply chain for long;
- product diversity and niche products;
- variety and interest in product categories;
- linking local consumers and producers;
- reduction in food miles (positive environmental effect);
- support for local economies.

Obstacles to local sourcing:

- quality control can be difficult to achieve;
- consistency of supply (which can be seasonal and risky);
- inability of suppliers to comply with requirements of the supply chain (which are geared up to larger suppliers).

Source: Abdy, 2001; Welsh Development Agency web site, accessed 02/09/04

In an apparent contradiction to the trend towards a more widespread search for suppliers, retail suppliers, whether they are wholesalers, agents, or the sales force of a direct supplier, are frequently geographically concentrated. This provides convenience and efficiency for the retail buyers, and a higher density of retail buyers are attracted by the critical mass of supply sources in one area. The wholesale market at New Covent Garden in the UK is a well-known example of this concentration of retail supply, whilst the showrooms of many of the retail clothing suppliers are located in the area north of Oxford Street in London's West End (the 'rag trade' area). In the US, 'market weeks' take place twice a year in Los Angeles and New York, which provides geographical and time concentration for both retailers and suppliers. The retailers know that the suppliers will have their full ranges of the latest products on show, and the suppliers are able to gain scale efficiencies by taking a large proportion of their orders at one time. Ultimately, geographical clusters of suppliers bring efficiencies which make the end product cheaper for the final consumer and provide the necessary means of distributing products to a wider customer base.

Trade shows

A trade show is an organised gathering of suppliers, who present samples of the products they are able to supply to retailers and take orders against those samples for supply at some stage in the future. Trade shows are organised on a product specific basis, and are usually held in a purpose built exhibition hall, such as the National Exhibition Centre, in Birmingham, UK (see Box 5.3).

BOX 5.3 THE LONDON INTERNATIONAL WINE AND SPIRITS FAIR

The aim of the London International Wine and Spirits Fair, which is held annually in the capital city, is to bring buyers and producers together in a single time and place. According to its organisers, the show provides 'a time-efficient means of seeing the entire world's wine producers'. With around 500 exhibitors and 15,500 visitors, the LIWSF allows key trade people to get together and discuss maximising opportunities in a fast moving and innovative product category.

Source: *Grocer*, 26 April 2003

Literature

The busy environment of the buying office is not exactly conducive to reading, but retail product management personnel make time to read relevant trade journals, and peruse any product catalogues that may be sent into the buying office. These secondary sources may therefore provide more supplier information for the buyer.

THE CHOICE OF SUPPLIER

In the traditional model of the buying process, shown in Chapter 2, the stage following the supplier search is the selection of the supplier. Having made the initial contact by way of an interview, or perhaps by meeting at a trade show, the retail buyer then has to assess a supplier's suitability to his or her company's needs. A product sample may appear very attractive in a showroom, but a retailer needs to be assured that the product will look as attractive to its customers when the product is on display in the store, or when the product reaches a consumer's home. Normally, a retailer will put a supplier through a number of assessment stages in order to appraise its suitability and will evaluate and monitor its performance.

Initial selection factors

A supplier's initial assessment will be made according to its ability to satisfy a retailer in four main areas. Table 5.1 shows a range of supplier assessment criteria, together with the kind of indicators that would determine the likelihood of a supplier meeting these criteria.

Much of this appraisal is really only possible once a supplier is 'live' and actually fulfilling an order. It makes sense therefore to begin a relationship with a supplier by conducting a low risk trial in the form of a small order or an order of a basic item that the retailer may already be sourcing from a number of existing suppliers. Before embarking on a trial order the retailer may take further steps to appraise a supplier. This might include: taking references from other retail customers (not always feasible due to competitive constraints); taking references from the supplier's sources of raw materials; conducting an analysis of the supplier's current customer list;

Table 5.1 *Supplier assessment criteria*

Criteria	Indicators
Product range and technical quality: The variety of products available, the quality standard achievable, the quality standard for the price, and the ability of the supplier to assure product quality (see Chapter 4)	Technical capability of machinery and workforce training, production specialisation and flexibility, access to raw materials, design capability, quality assurance procedures, nil defect delivery, ethical and socially responsible working practices and sourcing policy, accreditation by third party quality assessor
Price: The value of the product for the price, the discounts available for large quantities and for rapid payment, the profit margin envisaged on the product	Scale economies, experience effects, low cost raw materials and components, financial stability, willingness to negotiate, viability of cost structure and business plan
Delivery: The ability of the supplier to deliver according to the retailer's specification in terms of timing, quantities, and product variety	Capacity, minimum order quantities, production location, lead times (for initial and repeat orders), willingness and ability to collaborate on consumer-led response initiative (see Chapter 3), workforce stability, and the extent to which the supplier is involved with other retailers
Service: This could refer to a number of ways in which a supplier adds value through service to their retail customers; it would include both before- and after-sales service	Innovation, speed of new product introduction, sampling service, marketing support, handling of queries and complaints, exclusivity deals (regional or national)
General qualitative supplier assessment: In response to consumer's concerns about ethical and environmental issues that surround product sourcing and production, retailers are placing increased pressure on suppliers to conform to a variety of qualitative assessment criteria that relate to the general running of a supplier's business rather than specific products	Risk assessment and environmental assessment of production processes, staffing policy, training and development opportunities (e.g. 'Investors in People' award), ethical and socially responsible working practices and sourcing policy, willingness and ability to sign up to a retailer's code of practice

visiting the production units where the goods will be made; and inspecting and testing samples of products from the production line. Suppliers may have specific expertise, and therefore offer value for the production of part of a range whilst being inappropriate for others. For example, the machinery needed to sew fine fabrics for blouses and shirts would not be suitable for the production of heavy jeans.

In a multiple retailer a technologist is likely to become involved with the supplier appraisal, in order to assess the capabilities of the machinery and processes, to predict the likely product quality outcome. A small retailer may not have the resources to inspect a supplier in this way; therefore, a small trial order could be the most cost-effective method of assessing supplier suitability. A retailer does not generally pay for goods until they have been received and inspected, so no immediate financial loss is incurred if the goods have to be returned to the manufacturer.

Out-sourcing supplier assessment

Some large retail organisations contract out their supplier assessment monitoring to third parties. Here, the retailer engages the services of a third party specialist organisation that takes on the responsibility for checking, assessing and accrediting suitable suppliers according to the retailer's requirements. The accreditation usually involves quality checks which assess not only the supplier's machinery and technical capability, but also that the factory is able to follow a code of conduct and reach acceptable ethical standards. Once a factory is accredited it can be used to supply any relevant buying department within a retailer's organisation, and will be quality audited on a regular basis by the quality control organisation. The release of in-house technologist resources in the retailer enables a greater emphasis to be placed on product costing and price point engineering in the early stages of product development.

SUPPLIER DEVELOPMENT

Multiple retailers who produce product ranges under their own labels or brands will be interested in assessing a supplier's ability to be 'developed'. Most retailers will have a supply base that includes suppliers at different stages of development within their portfolio. Some will be relatively new, undergoing trial orders. Others will have completed their trial orders successfully and the volume of their orders will be increasing, or they might be being asked to supply a greater variety of product for the retailer. Other suppliers will be very well established, perhaps having grown with the retail business, and may be supplying a wide variety of products to many different buying departments. Table 5.2 illustrates the concept of a portfolio of different types of supplier in terms of their relationship with a retailer. Suppliers that fall into the top two categories, the core suppliers and supply partners, are sometimes referred to as 'preferred suppliers' as they would be the first choice for a retailer to place orders with; they are likely to have established accreditation for their processing methods and so less risk is involved when using them.

Table 5.2 *A portfolio of supplier relationships*

Supplier	Relationship
Core suppliers	Use on regular basis for specific skills Increasing business according to competence
Supply partners	Ongoing supply Shared strategic objectives Operational adaptations
New/intermittent suppliers	Emerging product markets Occasional purchase requirement (seasonal) Fads
Inactive suppliers	Dormant De-listed Emergency supply

SUPPLIER EVALUATION AND MONITORING

If a supplier has been dealing with a retailer for a long time, it can be assumed that they are reaching a high level of satisfaction with the retailer on the main assessment criteria of product quality, price, delivery and service. However, suppliers to major retailers are subjected to continual monitoring or regular evaluation to ensure that their standards do not fall. The buying department may carry out this analysis or it may be the task of a separate department or third party who are responsible for supply chain management. The most common method of supplier evaluation is the weighted multi-attribute evaluation system. Box 5.4 shows how this system of supplier evaluation works.

BOX 5.4 SUPPLIER EVALUATION: THE MULTI-ATTRIBUTE RATING SYSTEM

Suppliers to be evaluated: A, B and C

Supplier evaluation criteria to be used:

	Importance weighting (out of 10)
Innovative products	8
Short lead times	7
On time delivery	9
Nil defect delivery	9
Low prices	8

Marks (out of 10) for each supplier are given on the above criteria:

	A	B	C
Innovative products	5	7	9
Short lead times	6	7	9
On time delivery	9	5	7
Nil defect delivery	8	6	7
Low prices	7	8	7

	A	B	C
Composite ratings: (Multiply criteria weighting by individual score)	291	268	317

Result:
Supplier C has the highest evaluation and supplier B has the lowest evaluation.

Suppliers who do not achieve the required level of evaluation are likely to be subjected to financial penalty, or reduced orders in the future.

Supplier monitoring

Rather than taking a one-off evaluation, many retailers monitor their suppliers on a continuous basis. The supplier's performance is rated as a percentage on a set of performance indicators. If the percentage starts to fall a significant way below 100 per cent, remedial steps need to be taken by the supplier, otherwise penalties will be incurred, as described above. Performance indicators may encompass all the main evaluation criteria shown in Table 5.1.

The evaluation of a supplier's performance does not stop at the point where the product is delivered to the retailer's premises, whether that is at a distribution centre or at a store. A supplier is also evaluated according to the sell-through rate of the product. This refers to how quickly a product sells, how much volume is generated in a time period and how much of that volume is sold at full price. These factors have a direct relationship to the ability of a product to generate profit, and the more profits generated for the retailer from a particular supplier's product range, the more favourable the product manager will be towards that supplier in the future. The volume and value of returned goods, whether they are faulty or not, may also be used in the evaluation of suppliers. This is especially relevant to non-store retailing.

RETAILER–SUPPLIER RELATIONSHIP DEVELOPMENT

Most transactions that a retail buyer makes are not carried out with a new supplier. The majority of the transactions will be carried out within the framework of an ongoing business relationship between a retail organisation and a supply organisation. This reality causes problems when attempting to equate what actually is normal practice in the buying office with the traditional buying process theory outlined in Chapter 2. Very often it will be a supplier who makes a new product suggestion or who comes up with a product improvement; suppliers who wait passively to be found by a searching buyer will probably wait forever! This lack of emphasis on the influence that the supplying firm could have on the way in which organisational buyers actually behave, prompted a group of researchers in the early 1980s to revisit the buying process. The resulting interaction model (IMP Group, 1982) of organisational buying behaviour is adapted to the retail buying situation in Figure 5.1.

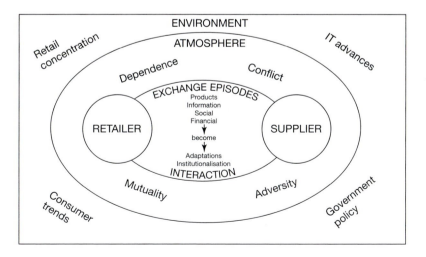

Figure 5.1 *The interaction model of retail buying*

THE INTERACTION APPROACH

The interaction approach recognises that transactions, or exchanges between a retailer and a supplier occur in a number of different formats. The most obvious is the transaction of goods for money. In a straightforward purchase of a box of one dozen cans of baked beans from the local wholesaler, money for goods might be the only transaction that occurs. In the case of a biscuit supplier developing a new chocolate biscuit bar for Tesco plc, however, it is likely that a number of prototype products will pass to and from each company, together with packaging ideas, promotional plans, costing information and sales estimates. The main purchase will occur at the end of a significant amount of discussion and negotiation. In this type of transaction there is a great deal of interaction between the two companies, involving personnel from a number of different departments. A technical issue may need to be resolved between Tesco's technologist and the supplier's product engineer. The supplier's packaging designers will liaise with Tesco's corporate design department to ensure that the packaging conforms to the corporate image, and carries all the necessary product information. Once the biscuit is on the store shelves and selling, Tesco's stock control team will discuss delivery schedules with the production controllers at the biscuit manufacturer, and the buyer will discuss any promotional price offers with the supplier's sales director.

Naturally, as time progresses the individuals from the two companies get to know each other and the contact changes from being purely business orientated to involve social exchanges. These social exchanges do not necessarily involve non-business communications nor do they have to take place off the work premises. They simply refer to the way in which people get to know each other in their work roles, which facilitates communication and eliminates the need for formalities that can take up valuable time and resources. The retailer expects the supplying company to learn how they like to work, and if necessary to adapt to their working methods. Once these procedures have been adopted they become what is referred to as institutionalised within the business, so that any other working methods become obsolete. In such a situation, individual exchanges or exchange episodes (as they are referred to in the original model) merge to become facets of the relationship.

Atmosphere

The IMP Group found that interactions between supplying firms and buying firms generally took place within a discernible atmosphere. The atmosphere could be one of trust and mutuality, or it could be one of conflict and antagonism. The atmosphere was seen to have an influence over the way exchanges were carried out. Where the dealings between two companies were geared to discrete transactions, it was more likely that the atmosphere would be confrontational, with little expectation of continuity in dealings. Where the relationship had developed over time, however, the atmosphere tended towards being trusting and co-operative, with an emphasis on continuity of a business relationship between the two companies.

Environment

Whilst the traditional buying process models (such as Webster and Wind, 1972) did acknowledge that business environment influences, such as technology, societal change, economic well-being and the political framework, could affect the buying process, these influences were only acknowledged to be of relevance to the buying organisation. In fact, a buying and a selling company operate in the same business environment, and so it is the combined response of the two organisations to environmental threats and opportunities that will have the most significant bearing on the interaction between the two. For example, in an economic downturn, a retailer is faced with more price sensitive shoppers. One response could be for the retailer to cut back order quantities as demand falls for products, with the possible result that a production plant may have to be closed and skilled operators laid off. When the economy improves, those skilled workers are no longer available for work, so the factory cannot be re-opened and the retailer has to source elsewhere. An alternative response could be a combined effort between retailer and supplier to investigate ways of reducing the cost of the item, thereby offering the consumer a lower priced product. Demand is therefore retained, the factory stays open, and the relationship between supplier and retailer is maintained. Co-operation between the two interacting companies allows threats to be challenged and overcome.

BOX 5.5 THE EFFECTIVENESS OF CODES OF PRACTICE

In 2000, the UK government's competition commission undertook an extensive report into the grocery retail sector. The general remit was to investigate the extent to which retail market concentration ('supermarket power') was affecting pricing policy ('ripping off the consumer'). Under the specific terms of reference one of the objectives was to investigate the extent to which supermarkets abused their power when it came to dealing with their suppliers. Overall, the commission found that the supermarket sector was working competitively but found evidence that the relationship that supermarkets had with their suppliers could work against public interest. One of the recommendations of the commission's report (Competition Commission, 2000) was that an industry code of practice should be drawn up to prevent suppliers being exploited by their powerful retail customers.

The code, drawn up in 2002, and updated in 2003, attempts to outlaw alleged anti-competitive practices used by supermarkets such as delaying payments, asking suppliers for retrospective reductions in prices during a period of contract and making lump payments as a condition of supply. Although the major supermarkets report that their buyers respect and implement the code of practice, and that they are proud of the good relationships they have with their suppliers, some industry forums suggest that it has made little difference and that suppliers are still subjected to unreasonable demands such as being paid the same or less than the cost of production for their produce, being forced to pay a rebate on previously agreed prices or for unsold goods, and being required to change transportation or packaging for products without being compensated for extra costs. The supermarkets point to the lack of complaints by suppliers as evidence of good relationships; however, groups like the National Farmer's Union and Friends of the Earth suggest that suppliers do not complain because they are afraid to, in case they lose their business; the concentrated nature of the industry means that alternative outlets for produce are not available.

Source: Lawrence, 2003; Denny and Moore, 2004; www.oft.gov.uk 2004

STAGES OF DEVELOPMENT IN RETAILER–SUPPLIER RELATIONSHIPS

Earlier in this chapter, it was suggested that a retailer might have suppliers at different stages of development within their supplier portfolio (see Table 5.2). Some retailers may have a supply base dominated by producers who have been supplying the retailer for many years. On the other hand some retailers may never develop very close relationships with suppliers, and may always deal with suppliers on a one-off basis. The extent to which the relationship between a retailer and a supplier has developed can be depicted on a continuum (see Figure 5.2).

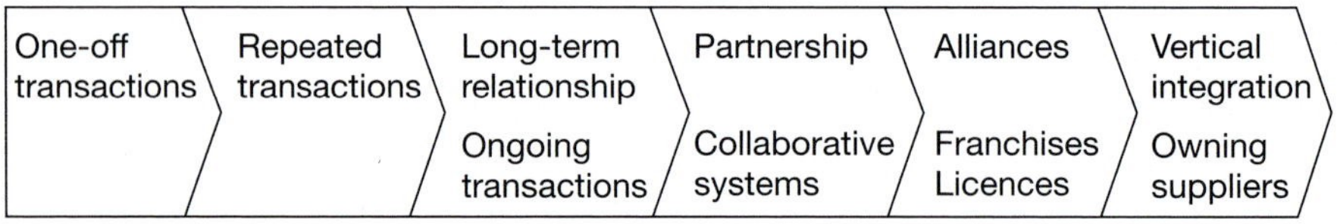

One-off transactions	Repeated transactions	Long-term relationship	Partnership	Alliances	Vertical integration
		Ongoing transactions	Collaborative systems	Franchises Licences	Owning suppliers

Figure 5.2 *A continuum of retailer–supplier relationship development*
Source: Adapted from Webster, 1992: 1–17

Although there are a number of retailers who are vertically integrated, most became so by moving forward into the distribution channel, that is, manufacturers opening up retail outlets. The number of retailers who have taken ownership of their suppliers is relatively small. The tendency these days is for retailer and manufacturer to retain their autonomy, yet move the businesses together by forming supply 'partnerships'. The characteristics of a supply partnership are contrasted with the characteristics of transactional supplier dealing in Table 5.3.

Table 5.3 *Transactional vs. partnership approach in retail supply*

Transactional	Short-term or one-off
	Many suppliers and buyers
	Disloyalty and lack of commitment
	Low switching costs, little or no investment made in relationships
	Loose or no procedures
	Exchange centred on single person in firm
	Changes in customer/supplier makes little difference
Partnerships	Long-term and ongoing
	Few suppliers and buyers
	Loyalty and commitment
	High switching costs, significant investments will have been made in the partnership
	Strict procedural guidelines
	Many people and departments involved in exchanges
	Change in customer/supplier causes disruption

There are some relationships between retailers and their supply sources that are best described as alliances; where there is some kind of legal arrangement that binds the channel members. An example of this kind of relationship is a franchising operation, where a central organisation allows an individual to run their own business, but has the legal right to insist that the business is conducted in a particular way, conforming to a central policy with regard to standardised product and service offers. Another example is a licensing arrangement, which is particularly prevalent in character merchandising (see Box 5.6).

BOX 5.6 CHARACTER MERCHANDISE

Licensing refers to an arrangement where manufacturers produce goods that have some reference to a popular character. In effect, it is the character, for example Mickey Mouse or Barbie, that becomes the brand, and it overrides both the retailer and the supplier. Character merchandise can be found in almost every retail sector, with food and clothing being the most important in a global market worth £76 billion (Mintel, 1999). Primary-school children are the main market for character merchandise. The children recognise the character, and subject their parents to 'pester power' for the product.

Although popular with the target market, licensing does have a number of drawbacks: the characters may become unpopular or perceived as 'too childish', restricting its appeal to a narrower age band; parents may feel children are being exploited, or they may disapprove of the character. In addition, character merchandise is usually premium priced because of the extra cost of royalties paid to the licensees, who may intervene in the retailer–supplier relationship in order to maintain their own quality standards. The success of licensing can change business priorities. For example, just over a quarter of Disney's US retail stores were closed in three years (to 2003) as direct links with leading retail chains like Kmart and Target and expanded product ranges have increased the availability of Disney merchandise in general retailers.

Source: Day, 1999; Parkes, 2003

SUPPLY CHAIN MANAGEMENT

Supply chain management (see Chapter 3) has provided retailers with the opportunity to obtain higher levels of operational efficiency through the alignment of suppliers' logistical systems with their own. This is only possible when a partnership approach is taken, and both parties stand to benefit from the results, as described in Chapter 3. The trend towards supply partnership development and the use of integrated information technology systems through the whole supply chain has resulted in retailers placing an increasing responsibility on suppliers for ensuring product availability. Retailers are also placing growing responsibility on their existing suppliers to increase the variety in the product offer. Rather than searching for and developing new suppliers when a product opportunity is identified, retailers are more likely to increase the business within the existing supply base, which has already made the adaptation and institutionalisation investment to service the retailer as they require. This strategy for new products should result in lower priced products from an experienced supplier. Low prices, however, are not the only benefit that can be accrued from taking a strategic approach to supply chain management. For example, in 2002 Marks & Spencer altered the supply chain strategy for its Autograph designer clothing range from using a variety of different manufacturers to a single, well established source. In the earlier stages of the collection's history, manufacturers for the garments were those that each member of the Autograph design team had used in the past for their own collections. However, a decision was taken for the Autograph Autumn/Winter 2002 collection to be made by one, well established Marks & Spencer clothing supplier: Courtaulds Ladieswear. Concentrating the supply of the range to one supplier helps to achieve styling and quality consistency across the brand. Control of product flow is also easier to achieve with a single source. However, a strategy such as this is only successful if the supplier's production facility is 'flexible and agile' enough to manufacture and respond to the sales patterns of a diversity of products. In the case of the Autograph label this includes tailored garments, knitwear and lightweight items, and so a dedicated production facility was established within the Courtaulds set up. Courtaulds' long relationship in many other departments of Marks & Spencer gave them a full understanding of the product and service requirements of the retailer (Clements, 2002).

Increased marketing and distribution efficiency as a result of supply chain management has been the focus of much strategic development of large retailers and their supply partners since the 1990s, but retailer–supplier partnering is not only available to large organisations. Examples of initiatives that will improve retailer–supplier relationships in any size of business are shown in Box 5.7.

BOX 5.7   FACTORS THAT WILL IMPROVE RELATIONSHIPS BETWEEN RETAILERS AND THEIR SUPPLIERS

- Understanding each other's strategic business aims, including an appreciation of target customer profiles and brand image. Mutuality in this respect will help the businesses grow simultaneously.

- Detailed feedback on sales from the retailer to the supplier. This is likely to include transmission of sales data via electronic data networks in large retail organisations. Qualitative feedback and discussion on poor sellers is likely to reduce mistakes in the future.

- Co-operation and co-ordination in marketing activities. Examples would include co-operative advertising, provision of promotional material by supplier for retailer's campaigns, store support for supplier's media campaigns, joint participation in charity-linked promotions.

- Sharing of information on relevant consumer trends and product/market trends and innovations.

- Commitment of businesses to one another, including combined forward planning, store space dedicated to supplier's ranges, provision of point of purchase materials and fixtures for the retailer, retailer involvement in product development.

- An understanding of the retailer's quality standard requirements, including product quality and compliance on service, delivery, and administration.

- Systems integration to facilitate information sharing, including sales data, stock and delivery information.

- Adoption of information management systems which underpin collaboration between retailers and suppliers.

SUMMARY

The supply base is increasingly being used to contribute to the value added to the product range by the retailer. Access to product sources around the globe and advances in logistics and supply chain integration have allowed retailers to improve choice and availability. Retail product managers are responsible for developing suppliers that meet a retailer's product and service requirements. They also need to monitor supplier performance to ensure those standards are maintained. The trend towards partnerships between retailers and their suppliers is allowing the two parties to combine their expertise to provide more flexible product assortments and faster new product innovations. Even small retailers are working more closely with their suppliers to gain a mutual understanding and a combined customer orientation.

CASE STUDY   RETAIL EXCHANGES

The idea of the retail exchange emerged as an application of internet-based information technology, in which retail buyers and suppliers would come together in a virtual market place. Participating members of the exchange are then matched in terms of capability (suppliers) and need (buyers). In order to be effective and derive the potential efficiencies offered by it, the exchange requires common tools and standards amongst participating organisations (Sparks and Wagner, 2004). These would include systems alignment and commonality in descriptive technical terms and data presentation. Some retail exchanges, such as Wal-Mart's Retail Link are private networks, owned and managed by the one retailer, to which suppliers are invited to join. Other well-known retail exchanges are formed by groups of collaborating retail companies, who combine buying power to obtain better terms from suppliers. This type of 'consortia' exchange includes GNX (Global Net eXchange) and WWRE (Worldwide Retail Exchange).

One of the benefits of a retail exchange is that it allows retailers and suppliers of different sizes and geographic locations to be linked and easily exchange information about products. Theoretically this then leads to greater objectivity in terms of prices and product selection, and collaboration opportunities for product development.

An important development that a retail exchange allows is an auction (often referred to as a reverse auction) whereby a retailer sets out their requirements in a product specification, against which suppliers connected to the exchange simultaneously provide their best bid. For members of the retail exchange an auction can bring the benefit of obtaining a wider supplier base, and access to highly competitive current market prices, very quickly.

The success of the retail exchange, however, has varied. Some of the drawbacks reported have been the difficulties in getting common terms, standards and processes between exchange members; the time it takes to prepare for an auction, which can include supplier training, and the fact that the lowest price supplier does not always live up to expectations in terms of other product selection criteria (such as product quality). Additionally, conducting a buying process with the major focus on price goes against the idea of retailer–supplier relationship development.

Another stalling block is that whilst collaboration on new product development potentially provides opportunities to share costs and access to new ideas, the reality is that the retail industry is highly competitive and historically secretive, with unique products being a source of competitive advantage. Retail exchanges, therefore, appear to be more attractive for buying business commodities (such as computers, stationery and only very basic retail outlet stock). Another potential difficulty with collaborative buying between large organisations is that it could be seen as unfair competition for smaller industry players, and therefore illegal, or in need of regulation. Retail exchanges are proactively developing ethical codes in order to deal with some of the problems that can arise, such as providing training for suppliers so that all have access and the opportunity to bid or respecting confidential pricing information that a supplier may give during an auction.

Source: Sparks and Wagner (2004); www.GNX.com; www.worldwideretailexchange.org

QUESTIONS

1   Review the various types of supplier that are available to retailers, indicating which type of supplier would be more suitable for the following retailer types: (a) a superstore group such as Tesco or Asda; (b) an independent gift shop; and (c) a medium sized regional department store chain.

2   Outline ways in which a supplier's potential and actual performance can be assessed.

3   Evaluate the benefits of (a) regional and (b) global sourcing for national retailers.

4   A partnership approach to retailer–supplier relations usually involves a reduction in the number of suppliers that a retailer uses. Suggest reasons for this trend.

5   To what extent do you think the large supermarket retailers in the UK consider their suppliers to be partners?

6   Assess the likely effect of retail exchanges on retail buying and merchandising practices.

7   Suggest ways in which a retailer's supply base can bring competitive advantage to the company.

REFERENCES AND FURTHER READING

Abdy, M. (2001) 'Pros and Cons of Keeping It Local', *Retail Week*, 21 August.

Bowlby, S.R. and Foord, J. (1995) 'Relational Contracting between UK Retailers and Manufacturers', *International Review of Retail, Distribution and Consumer Research*, 5(3): 333–360.

Butaney, G. and Wortzel, L.H. (1988) 'Distribution Power Versus Manufacturer Power: The Customer Pole', *Journal of Marketing*, 52 (Jan.): 52–63.

Clements, A. (2002) 'Designer Supplier', *Retail Week*, 12 December.

Dawson, J.A. and Shaw, S. (1990) 'The Changing Character of Retailer–Supplier Relationships', in J. Fernie (ed.), *Retail Distribution Management*, Kogan Page, London, ch. 1.

Day, J. (1999) 'Building a Strong Character', *Marketing Week*, 25 November.

Denny, C. and Moore, C. (2004) 'OFT Sends in Auditors as New Code Fails to Break Supermarkets' Armlock', *Guardian*, 21 February.

El Ansary, A.I. and Stern, L.W. (1972) 'Power Measurement in Distribution Channels', *Journal of Marketing Research*, 9 (Feb.): 47–52.

Ford, D. (1998) *Managing Business Relationships*, Wiley, Chichester.

Goldsmith, J. (2003) 'Joining Forces', *Retail Week*, 26 September.

Gregory, H. (2003) 'The Buying Game', *Grocer*, 26 April.

Grocer (2003) 'London Gateway to World of Wine', editorial 26 April.

Harris, L.C. and Ogbonna, E. (2001) 'Competitive Advantage in the UK Food Retailing Sector: Past, Present and Future, *Journal of Retailing and Consumer Studies*, 8(3): 157–173.

Hogarth Scott, S. and Parkinson, S.T. (1993) 'Retailer–Supplier Relationships in the Food Channel: A Supplier Perspective', *International Journal of Retail and Distribution Management*, 21(8): 11–18.

Hutt, M.D. and Speh, T.W. (2001) *Business Marketing Management*, Harcourt Inc., Orlando.

IMP Group (1982) in H. Hakanson (ed.), *International Marketing and Purchasing of Industrial Goods: An Interaction Approach*, Wiley, New York.

Kline, B. and Wagner, J. (1994) 'Information Sources and Retail Buyer Decision-making: The Effect of Product-specific Buying Experience', *Journal of Retailing*, 70(1): 75–88.

Lawrence, F. (2003) 'Farmers Still Exploited by Big Retailer', *Guardian*, 17 March.

Mintel (1999) *Character Merchandising Report*, Mintel International Group, London.

Murphy, C. (2003) 'Grocers Cook Up a Recipe for Growth', *Financial Times*, 13 November.

Parkes, C. (2003) 'Walt Disney Considers Sale of Its Retail Stores Chain', *Financial Times*, 23 May.

Retail Week (2004) 'B&Q in Focus on Direct Sourcing', editorial 2 February.

Sparks, L. and Wagner, B. (2004) 'Transforming Technologies: Retail Exchanges and RFID', in J. Fernie and L. Sparks (eds), *Logistics and Retail Management*, 2nd edn, Kogan Page, London.

Stern, L.W. and El Ansary, A.I. (1988) *Marketing Channels*, 3rd edn, Prentice Hall, Englewood Cliffs, NJ.

Thomas, D. (2003) 'Superpowers?', *Marketing Week*, 17 April.

Valsamakis, V. and Groves, O.G. (1996) 'Supplier–Customer Relationships: Do Partnerships Perform Better?', *Journal of Fashion Marketing and Management*, 1(1): 9–25.

Webster, F.E. and Wind, Y. (1972) 'A General Model for Understanding Organisational Buying Behaviour', *Journal of Marketing*, 36 (April): 12.

Welsh Development Agency (2004) 'New Markets for Welsh Ready Meals', press release, posted 13 February.

Web site

Welsh Development Agency: http://wda.co.uk/index.cfm, accessed 2/9/04

Chapter 6

Product quantity decisions and stock management

LEARNING OBJECTIVES

The purpose of this chapter is to:

■ Stipulate the objectives of stock management and the risks associated with getting buying quantities wrong

■ Introduce the principles of stock management, and become familiar with key terms that are relevant to this area of retail product management

■ Appreciate that different approaches to stock control are applicable in various retail contexts

■ Understand the relationship between sales, stock levels and ordering quantities, and how these relationships can vary in different product categories

■ Be able to account for the different influences that will determine the product quantity requirement in a retail organisation.

INTRODUCTION

Getting the right quantities of merchandise delivered into the retail organisation is necessary to satisfy basic customer needs and retail management goals. Too much stock threatens the profitability of the product range, while too little stock results in losses of sales and customers. The main aim of this chapter is to present an overview of some key principles associated with determining buying quantities that are used in the process of controlling the flow of product; which represents not only the physical stock, but also the financial investment.

STOCK MANAGEMENT

One of the fundamental questions for the retail product manager, whether carrying the title of buyer, merchandiser or category manager, is how much of a particular product line is needed? This apparently simple question needs further exploration and clarification within the context of the individual retail business. For example, quantities required may be calculated at different levels, such as by store, or by region, or by the whole organisation. The time dimension also needs to be stipulated, whether the quantity required is for a day, or for a week's trading or an estimate for a whole season.

If there is not enough of a product item, then there is a risk of unsatisfied customer demand, which means lost sales for the retailer. The extent of this loss is difficult to determine and may account for a much greater value than the loss of the one product item. Not only can a stock-out affect the sales of complementary goods (for example, a jacket may sell much better when matching trousers are available), dissatisfied customers may decide to take their custom to another store and never return. On the other hand, the penalties of having too much product are also great. The retailer has to bear the costs of carrying excess stock, in terms of financial investment, operational maintenance costs and the use of valuable space to store unproductive merchandise. It may also result in the retailer having to lower prices to stimulate demand for the overstocked item, resulting in reduced profit margins on the product.

An ideal situation in retailing would seem to be where quantities of merchandise, commonly referred to as a retailer's 'stock', are replenished exactly at the rate at which it sells. But even this does not always hold true; for example, which retailer would like to replenish Christmas decorations at the rate they sold them in the week commencing 19 December? Management of the quantity of product items in retailing is often referred to as stock control, because the flow of stock is controlled at a rate that is appropriate for the level of sales. However, the management of stock is also about managing the finance tied up in stock and so considerations other than the basic rate of sales have to be taken into account when determining buying quantities.

As well as the different variables that need to be considered in terms of consumer demand, there are also considerations about product supply that need to be taken into account when making decisions about order quantities; for example, the discount available for larger orders, the quantities in which products are delivered from suppliers (crate sizes, for example), the time between order and delivery, and the minimum quantities required by suppliers to guarantee exclusivity.

STOCK MANAGEMENT FOR STAPLE ITEMS

Within the product range offered by most retailers, there are some products that are termed staple items. These are the kind of products that need to be replaced at regular intervals. The consumption of these products is consistent, and so the derived demand is also consistent. Examples of this type of product are family shampoo, milk, bread, furniture polish, dishcloths, basic underwear and light bulbs. Over time the expected sales for this type of product become very predictable and could be expressed as a function of average per capita consumption and the number of customers who visit a particular retailer.

STOCK MANAGEMENT BY PERIODIC REVIEW

Control of stock, in the case of staple products, is relatively straightforward and the use of systems based on the periodic review process is commonplace for this kind of merchandise. The periodic review, as the name suggests, relies on the stock position being reviewed within a specific time period. The frequency of review depends on the shelf life of the product and the demand for the item. For example, a review by a grocer of the stock position of milk would take place at least once a day, whereas an electrical retailer may review the stock position of light bulbs once a week (see Figure 6.1).

When the electrical retailer reviews the stock position and realises that more light bulbs need to be ordered, an order is given to a supplier. The retailer then waits for the delivery. In the meantime light bulbs continue to sell, so the review period should be set at a time when the goods are unlikely to have completely run out, and the remaining stock, known as the safety, or 'buffer' stock, will cover customer purchases until the new light bulb delivery arrives. This might be a matter of days or it might be a week or so. The time between placing and receiving an order

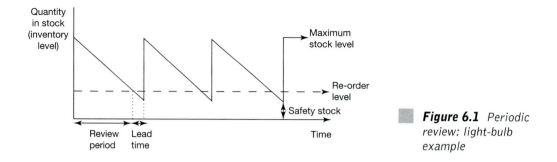

Figure 6.1 *Periodic review: light-bulb example*

is referred to as a supplier's lead-time. The longer the lead-time, the higher the safety stock level needs to be. The advantages of the periodic review system are that it is simple and easy to administer (and can be carried out at both store and warehouse level), but it is not very useful for fast selling merchandise or when large fluctuations in demand occur. For this type of merchandise, an ordering system that is based on the rate of sales, or the estimated rate of sales, might be more appropriate. These approaches are discussed later in this chapter.

The longer the review period in the stock control system described above, the larger the quantity required in order to prevent stock-outs. However, a large order quantity is likely to present the retailer with other problems, such as storage and handling costs, as well as the problem of financing such high stock levels. It may seem more cost-effective to order more frequently, in smaller quantities. The retailer therefore has not yet solved the problem of how much product to order at any one time. A principle that may help a retailer decide how much product to order is the economic order quantity.

THE ECONOMIC ORDER QUANTITY (EOQ)

One of the basic principles of stock management is that of the EOQ, and whilst the EOQ may not be theoretically relevant to many retail buying situations nowadays for reasons that will become apparent later on in this chapter, an appreciation of its principles will help product managers to see some of the hidden costs associated with their decisions about order quantities.

In the process of buying a product, there are a number of costs involved, some of which may be more apparent to the retail organisation than others. The costs involved in acquiring a product can include:

- the administration cost of placing an order, such as labour, paper, telephone bills. Many companies have been able to reduce this cost substantially by using electronic data transfer;
- the costs involved with supplier search and selection (see Chapter 5). This might include overseas sourcing trips, as well as the day-to-day costs of information exchange and negotiations between the retail buyer and their supplier base;
- once an order is placed, further costs might be incurred when expediting the order. This involves checking that the order is going to arrive on time and making alternative arrangements if there are problems with the delivery;
- the retailer may feel it necessary to inspect the product once it arrives, which can be an extremely costly exercise (see Chapter 4).

Clearly, some of these costs are easier to allocate to individual product lines than others, and often they will be absorbed under the general fixed costs of the buying department. However, the

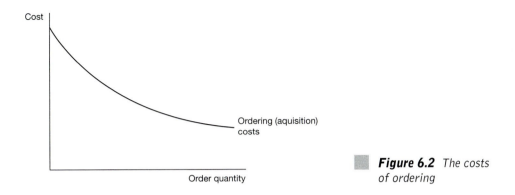

Cost

Ordering (aquisition) costs

Order quantity

Figure 6.2 *The costs of ordering*

smaller the quantity ordered, the more orders will need to be placed in any period of time, and therefore the higher the costs involved will be (Figure 6.2).

On the other hand, there are also costs involved with the possession of products. The largest cost to a retailer of possessing stock is the capital tied up in it, which is only released at the point of sale. This cost is relatively easy to allocate to individual product lines. There are other costs associated with the possession of goods that are less obvious and harder to allocate. Once the goods have been received, they will need to be handled, warehoused, picked, be prepared and packaged to be sent to stores, delivered to store and possibly be maintained in store (Figure 6.3). The economic order quantity is the point at which the cost of ordering equals the cost of possessing the stock, and is the point at which the total cost of buying is at its lowest (Figure 6.4).

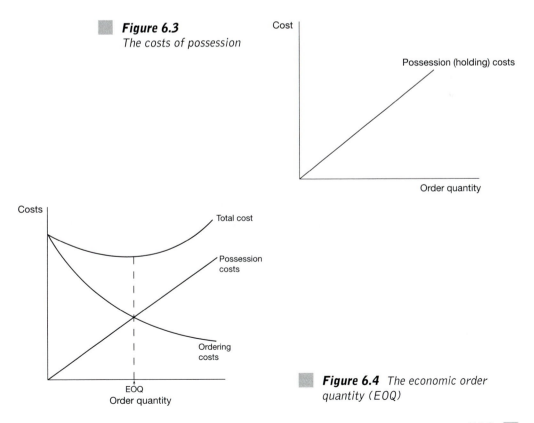

Figure 6.3
The costs of possession

Cost

Possession (holding) costs

Order quantity

Costs

Total cost

Possession costs

Ordering costs

EOQ
Order quantity

Figure 6.4 *The economic order quantity (EOQ)*

BOX 6.1 THE MECHANISMS OF THE EOQ

The following example illustrates the mechanisms of the economic order quantity (EOQ). A small hardware retailer places orders for cleaning products from XYZ supplier. The cost of acquiring the cleaning products is £6.00 per order. The cost of possessing the products is 7.5 per cent of the monthly stock value. The total order value for cleaning products for the year is £6,000 (12,000 items at an average price of £0.50) (Table 6.1).

Table 6.1 *Quantities and costs in the economic order quantity (EOQ) calculation*

Order frequency	Order quantity	Value of order (£)	Cost of ordering (£)	Cost of possession (£)	Total annual costs (£)
24	500	250	144	18.75	162.75
12	1,000	500	72	37.50	109.50
10	1,200	600	60	45.00	105.00
8	*1,500*	*750*	*48*	*56.25*	*104.25*
7	1,715	857	42	64.29	106.29
6	2,000	1,000	36	75.00	111.00
4	3,000	1,500	24	112.50	136.50
2	6,000	3,000	12	225.00	237.00

The economic order quantity, or the amount that retailer XYZ should order to minimise their costs is 1,500 items, at an order value of £750, and the order should be placed eight times a year.

The economic order quantity principle does have a number of drawbacks:

■ EOQ does not consider the need to react to unexpected sales fluctuations.

■ EOQ does not consider seasonality or perishability factors which could lead to product obsolescence.

■ EOQ does not consider the discounts that might be obtainable for ordering larger quantities.

■ EOQ does not consider the quantities a product is available in (for example, the product may only be available in dozens, or crates of 100).

■ The retailer may not have available space for the EOQ; it may not have any storage space.

■ The retailer may depend on the delivery of suppliers or distributors whose own delivery schedules may determine the order quantity placed by the retailer.

The practicalities of retailing that invariably lead to making decisions based on compromise, especially in the case of the small retailer, mean that the EOQ is better approached as a theoretical concept rather than as a buying aid for retailers. This is because in most product instances, the demand for an item is not constant, the shelf life of many products is very short, and the cost of maintaining and holding stock has risen much more steeply than the costs of acquiring stock.

Since the 1990s, many retailers have found that they have been able to lower substantially the cost of ordering, whilst the costs of holding stock have increased. This has meant that a much larger cost saving can be made by lowering the amount of stock held in the retail system than could be made by reducing the number of times orders are placed. Lower stock holdings have been one of the major benefits of the implementation of consumer-led approaches to product management (see Chapter 3).

Some of the methods retailers have adopted to reduce the costs of ordering are

- centralised ordering;
- the use of an order programme at the start of the season. This is similar in principle to a materials requirement plan (MRP) used in purchasing for production companies; it outlines the order quantities required for a future time period, and then schedules deliveries from suppliers to meet those requirements;
- the use of EDI and network systems to cut out paperwork and provide collated information quickly to other members of the supply chain;
- the use of sales based automatic replenishment systems (discussed in Chapter 7).

THE NEED FOR STOCK INVESTMENT

Service level

In Chapter 1 the concepts of variety and assortment were introduced as determinants of the retail offer. However the third facet of the retail offer, which plays an important role in determining the customer's perception of the product offer, is the service level that a retailer offers. In this context, service level does not relate to the level of personal service a customer receives in the shop, but refers to the stock service level or the amount of certainty customers have of finding the items they wish to purchase in stock. The ideal stock service level is 100 per cent, so that no matter how many customers come into an outlet for a product item, a stock-out will not occur. It therefore follows that the service level has a bearing on the financial and physical capabilities of the retailer. A very high service level maximises sales opportunities but runs the risk of having too much stock, which the retailer may not be able to pay for or have room for.

Variety requirement

The amount of choice that a customer requires when undertaking shopping activity can vary between product categories. For some products, consumers are not really interested in variety, they are happy to have a limited offering and will tend to buy the same product variation each time. For other categories the consumer would need a large selection from which to choose a product item. They will be looking for individuality and would not consider a limited retail offer to be satisfactory. Figure 6.5 shows how the variety requirement increases across different product categories.

STOCK MANAGEMENT SYSTEMS

Many large retailers use customised or proprietary computerised stock management systems, which help them to calculate buying quantities. These systems will help a merchandiser to maintain a detailed overview of the stock position of every item, and help them to manage the stock according to predetermined objectives. Most stock management systems issue reports which give the following information:

115

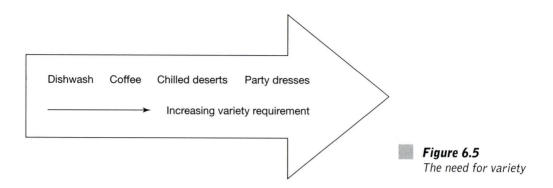

Dishwash   Coffee   Chilled deserts   Party dresses

Increasing variety requirement

Figure 6.5
The need for variety

- a list of product lines (by SKU);
- the sales of the product line (may be given over different time periods, for example, previous day, last week, last four weeks and so on);
- the turnover (the amount of sales within a time period, measured against the amount of stock);
- the amount of goods on sale, available to sell;
- the amount of goods on order, in the supply chain and immediately available from suppliers;
- the level of availability target;
- the sales forecast;
- the minimum stock level, the reorder level and the safety stock (see Figure 6.1 Periodic review).

The output of the system will be a suggested order quantitiy, taking into account the supplier's pack quantities.

Some of the inputs for this type of system may come directly (in an integrated system) from EPOS (namely sales data), but many of the inputs rely on a merchandiser's knowledge and experience. For example, the availability target will depend on the importance of the item to the retail organisation's offer as a core or peripheral product line. The sales forecast input will be dependent to a greater degree on previous sales figures, but may need to be over-written because of particular circumstances (see section on forecasting below).

SALES FORECASTING

An understanding of how products sell is the best basis for an effective stock control system within a retail business, and analysis of past sales to make predictions about future sales is the starting point for a sales forecast. Indeed for a staple product such as butter or flour or cereal, the fluctuations in demand over time may be so small that past sales alone might be enough to obtain an accurate sales forecast. The principle used for forecasting sales for staple items is to extend sales trends from the past into the future. A very simple approach would be to take the average sales from a number of previous weeks (say four or six) and use that as the forecast for the next week (case study at the end of this chapter). This technique, referred to as the moving average, would be fine if the demand for the product was consistent. In reality, from a stock control viewpoint, very few product items have really stable demand. Even very basic items such as milk, bread, and eggs tend to sell more towards the end of the week, in anticipation of increased consumption at the weekend.

EPOS systems have contributed enormously to a retailer's ability to improve stock control. Detailed information about past sales of each stock-keeping unit (SKU) has facilitated the job of predicting the future sales of each product line, which enables the retailer to be prepared with enough stock to meet sales. The data are captured at the point of sale and transmitted electronically, and therefore immediately, to a central data storage point, usually located in the retailer's head office. The retailer therefore can build up a very accurate picture of what is selling and how quickly in its outlets. The retailer can see sales patterns emerging on a seasonal basis, a weekly basis, or even at different times throughout the day, as shown in Table 6.2.

In reality, the sales of most products are influenced to a greater or lesser degree by a number of factors:

- seasonality;
- fashion;
- product endorsement;
- price fluctuations;
- likely product substitutions;
- complementary product sales;
- promotional activity.

Seasonality

The seasons in the year influence product availability and demand. At one time customers accepted that seasonal fruit and vegetable availability fluctuated throughout the year and consumption patterns reflected what was locally available. Global sourcing and improvements in logistics and transportation have allowed retailers to extend the selling season of many fresh items, such as strawberries and sweetcorn, by importing the produce from various countries around the world throughout the year. Despite the improvement in availability, however, demand for products still tends to peak at the time when the product was originally available in the local market, because of the seasonal associations, such as bowlfuls of strawberries and cream eaten during the Wimbledon Tennis Championship held in London in June.

Table 6.2 *Convenience store: typical daily sales pattern*

Time of day		Purchases
Early morning	(6–9 a.m.)	Newspapers, milk, cigarettes, bread products
Morning	(9–12 a.m.)	General groceries, household goods, stamps, fresh fruit and vegetables
Lunchtime	(12–3 p.m.)	General groceries, soft drinks, fresh fruit and vegetables
Afternoon	(3–5 p.m.)	Confectionery, milk, bread, cakes, tinned foods, fresh produce, soft drinks
Early evening	(5–8 p.m.)	Bread, confectionery, lottery tickets, pre-prepared meals, wines and spirits, video rentals
Evening	(8–10 p.m.)	Alcoholic drinks, confectionery, video rental, lottery tickets

Source: Mintel (1997)

Seasonal influences can be product specific or they can have a broader effect. The sales pattern for pumpkins, for example would be quite dramatic, as shown in Figure 6.6. Pumpkins are generally not a popular food in the UK, but are a vital ingredient for Halloween celebrations on 31 October.

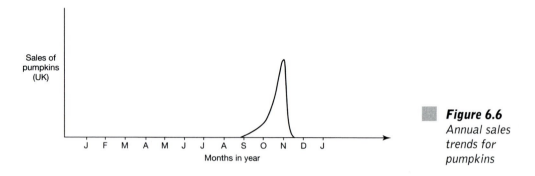

Figure 6.6
Annual sales trends for pumpkins

The most important seasonal influence on the UK retail market is Christmas. Marks & Spencer for example, break their annual sales reporting into three key seasons, spring, summer and Christmas. There are very few categories of merchandise that do not benefit from the Christmas season sales uplift. Even sales of swimwear increase at this time because people who can afford winter sun are likely to be giving their wardrobes an overhaul at this time of year. A hot Christmas present item can result in exceptional sales peaks and enormous strains on the supply chain. On 10 December 2003, it was reported that Asda flew in a jumbo jet full of DVD players from Singapore so that they could be in stores by the pre-Christmas weekend. Demand across the UK for DVD players had resulted in a shortage of the product in many retail outlets. As increasing numbers of children have their own TV sets in their bedrooms the demand for their own DVD will follow (*Retail Week*, 2003 web site). Table 6.3 shows some other seasonal peaks in different product categories.

BOX 6.2 GOING POSH FOR CHRISTMAS?

An interesting feature of the UK retail market is the tendency for consumers to 'trade up' during celebration seasons. Anyone would expect sales of chocolates, decorations, turkeys and wine to fly in the run up to Christmas, but even in the most mundane of categories a little Christmas sparkle can be found. It is the phenomenon of snob value; with impending visits from discerning guests and fastidious in-laws, sales of more expensive and quilted toilet roll replace the more basic version at this time of year. Branded dishwash, handwash and bubblebath are other categories that will be 'on show' and are where leading brand sales take a step up in pre-Christmas shopping baskets. Consumers also trade up to freshly squeezed orange juice and ground coffee.

Retail own-brand product development teams have responded to this trading-up opportunity by introducing novelty 'limited edition' products such as tangerine and cranberry dishwash and holly-printed toilet paper.

Source: theretailbulletin, accessed 18/12/03

Table 6.3 *Seasonal peaks in different product categories*

Product classifications	Seasonal peak
Gardening and DIY	April–June
Barbecue products	May–September
Toiletries	February (Valentine's Day), March (Mother's Day) and November/December (Christmas).

Fashion

Although seasonal features and fashion features of products, whether clothing or otherwise, have a combined effect on sales patterns, the effect that fashion has on a product becoming outdated and therefore obsolete, stimulates demand for new products in retail businesses. Fashion trends can be quite dramatic, causing a high peak in sales, followed by a steep drop as the 'fad' passes on to something new. Other fashion influences last one or more years, for example a trouser width or a shirt collar shape. Here are some examples of fashions and fads in different product categories:

- *Home furnishings*: Brabantia-type pedal bins, patio heaters, laminated wood flooring.
- *Food/drink*: Sushi, wild mushrooms, flavoured vodka, bio-culture yogurt drinks.
- *Toys*: Cyberpets, yoyos, alien eggs, Beyblades, Pokemon cards.

Product endorsements

When the famous TV cookery presenter Delia Smith showed the British nation how to cook a boiled egg in 1999, she used white hens' eggs. A day later, the BBC was inundated by calls from viewers demanding to know where they could buy white eggs. Supermarkets had long since phased out white eggs in favour of the more homely looking brown egg. Such is the effect of product endorsement by a famous and trusted figurehead. The effect of Delia Smith's following is so great that supermarkets are notified in advance of the ingredients used in her recipes so that huge quantities of the items can be distributed to stores. Product endorsement in itself can create a fashion, such as hair accessories for men, endorsed by David Beckham. Although the footballer celebrity has earned a fortune with formal advertising contracts for sunglasses, mobile phones, and boys' clothing, his hairstyling and accessories have helped to generally endorse a variety of men's grooming products without being paid to do so. In December 2003, JJB sports, the UK's largest sportswear retailer sold twice as many replica rugby shirts as football shirts; a response to the success of England's rugby team in the World Cup. Sales of rugby clothing and equipment increased tenfold during the time of the tournament (www.theretailbulletin, 15/12/03).

Other influences

The three factors, seasonality, fashion and endorsement, can stimulate demand for specific products within a time period. However, demand for products can also be stimulated by other factors. Price reductions are introduced to stimulate sales, whether they take the form of a short-term and product specific reduction, or a longer-term, general reduction, as in the case of an end-of-season sale. The role of price in the product management process is examined in detail in Chapter 12, but the effect of price changes on sales patterns and the expectation of seasonal price reductions cannot be overlooked at this stage. Product substitutions also have a role to play in

119

sales forecasting. Lack of availability of one product, or brand of a product, is likely to increase the likelihood of a competing item being purchased as a next-best alternative. Even though the nation was not able to buy white eggs after the Delia Smith demonstration, the demand for brown eggs increased substantially. Similarly, an increase in demand for one product can lead to increased sales of a complementary product (see Chapter 8).

Exponential smoothing

Exponential smoothing is a technique that attempts to make a forecast more accurate than one that is based purely on sales averages. It aims to fine-tune a sales forecast based on current trends by weighting previous sales history according to its likely influence on future sales. For example, whilst the sales figures of butter for the previous few weeks are the most likely indicator of sales of butter for the next week, the issuing of a health report that puts butter in a negative context might cause sales of butter to fall. By giving greatest weight to the most recent sales history (a downturn for butter, for example) the sales forecast reacts to the current trend, but the value of the weighting is adjusted so that stores are not left without butter on the shelves. Exponential smoothing aims to provide a sensible forecast that is based on the previous sales trends with the distorting effect of any exceptionally high or low figures being effectively managed by subjective weighting (see Exercise at the end of the chapter for further explanation).

BOX 6.3 SALES IN THE CITY

Trading in the centre of a city has traditionally been extremely profitable, with the concentration of office workers, the influx of shoppers on day trips and tourists all adding to a high footfall potential. City centres, however, rely on public transportation, and the concentration of people has made city centres the unfortunate target of real and threatened terrorist attacks. Sales forecasts can go awry when the stability of a shopping area is hampered by events that are entirely out of the control of retail managers who may need to adopt a contingency planning approach to sales forecasting in the future.

In March 2003, the department store John Lewis, which is located on Oxford Street in the centre of London's busiest shopping district, reported that overall store sales had declined by 12 per cent in the wake of the closure and repair of the Central Line, an arterial route within London's underground transport system. In the first full week of closure, following a derailment at one of the city's stations, turnover collapsed by 44 per cent.

Source: Finch, 2003

THE INVOLVEMENT OF BRANCH STORES IN DETERMINING QUANTITIES

Although it is unlikely that branch managers in most multiple retailers will be habitually placing orders directly with suppliers, in many retail situations sales forecasting has a significant input at local branch level. It is the branch managers who know the characteristics of the catchment area and its influence on customer needs and preferences. They will also know the effect of local competition on sales and how this may affect the sales estimate for different product categories.

The method of formulating a forecast that is amalgamated from the forecasts of individual stores is the 'base-upwards' approach to sales forecasting. The forecasts from the stores may then be collated at regional level (possibly distribution centre region) and then split down according to departments from which the buyers or merchandisers will forecast the business for the whole retail company.

An alternative method is the 'top-down' approach where the higher echelons of retail management make an overall company target and subsequently split the forecast by department and by store, and then set the buyers and branch managers the challenge of meeting their targets by whatever means they can. Difficulties with the top-down approach are as follows.

- *Motivation*: Associates at all levels prefer to be consulted about their own performance. If they have set their own targets, they are likely to feel more motivated to achieve them.
- *Lack of knowledge about the local catchment's profiles*: It is the person who has the knowledge about the opportunities and threats within the local business environment who is most likely to give an accurate picture of what the outcome will be for the retailer.
- *Lack of appreciation of category lifecycles or trends*: These factors, which have a bearing on the long-term growth or decline of a product category are best assessed by the buying departments, which are the most likely to have immediate product and market expertise.

Top-down forecasting, on the other hand, allows a retailer to benefit from the judgement of experienced managers, and may prevent the over-ambitious buyer or branch manager being dangerously optimistic in forecasting.

FORECASTING AT DISTRIBUTION CENTRE LEVEL

In most large retail companies, orders from the stores are sent electronically to a distribution centre, which replenishes the stores on a regular basis. The use of distribution centres in the supply chain has a useful smoothing effect on sales forecasting. By combining the sales forecast for a number of stores in a retailer's network, a more accurate forecast at regional level is established.

Having considered the complexity of a sales forecast we will now use it in a merchandise management technique that has for many years been employed to control stock investment in product categories that are susceptible to considerable demand fluctuations, such as fashion merchandise.

THE MERCHANDISE BUDGET PLAN

Merchandise budget plans are concerned with the financial planning of merchandise ranges, rather than the control of the physical number of items. For any retailer (of any size) it is vital that a balance is achieved between the amount of money going out of a business to pay for supplies of stock, and money coming into the business from sales to customers. Even though there are various accounting methods that allow a little flexibility (for example, extended credit terms), this balance is key to the liquidity of the business. A merchandise budget plan is difficult to accomplish without the benefit of previous experience and internal records; however, relying on historical data alone can lead a buyer or product manager into repeating previous mistakes, including missed opportunities.

The first step of the plan is a realistic sales forecast, the principles of which were discussed earlier in this chapter. The time period for the plan will vary according to the individual needs of the retail business, but a six-monthly plan is common for many seasonal products. The sales forecast shown in Table 6.4 is for a relatively seasonal product – women's toiletry gift packs. The

Table 6.4 *The first stages of a merchandise budget plan*

Category: toiletry	Jan.	Feb.	Mar.	Apr.	May	Jun.	Total
Gift packs (women's)							
Forecast sales (%)	19	13	21	16	14	17	100
Forecast (£)	11,400	7,800	12,600	9,600	8,400	10,200	60,000
BOM stock: sales ratio	2.8	3.3	2.9	2.8	3.1	3.1	3.0 (average)
Beginning of month (BOM) stock (£)	31,920	25,740	36,540	26,880	26,040	31,620	N/A

sales are above average in January, because of all the reduced Christmas stock, in March because of Mother's Day and Easter (which usually fall in this month), and in June due to pre-holiday purchases. The forecasted sales are shown as a percentage of the total season's sales estimate, and at retail selling value.

The second step of the plan is to consider how much stock is needed in the stores in order to achieve the forecasted level of sales. Arriving at this stock to sales ratio will need consideration of the following:

■ How fast can replacement items be supplied?
■ How fast will the item sell out, and how important is it to keep the product in stock?
■ How much choice does the customer expect to find in the store, in order to make a purchase?

For a relatively slow selling, specific product item that can be restocked by a local distributor (power tools, for example), the stock to sales ratio can be kept low; but for party dresses, where lead-times might be three weeks or more and customers require an extensive selection of styles and sizes to choose from, the stock to sales ratio needs to be higher. Usually these factors are considered collectively for the category of merchandise being planned, and an average stock to sales ratio is arrived at for the planning period. Thus, an average ratio of 2 might be sufficient for power tools, but may be as high as 10 for party dresses. This average is then raised or lowered through the selling season to reflect the effect of differing sales rates on the stock position: when sales peak, the stock runs down quickly and the stock to sales ratio drops down from the average; but when sales are slow, the stock to sales ratio rises. For seasonal goods it might be necessary to 'stockpile' in order to cope with subsequent surges in demand; again this is reflected by an increasing stock to sales ratio. In the example of women's toiletries, the average stock ratio is 3.0 and is raised and lowered according to the rate of sales.

The stock required to achieve the sales during the month should ideally be present at the beginning of the month; therefore, the stock position refers to the beginning of month (BOM) stock level. As sales progress through the month, the stock level drops, so that by the end of the month the stock position could be expressed as (BOM stock – sales). However, in reality, as well as selling stock, the retailer will also be receiving stock, in order to build the required level of stock for the next month, so that the stock position at the end of a preceding month should be the required BOM stock of the next month. The difference between the (BOM stock-sales) figure and the EOM stock figure will be the purchases that have arrived during the month. Figure 6.7 illustrates this process.

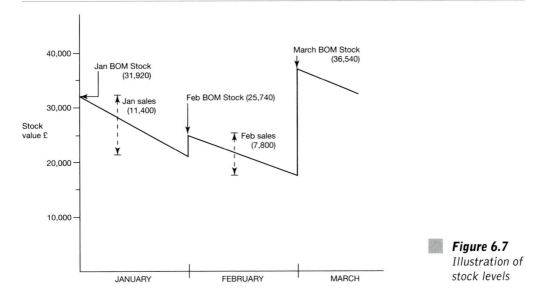

Figure 6.7
*Illustration of
stock levels*

If the plan started in Table 6.4 is continued, we can see how this process works through the season (see Table 6.5). Expressed as an equation it is as follows:

Planned purchases = EOM stock + sales – BOM stock

The planned purchases for each month represent the value of stock (at retail price) that the buyer needs to bring in from suppliers. Some goods may need to be ordered in advance of the season, whilst others can be topped up immediately; therefore, it is likely that some of the planned purchase figure will have already been committed to pre-ordered goods suppliers. The remaining funds are what are left 'open' for the buyer to spend on fast lead-time stock. In this way the stock level for the next month is achieved.

Table 6.5 *Arriving at the planned purchase figures*

Category: toiletry	Jan.	Feb.	Mar.	Apr.	May	Jun.	Total
Gift packs (women's)							
Forecast sales (%)	19	13	21	16	14	17	100
Forecast sales (£)	11,400	7,800	12,600	9,600	8,400	10,200	60,000
BOM stock: sales ratio	2.8	3.3	2.9	2.8	3.1	3.1	3.0 (average)
Beginning of month (BOM) stock (£)	31,920	25,740	36,540	26,880	26,040	31,620	N/A
End of month (EOM) stock (£)	25,740	36,540	26,880	26,040	31,620	—	N/A
Planned purchases (£)	5,220	18,600	2,940	8,760	13,980	—	N/A

Open-to-buy

Buyers do not pay their suppliers retail selling prices however, and so the planned purchase figure must have the gross profit margin removed in order to give the buyer the true 'open-to-buy' figures. For planning purposes, an average gross margin for the category might be used, even though the retailer may vary the margin on the products within the range (see Chapter 12). The sales and stock figures in the plan should always be planned at retail selling price, so that actual and planned figures can be easily compared.

Reductions in stock value

Unfortunately, sales are not the only reasons for the removal of stock from retail businesses. There are a variety of reasons why a stock value position falls, and these have to be accounted for in order to give a true reflection of value of stock. Stock reductions include:

- external theft;
- internal pilferage;
- shop soiling and damage;
- markdowns.

Discounts may also be given to customers (for example to store card holders) and to staff (as an incentive), and so all of these reductions in the value of stock have to be reflected in the budget plan. Historical figures will be useful in terms of setting a realistic reductions level for a category of merchandise; however, the following guidelines should be used when it comes to detailed planning:

- *Shrinkage* (theft and damage) tends to follow the same pattern as sales: the more people in the store, the more shop soiling and damage of goods is likely to occur, and the easier it is for thieves to operate amongst the crowds. In addition, a thief's needs tend to coincide with those of an honest shopper, so the retail crime rate peaks in the Christmas build-up.
- *Markdowns* may be taken as part of a planned, offensive promotional strategy or as a defensive reaction to competition or poor sales performance. If the general economic forecast is poor, it may be prudent to plan a higher than average markdown figure, for example.
- *Staff discounts and customer discounts* tend to be taken slightly ahead of the normal sales peak. This is because it is more likely that staff and regular customers will be enticed by new merchandise offerings at the start of the season. They may also be swift to take advantage of end of season price-cutting.

If these various reductions to the value of stock were not taken into account, the stock value on the retailer's stock control system would be very different to the actual value of the physical stock present within the retail business. The only way to reconcile the two would be to undertake a physical stock-take. This will confirm whether or not the planning and monitoring systems are showing an accurate representation of business reality.

In terms of dealing with reductions in the merchandise budget plan, they have to be planned into the stock equation as shown in Table 6.6; in effect, a retailer has to buy extra stock into the business in order to compensate for the falling value of stock through reductions. In this case the total reduction in stock value through the season averages to 10 per cent of the total estimated sales for the category. The equation for calculating the planned purchase figure, taking reductions into account is:

Planned purchases = EOM stock + sales + reductions − BOM stock

Table 6.6 *A full merchandise budget plan*

Category: toiletry	Jan.	Feb.	Mar.	Apr.	May	Jun.	Total
Gift packs (women's)							
Forecast sales (%)	19	13	21	16	14	17	100
Forecast sales (£)	11,400	7,800	12,600	9,600	8,400	10,200	60,000
Forecast reductions %	21	13	21	14	15	16	100
Forecast reductions (£'000)	1,260	780	1,260	840	900	960	6000
BOM stock: sales ratio	2.8	3.3	2.9	2.8	3.1	3.1	3.0 (average)
Beginning of month (BOM) stock (£)	31,920	25,740	36,540	26,880	26,040	31,620	N/A
End of month (EOM) stock (£)	25,740	36,540	26,880	26,040	31,620	—	N/A
Planned purchases (£)	6,480	19,380	4,200	9,600	14,880	—	N/A

SUMMARY

The purpose of this chapter has been to explore the various principles associated with the management of products, from a quantitative viewpoint, both in terms of the physical volume of products for ordering quantities and providing stock cover, and the value of stock investment. Having the right amount of product allows a retailer to maintain its customer service objectives with high availability levels and extended choice. Having fast selling items well supported and less money tied up in slower lines means that a retailer is making their selling space productive. Too much of the wrong type of product results in low profits, cluttered retail outlets and dissatisfied customers. This chapter has sought to give the reader an insight into the complexities of stock management and to show how stock control challenges for retailers start to become more difficult when products have a high seasonal or fashion factor: forecasting becomes more difficult, sales patterns become more varied and extreme, and the risk of having too much or too little product becomes much greater.

The number-crunching abilities of modern stock management systems have taken much of the drudgery out of stock management, and merchandisers have much better information upon which to base stock management decisions. Highly seasonal and fashion influenced products continue to be a challenge for retail product managers, however, it is these products that provide the opportunities to create interest in product ranges and to report an exceptional sales reaction.

EXERCISE FORECASTING THE SALES OF A STAPLE PRODUCT

The following table shows the sales figures (in numbers of products sold, i.e. volume) for product A

Weeks	1	2	3	4	5	6	7	8	9	10	11	12
Actual Sales of product A	70	68	70	72	75	77	78	70	?	?	?	?
4 weekly totals				280				300			Forecast?	

You need to produce a forecast for the next 4 weeks (weeks 9–12)

A simple approach would be to add the sales for weeks 1–8 together, and then divide that total by the number of weeks (8). This would give you an average sales figure over the specified time period. In this case the average weekly sales figure is 72.5 items, and so the forecast for the next four week period would be 290. This type of approach is sometimes referred to as the moving averages forecasting technique.

However, we can see that, although this product is classed as a staple product, sales are not absolutely flat. In the weeks 1–4 sales were gently fluctuating and then in weeks 4–7 sales started to increase slowly, but in week 8 the sales figure dropped relatively significantly from week 7. What if this is the start of a downturn in sales, reversing the longer-term, upward trend that was apparent in weeks 3 to 8? A forecast of 290 based on the average sales figure would be too high.

In the exponential smoothing technique the most recent sales performances are taken to be those which will have the most bearing on the future. The sales in previous time periods are weighted to forecast future periods.

The sales for product A over the previous 4 weeks (5–8) were 300 in total. Sales for weeks (1–4) came to 280. When producing the forecasts for the next 4 weeks, the product manager wants to be optimistic about the long-term sales trend, but is concerned about the drop over the last week from 78 to 70.

The exponential smoothing technique introduces an 'alpha factor' that determines the extent to which actual demand should have an influence on a new forecast. The alpha factor can vary between 0 and 1 and can be set high (e.g. 0.5) when demand is changing rapidly, but when demand is changing slowly the alpha factor can be set low (e.g. 0.2). The new forecast is calculated by taking the forecast for the previous period and adding it to the alpha factor multiplied by the difference between actual demand and the old forecast.

If the product manager (PM) considers last week's drop in sales to be a 'blip' in a healthy upward sales trend, then a higher (say 0.4) alpha value can be set. The PM believes that the sales trend will continue to change for the better. If, on the other hand, the PM thinks the lower weekly sales might be the start of a slowdown in sales, or that sales may return to a more flat pattern, a lower (say 0.2) alpha value can be set. The two forecasts for the next four weeks will be as follows.

The 'old forecast' used in this calculation is a given value of 280. This was a forecast based on the sales for weeks 1–4 and was used for the following 4-week periods.

Old forecast	Alpha factor	Difference between actual demand and old forecast
280 +	0.4 ×	(300 − 280)
280 +	0.2 ×	(300 − 280)

The more confident forecast comes out as 288. The less confident forecast comes out as 284.

Although the difference is quite small, the forecasts reflect the difference that two alpha values (set by the retail product manager and based on experience) can make to a forecast. What is also interesting is that when we compare these forecasts with the one that was generated using moving averages both the values are lower. The moving average technique in comparison with the exponential smoothing technique is somewhat crude, whereas, with experience, the alpha values and the levels of confidences can be fine tuned to produce a forecast that is most likely to reflect retailing realities. The moving average forecast was not sensitive to the sudden downturn in sales and was in danger of causing an overstock.

This example has taken a simplified approach to explain the principles of exponential smoothing. As the figures for actual demand move into forecasted figures, new forecasts are continuously being produced. An automated forecasting programme within a stock control system will output suggested forecasts until a product manager overrides with any new input, like a different alpha value.

QUESTIONS

1   Explain the principles of the economic order quantity. Suggest reasons for the diminishing use of the EOQ in retail stock control operations.

2   Analyse the seasonal, fashion and endorsement influences on the demand for the following product categories: (a) soft drinks and (b) wines.

3   For a number of chosen categories, think of the sales distribution over the year. To what extent are your products seasonal, and when would be a good time(s) to launch a product related promotion in each category?

4   Refer back to Table 6.6 when attempting this exercise.
    Some additional information concerning the orders that the buyer of the women's toiletry department has provisionally booked with suppliers for the spring season has been provided:

- Beauty Pack Ltd: £3,000 order, delivery February, March.
- Handy Gifts & Co: £6,000 order, delivery February, March.
- Gift Bag Ltd: £4,000 order, delivery January, February, March.
- Scents and Sense: £2,000 order, delivery March, April.

NB: deliveries are split evenly across the months, unless otherwise stated.

The average gross margin for this category is 45 per cent.

Task: Calculate the open-to-buy figures that will be left for each month, when all the orders have been confirmed.

5   Refer back to Table 6.6 when attempting this exercise.
In order to show how the open-to-buy changes when actual sales do not exactly meet forecasted sales, make the following actual figure substitutions on the plan shown in Table 6.6:

■ The March promotion was more successful that anticipated, and sales peaked at £15,000.
■ May was very cold, which slowed holiday purchases, resulting in sales only reaching £7,000.

6   On a merchandise budget plan, what would be the significance of a negative figure in the Open-to-Buy figures as shown in March using Table 6.6 and the order values given in question 4. Suggest how a buyer might deal with this situation.

7   The following exercise involves drawing up a merchandise budget plan, based on an abstract from the merchandisers report for the 'Novelty Socks' category, which falls within the hosiery department of Harvey and Aldred Department store:

As one might expect, the sales of this type of merchandise are highly seasonal. Socks are favourite stocking fillers at Christmas, and are often bought at the last minute when no better idea has emerged! In fact, we take almost half the season's money in the month before Christmas. We do, however, keep a small range to sell the year round, with an average beginning of month stock/sales ratio of three. There are two reasons for this; there are Birthday gifts, of course, and it also enables us to join in any 'themed' promotion that is being planned storewide. This year, for example, we are doing a 'Tartan Promotion' in early October, which will be good for all men's accessories. In the week of November 5th, the whole men's wear floor has a celebration event, where we offer a 20 per cent discount on all customer purchases over £50. Socks often do well in this week as they are used to 'top up' the sales to get the discount. This year our total season's sales forecast is £18,500, and reductions normally average out at 10 per cent of sales.

REFERENCES AND FURTHER READING

Baily, P., Farmer, D., Jessop, D. and Jones, D. (1998) *Purchasing Principles and Management*, 8th edn, Pearson Education, London.
Fernie, J. (ed.) (1999) *The Future of UK Retailing*, Financial Times Retail and Consumer Reports, London.
Fernie, J. and Sparks, L. (2004) *Logistics and Retail Management*, 2nd edn, Kogan Page, London.
Finch, J. (2003) 'John Lewis Tots Up Bill for Central Line Closure', *Guardian*, 7 March.
Harris, D. and Walters, D. (1992) *Retail Operations Management: A Strategic Approach*, Prentice Hall, Hemel Hempstead.
Hart, C., Kirkup, M., Preston, D., Rafiq, M. and Walley, P. (eds), (1997) *Cases in Retailing: Operational Perspectives*, Blackwell, Oxford.
Lysons, C.K. (1991) *Purchasing*, Pitman, London.

Mintel (1997) *Convenience Retailing*, January, Mintel Report, London.

Wills, J. (1999) *Merchandising and Buying Strategies: New Roles for Global Operation*, Financial Times Retail and Consumer Reports, London.

Chapter 7

Managing the response to sales

LEARNING OBJECTIVES

The purpose of this chapter is to:

- Understand the concept of response within a product management system.
- Become familiar with information based systems that allow retailers to respond to sales with product replenishment.
- Understand the relationship between sales response and the management of supply.
- Appreciate the contribution that management philosophies such as quick response (QR) efficient consumer response (ECR) and collaborative planning, forecasting and replenishment (CPFR) have made to efficient product replenishment.

INTRODUCTION

Understanding the principles of the stock management techniques discussed in the previous chapter will help a retail product manager to appreciate the challenges that surround the objective of getting the 'right' quantity of product at the 'right' time into a retail business. The application of information technology and the resulting changes to business cost structures, however, has meant that buying practices have changed in many modern retail organisations: orders are communicated in paperless form, sales data is immediately available and goods are electronically tracked through the supply pipeline. Better and faster information has meant that retailers have been able to virtually turn stock management on its head; the approach now is not to manage stock, but rather to manage demand for products and respond to that demand with a flowing supply of goods. The aim of this chapter is to build on the reader's understanding of the concept of consumer-led product management and explore the notion of efficient replenishment, introduced in Chapter 3 under the auspices of category management within an ECR (efficient consumer response) system.

RESPONSE

With the exception of highly seasonal products like pumpkins or Father's Day cards for example, the 'ideal' situation for most products within a stock management system is that when one product is sold, that product is replenished. The ubiquitous EPOS (electronic point of sales) system, in principle allows this to happen. Sales are recorded at the checkout electronically, and detailed information about what has been sold is now available. It is unrealistic, however, to organise physical product replenishment on an individual item basis; customers would not be able to get around a store for people stacking shelves. The EPOS system therefore can be integrated with a stock control system, so that only when the number of products sold reaches a pre-set level does the system trigger a request for product replenishment. The request for more products is sent either to a distribution centre or warehouse, where a retailer is holding back-up stock, or in a small retailer where no warehousing facilities exist, the message is sent to the retailer's buying office, so that an order can be sent to a supplier for more products.

A responsive stock management system will be able to replenish the goods automatically, either from the retailer's distribution centre or from a supplier's warehouse. It is the fine-tuning of this response that has made modern-day retailers so efficient. They are able to keep products in stock whilst organising their supply chains in a way that keeps costs to a minimum. Response is all about maintaining high levels of availability. As we saw in Chapter 6, this is much easier to do with products with a relatively stable demand pattern. It is therefore with this type of product that much of the fine-tuning has taken place so that for a number of product categories response to sales in terms of replenishment can be automatic.

More recent approaches to stock control are ones that aim to cut all stock holding by retailers to the absolute minimum. This is achieved by having a replenishment system that only responds to actual sales. A stock plan is prepared in advance for a time period, but instead of stock being ordered according to forecast, it is called up in response to actual sales. These systems are the basis of efficient consumer response (ECR) systems in the food and fast moving consumer goods sectors and quick response (QR) systems in non-food sectors.

SALES-BASED ORDERING (SBO)

For goods with a relatively stable demand, multiple retailers can use a system of automatic ordering and replenishment based on previous sales. This system is based on the principle of exponential smoothing (see Chapter 6), which uses recent sales as a basis on which to forecast the sales in the next period. The SBO system orders directly against this forecast, but can be managed by exception if required, according to the current trading environment. For example, the demand for bottled water is relatively straightforward in that it is stable until warm weather occurs, when demand rises and falls according to the heat. As the temperature rises, the sales-based order is amended upwards until the heat wave breaks, at which point a product manager swiftly amends the sales-based order downwards to slow the flow of bottled water product. Managers of grocery stores in university towns have to swiftly increase the sales-based order for pizzas and cheap wine when term begins!

AUTOMATIC REPLENISHMENT

An automatic replenishment system relies on a supply source, whether a retailer's distribution centre or a supplier's depot, being able to respond directly to the demand for a product, shown in sales figures, with immediate supply. Many large multiple retailers have a network of regional distribution centres or warehouses that can replenish a store within a 24-hour cycle. Should the distribution network be experiencing difficulties with the supply of a product line, then store personnel can be advised via the same management information system about why a delay in replenishment might be occurring and what action they should take.

BOX 7.1 RETAILERS LOVE TO BLAME THE WEATHER

It is ironic that as retail product management becomes more reliant on information technology to drive the operations that get a product from a producer to a retailer's shelf, one of the fundamental challenges retailers face seems to be, if anything, making things even more difficult. It is still the most commonly cited reason for poor retail performance, and in the UK at least it is a national obsession. We are, of course, talking about the weather. Within the same week in early June the UK weather can vary by at least 15 degrees, with anything from drought to torrential rain.

Unpredictable weather means unpredictable demand, which means for some systems a breakdown in efficient response. Warm weather boosts sales in barbecues and garden furnishings; it encourages people to spend their holidays in the UK, while demand surges for light beer, soft drinks and ice cream. This is not unexpected, but warm weather also boosts sales of less obviously weather-sensitive products like baby wipes, shower gel and women's shavers. In contrast, warm weather in autumn can be disastrous for sales in the fashion trade, and makes us postpone our Christmas shopping.

The Meteorological Office estimated the cost of weather uncertainty to the retail trade to be £4.5 billion (Denny, 2003), with the food and clothing sectors being the most badly affected. Restaurants can also suffer, as people choose picnics and patio dining in place of a hot meal indoors.

Source: *Retail Week,* August 2003 and Denny, 2003

EFFICIENT CONSUMER RESPONSE (ECR) AND QUICK RESPONSE

The principles of the efficient consumer response (ECR) approach to product management were outlined in Chapter 3. The alignment of supply management with demand management in product categories relies on information sharing and collaboration between retailer and suppliers, and so an efficient sales reporting system is a fundamental requirement for setting a responsive supply system in motion. A retailer's logistical operations in their supply chain are heavily dependent on information technology, and in particular on the large integrated stock replenishment systems that control the movement and storage of an enormous number of separate products (Mackinnon, 1996, cited in Fernie and Sparks, 2004).

The key difference between an ECR system and a quick response (QR) system is determined by the nature of the products involved: ECR systems generally concern food and fast moving consumer goods, which have relatively stable demand patterns and higher volumes. The demand management is normally performed at distribution centre level and in higher unitisation than the single product item, for example the 'crate-load'. Quick response systems on the other hand deal with units, and therefore are concerned with higher value, lower volume product (typically clothing and home furnishings). They also involve supply techniques that allow retailers to respond more effectively to fashion and seasonal sales variations (Fiorito *et al.*, 1995). This is referred to as having 'agility' in the supply chain, which for some product markets is more important than efficiency. Agility allows a retailer's suppliers to respond quickly to unpredictable demand to avoid stock-outs, whilst minimising markdown and product obsolescence (Fernie and Sparks, 2004). Agility can also help retailers to respond quickly to new product market opportunities, and respond fast to customer orders, which is especially important for home deliveries.

In quick response systems sales information is sent electronically to the supplier without intervention from the buying office, so that the supplier is as up to date as the retailer on what is selling. The supplier replenishes the item directly to the store in accordance with a predetermined seasonal stock assortment plan (see Chapter 4). A quick response system means that stock is eliminated from the retailer's holding system (apart from what is on display in the store) but it does rely on a willingness of the supplier to hold a small amount of stock (possibly in a semi-finished state), to enable them to react immediately. This is supported by swift and flexible manufacturing systems, with production planned according to the requirements of the assortment plan and the sales information received. In an ECR system, the need for a predetermined stock assortment plan is effectively eliminated; the assortment plan exists for an indefinite period, and then is subject to a constant fine-tuning process in response to consumer demand patterns.

SUPPLIER INVOLVEMENT IN RESPONSIVE REPLENISHMENT SYSTEMS

The advantage for suppliers who are involved in a sales responsive system is that it gives them real-time sales information, which helps them to plan production for the back-up stock. The supplier will be able to spot fast and slow sellers and react swiftly by swapping production from slow to fast sellers. The sales information will also help the supplier schedule orders for raw materials more effectively (see case study at the end of this chapter).

A considerable commitment is required to make a sales responsive replenishment system work:

- The supplier and retailer must have compatible information systems to allow for electronic transmission of data.
- Distribution from supplier to retailer must be reliable and cost-effective.
- In a QR system, suppliers must perform functions that might otherwise take place at a retailer's distribution centre (DC). These functions are often referred to as pre-retailing and include: ticketing or labelling, preparation of stock (folding, hanging on retailer's hanger, pressing, stacking into predetermined quantities and so on).

In addition to these operational requirements, demand responsive systems only function properly if retailers and suppliers work together in an atmosphere of co-operation and trust. For example, the retailer must trust the supplier to treat potentially sensitive sales information in confidence, and they have to have faith in a supplier's willingness to hold stock or be able to replenish very quickly. The supplier adapts their systems to the requirements of the retailer in the belief that the business relationship will continue into the next season and beyond, and by giving a good service to the retailer, becomes part of a supply chain that provides high levels of customer satisfaction.

COLLABORATIVE PLANNING FORECASTING AND REPLENISHMENT (CPFR)

CPFR is a formalised management support system that helps retailers and their suppliers to work in partnership on stock management. CPFR encourages the sharing of information on market demand, and all the factors that influence demand, so that forecasting is more accurate, and production is more closely matched to sales. This, as we have seen, is more difficult to achieve in markets like clothing where fashion trends and seasonality cause fluctuating demand patterns, and so it is particularly useful when used in conjunction with quick response supply chain management.

Collaborative planning pools the resources of the experts from both organisations so that both retailer and supplier have a mutual understanding of the optimum product assortment and the means by which that assortment is going to be most efficiently maintained and managed through its demand cycles. In large retail organisations, not only retailers and their suppliers may be involved in CPFR, but also other entities in the supply chain such as logistics service providers. These partners develop joint business plans, contribute to what are often subjective forecasts, and agree on actions and financial remedies (such as markdowns) should sales fail to meet forecast.

CPFR is also very applicable in the product management of categories where a high level of promotional activity takes place, which results in significant demand fluctuations at SKU level. By collaborating on, and planning promotional activity together, retailer and supplier can ensure that promotional activity is supported with good product availability and rapid replenishment (see Chapter 10). Internet exchanges have helped to foster CPFR initiatives, with their ability to share large amounts of information from a variety of sources (see Chapter 5).

DRAWBACKS OF SALES RESPONSIVE REPLENISHMENT SYSTEMS

One of the drawbacks of a QR system is associated with the small, frequent delivery pattern. The extra transportation costs and pre-retailing function will eventually be paid for in the cost of the goods to the retailer and this may outweigh the benefit of the leaner stock holding levels. The logistical problems encountered when a number of suppliers are responding quickly may make store operations difficult. Where retailers have a very large product range, and an associated large number of suppliers, the quick response philosophy has only been partially adopted. In this case, automatic replenishment in response to sales is still part of the system, but instead of delivering direct to stores, the distribution centre retains its role, and ready prepared store deliveries from suppliers are collated onto lorries. Some retailers have found that they can improve stock replenishment by sharing logistics facilities with other retailers at a shopping destination (see Box 7.2).

BOX 7.2 CONSOLIDATION CENTRES

In spite of high levels of competition at the front end of the retailer outlet, retailers are sometimes able to enjoy significant benefits by collaborating in areas generally unseen by customers. Broadmead shopping centre in Bristol, for example, has a consolidation centre, run by the local city council and funded by the European Union, which aims to cut down town centre congestion and pollution. Retailers from the shopping centre, including Accessorize, Carphone Warehouse and Lush are therefore sharing a logistics facility that takes in deliveries for the various shops from their suppliers, then sorts them onto pallets for the shops and delivers them together. This helps the retailer by giving one delivery; they can schedule staff to be available to manage the stock intake, thereby improving the productivity of the replenishment process and reducing the likelihood of sales staff ignoring customers because they are busy with stock. Similar schemes are run at Heathrow, where flight terminal retailing is huge business, and at the busy purpose-built regional shopping centre at Meadowhall, Sheffield. The consolidation centres not only sort packages, but they can also offer retailers additional services such as unpacking, price tagging and even shelf stacking at the store. The contribution to efficiency in response is shown by the name given to the consolidation centre at Meadowhall: the ARC (Accelerated Response Centre).

Source: Lyster, 2004

Other drawbacks relate to both QR and ECR and include the difficulty in establishing real partnerships between retailers and their suppliers and the lack of appropriate structures within the retailer and supply organisations to allow the systems to operate to their full potential (see Chapter 3).

SUPPLIER-MANAGED INVENTORY

It is possible that, where appropriate, a retailer may relinquish the stock management operation completely to suppliers. In its true form a supplier or vendor managed inventory (VMI system) passes the responsibility for managing stock levels within a retail outlet to the supplier, with the retailer providing the information that allows the supplier to schedule their production and finished stock level so that automatic replenishment is guaranteed. In certain instances, it makes sense for a supplier to provide a stock filling service. For example, with small item merchandise such as batteries, spices or stationery, it is not unusual for the supplier to offer a replenishment service as part of their cost price to the retailer. The supplier simply invoices the retailer for the stock that is replenished on each visit. However, VMI is more complex than a shelf-stacking arrangement, with a supplier taking on the strategic development of a product category as well as providing the operational stock-servicing role. In a VMI system the retailer and the supplier agree to a forward planned assortment, and then the supplier is provided with real-time sales information, so that they can replenish automatically and spot the sales trends. This allows them to plan production in a way that means fast selling goods can be replenished without delay and the build-up of unwanted merchandise at the end of a season is reduced. The retailer provides seasonal promotional plans, and the supplier produces sales forecasts and replenishes according to agreed availability and inventory turnover targets.

In principle, VMI is similar to a QR system supported by CPFR, but with VMI the supplier has more control over range development. In effect, suppliers rent shelf space, and if they see a trend developing for a particular type of merchandise, then it is expected that they, rather than the retailer, will make the decision to offer increased variety in that type of product. As with other highly integrated stock management systems, VMI cannot work without a true partnership existing between retailer and supplier; it takes the role of category captain one stage further. Without this, VMI is open to abuse and some so-called VMI systems simply push the stock holding burden up the supply chain to the supplier, relieving the retailer of any end of season over-stock. Information is, again, the key, and must be openly shared if suppliers are to take on such a strategic role in product management. Only when a supplier can see the pattern of sales developing, can they react efficiently to demand. If they are not able to supply efficiently, then the costs will end up being passed back to the retailer in higher prices for future merchandise.

Achabal *et al.* (2000) summarised the advantages of VMI as: giving a retailer's customers the best opportunity to buy from a supplier's product range; helping a retailer to manage their stock more effectively; and assisting a supplier to schedule their production which is crucial for better long-term availability for customers. Suppliers may be better equipped to interpret the sales information they receive into demand patterns and be prepared with a more responsive replenishment, after all they may well be more motivated to keep their products in stock than a retailer, who may have substitute brands within the assortment.

STRATEGIC RESPONSE TO SALES

So far in this chapter a number of 'systems' have been explored, which have been instigated to help retailers and their supply networks respond to consumer demand. However, the discussion has focused on the methods retailers can employ to try to maintain a good flow of products in order to provide high levels of customer service and maximise sales opportunities. This is all very well, assuming that the assortment is correct in the first place and that the selection of goods on the shelf represents the best choice for the customer. This is where the concepts of efficient replenishment and efficient assortment meet. High customer service quality can therefore be derived from good availability measured at two levels. First, the extent to which stock of the planned assortment is available for purchase, and second, the extent to which a customer is satisfied by the category mix and the brands on offer within the planned assortment.

The extent to which a customer shares their spend amongst different retailers is an indication of satisfaction with the product assortment. For some shopping tasks, such as buying shoes or kitchen furniture, visiting a number of different retailers is part of the shopping process; consumers will carry out an extensive search to find the product that is 'right' for them, and be convinced that they have made the best choice. Other shopping tasks, such as grocery shopping, are considered a chore and the consumer wishes to buy as many products as possible under one roof, and so in order for retailers to generate loyalty in this type of shopping situation they must ensure that the product range matches the needs of the customer who visits.

Micro-marketing techniques, using systematic data analysis of personalised purchasing data (generated by the loyalty card) have allowed retailers to gain insights into the way customers use stores and how they shop in them. Ranges can then be adjusted according to purchasing patterns and the share of a customer's spend (Ziliani and Bellini, 2002). For example, by analysing customer data and shopping tendencies a leading grocery multiple was able to respond to a cash rich, time poor customer whose main concern while shopping was seeking out meal solutions by tailoring the product range in store. This resulted in an increase to fresh produce ranges, core grocery ranges more focused on top-up, e.g. less depth, wider variety, less promotional ranges, a coffee and deli counter at the front of the store, and expanded ranges in giftware, health and beauty.

Many smaller retailers do not have the resources to undertake the level of sophisticated data analysis indicated above. There are however, other methods that can be used to help a retailer be responsive to customers' product preferences. Some of these are as follows:

- listening to customers;
- encouraging sales staff to feed back customer reaction to product ranges;
- being aware of category lifecycle trends;
- consulting product market research reports;
- analysing the ranges of competitors;
- listening to suppliers.

All of these practices can help a retailer get a really good idea of what customers want and when they are likely to want to buy it, which will help them to plan their assortments and stock cover to achieve maximum availability.

SUMMARY

As retailers have become more adept at reading sales patterns and fine-tuning sales forecasts, they have been able to use this knowledge to gear up the supporting supply chain so that it is able to respond very quickly and without huge costs, to consumer demand. More recent approaches to retail stock management have taken two traditional, seemingly contradictory, aims, and have devised ways of achieving them simultaneously. These aims are to keep stock holding low and maintain a high level of stock service levels for customers. The essence of combining these objectives is to respond to, rather than predict and run the risk of being wrong about, demand for products. Responsive stock management involves supply partners that are willing to play their supporting role in the replenishment process. As relationships between retailer and supplier become more integrated, further developments such as CPFR and VMI combine the efforts of both parties to achieve high levels of availability and strategic response to customer needs. The development of integrated information and distribution systems that allow retailers immediate access to the knowledge of where and how much of any product is available at any point in the supply chain have made a really important contribution to the process of effective stock management.

CASE STUDY   QUICK RESPONSE IN FASHION RETAILING: THE PRINCIPLES AND THE PRACTICE

One of the first protagonists of the quick response approach to retail supply was Benetton. As a vertically integrated manufacturing and retailing company they were quick to see the benefits of setting up systems which enabled the manufacturing end of the business to react as swiftly as possible to consumer sales patterns. Forward ordering of stock can make stores vulnerable by causing them to carry styles and colours that prove to be less popular, whilst running out of the bestsellers quickly, with long lead-times for replenishment. Traditionally, sweaters and cardigans were produced by knitting up coloured yarn; however, Benetton's quick response system uses a 'garment-dyed' process, whereby uncoloured (grey) yarn is knitted up into the garment style. The finished article can then be 'piece-dyed' to whatever colour is selling well. In some cases two colour effects can be introduced using dye-resist and dye-attract yarn in the garment. The system prevents the build up of unwanted stock of both garments and yarn, as the finished article is produced according to the need for replenishment, and can be delivered to stores within a matter of days. The transfer of sales data via EDI to the manufacturing units is essential for this speedy process.

Oasis has also used quick response systems in its fashion supply chain. These include ordering fabric as late as possible, and then only finalising the style of garment to be cut out of the fabric 2–3 weeks before delivery is due into the stores. Using multiple suppliers for one product helps to prevent gaps in a range of co-ordinating pieces, whilst fast turnaround of goods in the distribution centre ensures the product is not stuck in non-retail space. Suppliers need to be able to understand the way Oasis works, and be able to provide the flexibility and quick changes that fashion retailing requires. Joint planning helps, but ultimately the suppliers have to understand that reacting to sales is always going to be necessary, and no amount of pre-planning will tell you what the fashion-led customer will end up buying. Past sales patterns only give an indication, and relying too heavily on what has done well in previous seasons runs the risk of producing stale product ranges. A high fashion product has a shorter shelf life than a packet of biscuits, and so needs to be treated as a perishable item.

137

Many of Oasis' suppliers have grown with the company from early days, and so they have a keen awareness of the retailer's need and have adapted their production facilities accordingly. They are rewarded for their service by loyalty from the retailer. Negotiations between the retailer and its suppliers are tough, but they are conducted with a mutual understanding that they are both continually striving towards the same aim, which is to sell more garments in Oasis stores to Oasis customers.

New Look and Zara are two other fashion retailers that have used QR to help them translate fashion ideas into garments in store at record time. Zara in particular have had their supply chain activities dissected by various observers in order to reveal their recipe for international success. Zara combine in-house production activities with subcontracted work to minimise costs at all stages of manufacture: dyeing, cutting, labelling and packing represent where the Zara organisation in northern Spain can achieve economies of scale; whereas other, more labour intensive activities like sewing and finishing are performed by a network of subcontractors who specialise in manufacturing a particular garment type. The centre for product management is the design department where trend knowledge is combined with sales data from each international market served to produce a flow of fashion ideas; the best of these are then put into production, and then trailed in a group of test stores, before stock allocations for the rest of the stores in the chain are finalised. Zara's supply chain combines efficiency with agility to give the company time-based competitive advantage; design ideas can turn into garments on shelves in less than two weeks. Zara does not lose any sleep when availability is low; it is their policy to under-supply to lessen markdown burden, and fresh stock is delivered to stores every two days. For the young fashion-conscious Zara customer, this is far more important than always having the right size for everybody.

Source: Jack, 1995; Christopher *et al.*, 2004; Clements, 2000; Fernie and Sparks, 2004

QUESTIONS

1   Discuss the notion that understanding consumer purchase patterns is the underpinning of any efficient stock control system.

2   Discuss the contribution that sales reactive stock control systems have made to leaner stock holding in retail organisations.

3   Referring to the case study at the end of the chapter, explain how a quick response system can help a fashion retailer to have the 'right' quantity of products in its stores.

4   Consider the advantages and drawbacks associated with CPFR and VMI stock management systems. How applicable are they to all retailers?

5   Explain the meaning of 'agility' in the context of retail supply chains, and assess how important it is for today's large multiple retailer.

REFERENCES AND FURTHER READING

Achabal, D.D., McIntyre, S.H., Smith, S.A. and Kalyanam, K. (2000) 'A Decision Support System for Vendor Managed Inventory', *Journal of Retailing*, 76(4): 430–454.

Christopher, M., Lowson, B. and Peck, H. (2004) 'Fashion Logistics and Quick Response', in J. Fernie and L. Sparks (eds), *Logistics and Retail Management: Insights into Current Practice and Trends from Leading Experts*, 2nd edn, Wiley, London, ch. 5.

Clements, A. (2000) 'Zara Leads Conquering Armada', *Retail Week*, 14 April.

Denny, N. (2003) 'Retailers Can Always Blame the Weather', *Retail Week*, 20 June.

Fernie, J. and Sparks, L. (eds) (2004) *Logistics and Retail Management: Insights into Current Practice and Trends from Leading Experts*, 2nd edn, Wiley, Chichester.

Fiorito, S.S., May, E.G. and Straughn, K. (1995) 'Quick Response in Retailing: Components and Implementation', *International Journal of Retailing and Distribution Management*, 23(5): 12–21.

Jack, S. (1995) 'All Together Now', *Drapers Record*, 11 February.

Lowson, B., King, R. and Hunter, A. (1999) *Quick Response: Managing the Supply Chain to Meet Consumer Demand*, Wiley, Chichester.

Lyster, S. (2004) 'A Load off Retailers' Minds', *Retail Week Supply Chain Guide*, September.

Wills, J. (1999) *Merchandising and Buying Strategies: New Roles for a Global Operation*, Financial Times Retail and Consumer Report, London.

Ziliani, C. and Bellini, S. (2003) '*Retail micro-marketing strategies and competition*'. Proceedings of the 12th EAERCD Conference, ESCP–EAP European School of Management, Paris, July 2003.

Web site

Voluntary Interindustry Commerce Standards (US): www.cpfr.org, accessed 09/05/05

Part III

The retail product management process
Implementation and evaluation

Chapter 8

Allocating retail space to products

LEARNING OBJECTIVES

The purpose of this chapter is to:

■ Gain an understanding of the concept of retail space, including how it is evaluated, what it represents in different retail contexts and why it is often constrained.

■ Become familiar with the space allocation process, and be able to indicate the stages involved for retailers.

■ Appreciate what a retailer's objectives might be when formulating space allocation plans.

■ Understand the relationship between retail space, sales turnover and profitability.

■ Have an appreciation of some of the practical challenges associated with space planning and allocation.

■ Assess the contribution of information technology to the space allocation process by understanding the principles of a space allocation system.

INTRODUCTION

In an era when physical retail space is still at a premium, constrained by planning restrictions and rising costs, productive use of space is a key indicator of buying and merchandising success, and high space productivity depends on offering the right range, in a logical layout, with products available and easy for the customer to find. Decisions about how much space to devote to each product line and its location in the store play an important role in the pursuit of merchandising success. The aim of this chapter is to provide an insight into this process.

SPACE MANAGEMENT

Space constraint applies to all retailers, but in non-store retailing the constraints are different. A mail order retailer, for example, has page space and the number of pages in a publication as constraining factors, whilst a TV shopping channel needs to break down the airtime to different products. However, internet retailing offers great opportunities for adding space without much additional resource input. The main constraint on the amount of space used in a virtual outlet is the customer's attention span. In spite of this additional freedom, the objectives of space allocation are essentially the same no matter which retail format is used.

The management of retail space is concerned with a number of key objectives. The first is to optimise both short-term and long-term returns on the investment cost of retail space. The second is to provide a logical, convenient and inspiring interface between the product range and the customer. This can be particularly important in a large store, where customers can quite easily become overwhelmed and lost. Another objective is to make sure that the right selection of products is available; that products fit into the retail space and that stock-outs are avoided. Choice for the customer is maximised when the best selection for them is put into the available space. Space allocation also has an important role to play in communicating the retail brand. When space is managed centrally it helps a chain of retail outlets to achieve visual consistency, so that customers are reassured by the similarity of the store layout and shelf appearance.

THE SPACE MANAGEMENT PROCESS

A retailer goes through a number of stages when allocating space to products. These are shown in Table 8.1. These four stages will be used as a framework for the inclusion of discussion topics within this chapter.

STAGE 1: MEASURING RETAIL SPACE

Although space in a store outlet is three dimensional, retail space is often measured in square, rather than cubic units. Square units are appropriate where, for example in fashion retailing, a variety of single tier fixtures stand on the shop floor (see Figure 8.1). Many fixtures, however, are multilevel and so more appropriate ways of measuring space to allocate might be on the basis of linear or cubic footage (see Figures 8.2 and 8.3). Measurements of space that are more specific to individual retailers might be useful, such as the number of pages to be published in a catalogue or the total number of fixtures available in an outlet.

Space productivity

The two principal measures of retail success are sales and profits. Sales volume and profitability can also be measured in relation to the amount of space used to generate those levels of sales and profits. This can then be compared with the level of financial investment in that space. The resulting measures express the productivity of retail space. Sales (or profits) per square metre is a commonly used measure of retail space productivity, which is an important concept in the evaluation of retail product management performance (see Chapter 12).

STAGE 2: DIVIDING THE SPACE INTO SELLING AREAS

At this stage, space management is concerned with allocating space to different product areas, defined according to individual retail businesses, but usually on the basis of product department or category. The amount of space will be determined to a greater extent on previous performance indicators, typically sales values. However, some products, because of their physical character-istics may need disproportionate amounts of space in relation to sales. In a department store, home furnishings may need a relatively large amount of space to generate a good level of sales because the products are bulky, a large variety of merchandise is needed for customers to choose from and a lot of display space is needed to do the product justice.

On the other hand, jewellery is a high value product category that needs relatively small amounts of space for display and selling purposes. The stage a product category is at in its lifecycle is likely to influence the space allocation at this level. If a category is growing, then more space should be allocated, whereas a declining category needs to have its space rationalised. For example

Table 8.1 *The space management process*

Stage 1   *Measuring space*: The total amount of space should be measurable. In store terms this would be physical space, the width, length and height should be taken into account. In non-store terms this would be the target number of pages in a catalogue or on a web site

Stage 2   *Dividing the space into selling areas*: At this stage the process is concerned with dividing the total retail space into selling areas, usually defined by product category or department. The space devoted will normally be determined by historical estimate of forecast category/department performance and will be expressed as a total spatial measure (for example, number of square metres). Sometimes the space will be allocated on the basis of the number of fixtures that will be given to each category

Stage 3   *Determine the layout*: At this stage product adjacencies will be decided, and the location of the selling areas will be determined. Individual outlet characteristics will influence this stage of the planning process; for example, location of entrances, set walkways around the store, lift and escalators, pillars and divisions all need to be taken into consideration in a store plan. In a catalogue the product categories that are going to go at the front of the book need to be decided. The relationships between one product category and another also have to be considered when determining the layout

Stage 4   *Determine the space allocation of product lines*: This involves the allocation of space on individual fixtures to each product line or stock keeping unit. The availability and characteristics of fixtures, individual product performances, product features and characteristics and the compatibility of products will all have a bearing on these decisions. Many retailers use sophisticated computerised space allocation systems at this stage

in December 2002 it was reported that Asda would be allocating more space to chilled foods, including ready meals, juices and dairy products in the coming year, as these were seen as growth categories for Asda. In the past they had allocated less space than their competitors to these product ranges (*Grocer*, 2002).

Home furnishings retailers, on the other hand have increased the space devoted to laminate flooring in response to the growing popularity of wood flooring. Although sales per selling space are the most commonly used indicator of departmental productivity, the profitability of the department or category may also have a bearing on the amount of space allocated at this level, so that, for example, the higher the profit margins on the products within a product range the more space is given to those products. The arguments for and against using both sales and profits to guide space allocation decisions are examined in detail later on in this chapter, when the space allocation given to individual product items is discussed, but they are also relevant at this level.

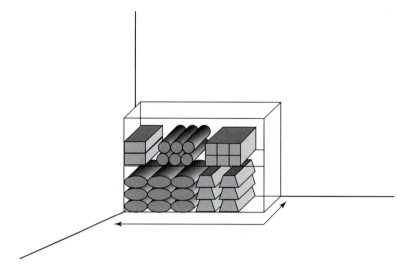

Figure 8.1 *Measuring retail space using square metres*

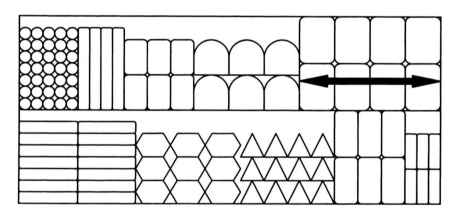

Figure 8.2 *Using linear measurement for retail space*

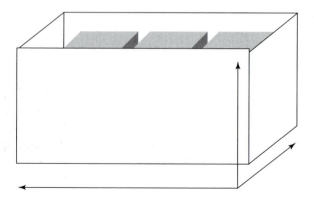

Figure 8.3 *Using cubic measurement for retail space*

STAGE 3: DETERMINING THE LAYOUT AND DECIDING ON PRODUCT ADJACENCIES

At this stage the numerical calculation of the selling areas is converted into a workable retail outlet layout. Having determined the amount of space that each department or category should be given based on their individual productivity, the areas have to be fitted around and into the actual space available. Some outlet space may be flexible, but some elements are immovable, such as checkout areas, entrances, walkways and so on. As well as these constraints, space can vary in terms of its 'quality', or potential to generate high sales, and product departments need to be organised so that there is some logical shopping flow through the outlet, and complementary categories are placed close to one another.

Space quality

When evaluating the level of productivity that retail space is generating, some consideration of the quality of the retail space should also be given, because within any retail outlet, some space will be better for selling from than other space. Every shopper for example has to pass an entrance, so this is a key area for promoting not only fast selling items, but those that play an important part in the overall retail brand image. High quality items, seasonal goods and the latest fashions are good choices for selling areas near entrances. In contrast, some areas, like the back of the store, need to have products that are particularly interesting so that customers are pulled into areas that would normally have low traffic. Discounted merchandise is useful for pulling customers to quieter areas. Till areas offer a retailer last minute purchasing opportunities, so impulse items are often located here.

The financial value of retail space is usually expressed in square metres. Rent and local government rates are usually charged at a rate per square foot or metre, and although alternative measures of retail space productivity are useful for retail product management, sales per square metre, otherwise known as sales density, is the measure most commonly used to compare the productivity of different retail outlets. Richer Sounds and Next, for example, are well known for having very high sales densities in their outlets.

Ground-level space is more valuable than other floors because it is more inconvenient to customers to get themselves to a different level. In a multi-level shopping centre, this becomes evident when the rent values of ground level outlets are compared with those of basement or upper levels. It is generally accepted that the value of space reduces from front to back of the store and increases when close to high footfall routes. The following elements of a store's design will therefore influence the value of space:

- entrances;
- lifts and escalators;
- service departments (toilets, cafés);
- destination product areas (for example a delicatessen counter in a supermarket);
- payment areas.

Areas of a retail outlet that are particularly effective places for selling are sometimes referred to as 'hotspots'. Exactly where these 'hotspots' are in any particular store will depend on the physical characteristics of individual outlets. Figure 8.4 shows the likely hot spots in a typical supermarket layout.

Retail management can also manipulate the customer flow in an attempt to maximise space productivity by allocating poorer retail space to 'destination' products and services. This is

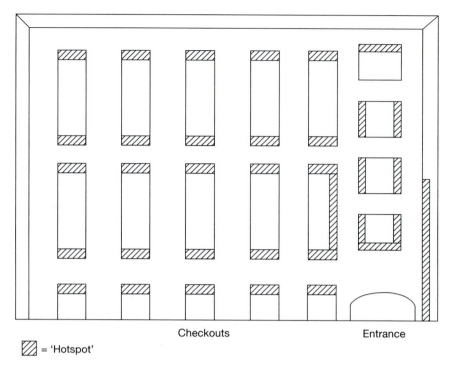

Checkouts   Entrance

= 'Hotspot'

Figure 8.4 *Typical 'hotspots' in a retail store*

particularly evident in department stores, where specialist products such as furniture and home entertainment, as well as hairdressing salons and customer service departments are located on basement or upper floors. Customer flow can also be encouraged by locating high demand items throughout the store layout, with plenty of impulse items located in between. Retailers need to find a balance between maximising sales of high demand products, generating flow around slower selling products (which may have higher profit margins), and providing logic and convenience in the layout for the customer.

Product adjacencies

A logical route through the different product categories or departments is part of a customer-focused offer, and can encourage linked sales. For example, in a baby equipment retailer like Mothercare it makes sense for merchandise to be grouped into themes for space planning purposes as shown in Table 8.2. These product themes are then presented in a logical way to the customer as they move through the store. Products for immediate needs, such as feeding and general baby-care come first, followed by bath-time and clothes; and then on to the more expensive, one-off purchases in the travel and nursery departments.

Table 8.2 *Product groups in a baby equipment retailer*

Feeding	Baby care	Bath time	Clothes	Travel	Nursery
Bottles	Nappies	Baby baths	Sleepwear	Prams	Cots
Sterilisers	Wipes	Soaps/liquids	Daywear	Pushchairs	Bedding
Formula milk	Change mats	Towels	Shoes	Strollers	Toys
Bottle warmers	Travel bags	Toys	Outerwear	Car seats	Travel cots
Bibs				Furniture	

BOX 8.1 PRODUCT ADJACENCIES: BEER AND FIRELIGHTERS?

The barbecue season provides a good opportunity for retailers to generate interest and sell distinctive groups of complementary products. Some of these products are strictly seasonal: the barbecues themselves and the briquettes for example. However, other products can be given additional space allocations in the seasonal aisle as part of the 'barbecue category'. Firelighters, matches, marinades, sauces, disposable tableware and beer are products that are found around the supermarket throughout the year, but are given a boost in the barbecue season by being merchandised as complementary goods.

It is estimated that guests take an average equivalent of eight drinks when they are invited to a barbecue, and 'stubbies' (bulk packed small bottles of beer) are particularly popular for barbecues as they are easy to handle, 'women friendly', and easily chilled. Whilst the majority of barbecue beer is bulk purchased in advance from supermarkets, and then chilled down at home, convenience store retailers are often used for guests to buy drinks en route, and so providing chilled beer becomes important for this type of retail format.

Source: *Grocer*, 2003

STAGE 4: ALLOCATING SPACE TO INDIVIDUAL PRODUCTS

Having made a plan for the layout of departments or categories within the retail outlet, the next stage is to make a decision about exactly how individual product lines should be displayed within the outlet, whether the product is going to sit on a fixture, or be represented by a photograph within a page spread. Various approaches to space allocation are discussed, for example by using sales or profits as a guideline, some practical challenges are considered, and the relationship between category management and space allocation is explored in this section.

Allocating space on the basis of sales

The guiding principle here is the more a product sells, the more space it should be given. Retaining a high stock service level will depend on retailers ensuring that they devote enough space to a high demand product, such as milk, to prevent replenishment of that item becoming inefficient and inconvenient to the customer. A fast selling item however, may not be one that a retailer makes much profit on (again milk is a good example), and so they may decide to allocate more space to their profitable lines. In taking this approach, however, the retailer is likely to encounter the problem of not devoting enough space to fast moving lines, so a balance has to be achieved.

Another decision that has to be made is which 'sales' figure should be used for the allocation exercise. Alternatives are historical sales figures (for that outlet); market share figures; or projected sales figures. The advantages and disadvantages of these methods are outlined in Box 8.2.

BOX 8.2 COMPARING ALTERNATIVE APPROACHES TO ALLOCATING SPACE ACCORDING TO SALES

Historical sales data

Advantages

- Easy to access
- Will indicate local preferences and influences

Disadvantages

- Will not allow for the potential of product lines that the store does not carry or for new products
- Does not allow for current and forecasted changes in trading environment
- Sales data may be net of returns, therefore where stores have a high level of returns from other branches or non-store channels, this will distort the sales figure recorded and could undermine the potential sales of product categories (see Box 8.3)

Market share

In this case the sales figures relate to the sales of that particular product in all retailers in the market. This approach is sometimes referred to as the level run down principle, and it assumes that individual products sell at the same rate in all retail outlets.

Advantages

- Easy to access (from published market reports)
- High demand products will be well supported, which is likely to appeal to the mass consumer
- Provides some indication of space allocation that is appropriate for products that are new to a given retailer, although not new to market

Disadvantages

- New or emerging products and categories will not be given the space allocation that their potential could warrant
- The product selection may appear mundane, or non-specialist, as it reflects the mass market rather than being tailored to individual store/outlet catchment profile
- Local preferences are not catered for

■ It may be appropriate to shrink the space of a declining category faster than sales would indicate to prevent the product selection looking outdated

Projected sales

Advantages

■ Projected sales are likely to be based on historical sales as far as possible, and will therefore reflect individual outlet characteristics
■ Incorporates (estimated) sales figures for new products and categories
■ Historical figures may have been affected by stock control or quality problems, which can be accounted for in the projected sales figure

Disadvantages

■ Actual sales may not meet projected sales, resulting in space being devoted to slow sellers while the faster selling products are underrepresented

BOX 8.3 THE EFFECT OF RETURNS ON SALES FIGURES

Store A is a branch of clothing retailer XYZ in a medium sized town centre. Ten miles away there is a regional shopping centre where branch B is located and twelve miles in the opposite direction, branch store C is located in the heart of a city centre shopping complex. The policy of retailer XYZ is to offer a returns policy in all of its stores for products bought in any outlet nationwide (including those purchased from its web site). Shoppers from the town where store A is located, often take shopping trips to the neighbouring centres, where B and C are located, especially if they are wanting to make a major purchase such as a coat or a suit, and require a wide choice of retail stores to select from. Unfortunately for store A, any unwanted products usually end up being returned to the customer's local store. This has the effect of distorting the sales figures for store A, upon which space allocation decisions are made. Unfortunately, the retailer's information system does not recognise the difference between a returned garment from the original store and one returned from a different outlet.

In order to counteract this problem, which can be quite widespread, a retailer would need to allocate space on the basis of estimated sales rather than historical sales.

Space elasticity

Allocating space according to a measure of sales assumes that there is a relationship between the amount of space and the rate of sales. This relationship is termed the space elasticity of a product and it refers to the extent to which the sales of a product will change in response to a change in the amount of space allocated to that product. Research suggests that space elasticity is not uniform amongst products, or across stores or departmental locations (McGoldrick, 2002: 478). In particular, the extent to which a product is bought on impulse will affect its space elasticity. If our attention is grabbed by a tonnage (high volume) display of a product such as cereal, or wine, we may succumb to an impulse purchase, but we are unlikely to respond as positively to an increase in display space of a staple store cupboard item such as salt or sugar.

The influence of other products in the retail offer

The sale of one product can be influenced by the sales of other products in a number of ways. Cross-elasticity is the direct relationship between a change in the sales of product A caused by a change in sales of product B. For example, if there is a promotion on pasta sauces which increased sales, the rate of sales of pasta is also likely to increase. If brand X has a price reduction, the sales of directly competing brand Y would decrease. Therefore space allocations of complementary and substitute products may have to be adjusted according to any changes to the marketing of a separate, influencing, product.

BOX 8.4 CLIP STRIPS: STORE CLUTTER OR HELPFUL SUGGESTIONS

Some retailers use clip strips to boost impulse purchases of related merchandise. Clip strips are plastic strips that clip onto store shelving and display small items, which complement the merchandise in the main display area. Too many clip strips may create the impression of a cluttered shelving display, but they allow a retailer the opportunity to give hints and suggestions to customers. From a practical point of view, clip strip products need to be small and lightweight. Some examples of shelf/clip strip combinations are found below:

Main shelf product	Clip strip product
hot dogs	instant mash potato
stock cubes	cornflour
tinned soup	croutons
cereal	ready-to-eat dried fruit
boxed chocolates	gift wrap
fresh meat	vacuum packed marinades
coffee	milk frother
coffee	wafer thin biscuits
paint	brushes

Clip strips can also be used to promote trial-size packs of new product variations.

Allocating space according to product profitability

Allocating space by any of the sales-based methods is likely to result in sales, rather than profits, being maximised and, if strictly implemented, would not take into account some of the more practical considerations about allocating retail space into account. Therefore an alternative approach would be to use the profits generated by each product as the basis on which to allocate space. Using profit measures as a basis for space allocation will prevent a retail manager from allocating large amounts of best quality retail space to unprofitable products. It could mean, however, that a retailer was allocating unnecessarily large amounts of space to products that would sell as well with a smaller space. Profitable lines may not in fact sell very quickly at all, and allocating extra facings or shelves of the product may have very little impact on the sales of the product. In this case the quality of the space becomes important, so the retailer can locate high profit items in locations around the store that are better for selling. Figure 8.5 illustrates the relationship between the sales and profits generated by different products, and suggests how space and ranging decisions should be made accordingly.

Allocating space according to sales, and in particular, product profitability, is working with the interests of the retailer, and not the customer in mind (Sanghavi, 1988) and therefore may suggest an illogical and confusing presentation of products. Long-term profitability depends on customer loyalty, which is dependent (among many other things) upon being satisfied with the presentation and assortment of products. Fine-tuning the allocation of space within a retail outlet therefore requires extensive amounts of high quality data, together with a pragmatic and customer orientated managerial approach at store level.

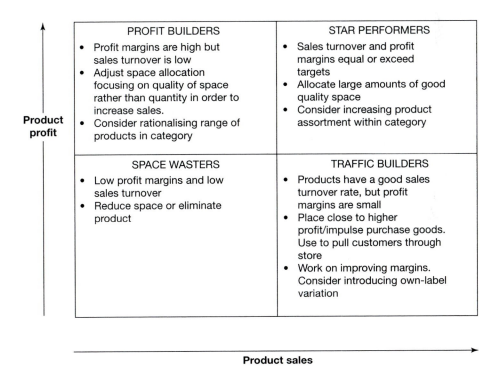

Figure 8.5 *Space allocation alternatives*

PRACTICAL AND CUSTOMER CONSIDERATIONS

Seasonality

Seasonal products need to be allocated more and better space at their peak selling periods. It may be necessary to allocate larger amounts of space to keep pace with customer demand; and allocating the best quality and increased quantities of space in line with seasonal events also has a reminder effect on customers and increases impulse purchases. High profile seasonal displays also have the more general positive effect of giving the perception of an interesting and relevant product selection overall. Examples of seasonal products in a home and garden improvement retailer that could be promoted are as follows:

- *summer*: garden furniture and barbecues;
- *autumn*: garden vacs, rakes, compost bins and bulbs;
- *winter*: heating products and fireplaces;
- *spring*: cleaning products, paint and seeds.

Product characteristics

The characteristics of the product itself may determine its space allocation in terms of both quality and quantity of space. Slim nappies are not only convenient for parents: smaller packs are welcomed by the retailers in order to offer more choice within the same space. Heavy and hazardous products (such as large bottles of bleach or bags of charcoal) should not be located on high shelves because of the increased danger and difficulty of handling for customers. Some products have special requirements of the display space that is allocated to them, which add further complications to space decisions. Chilled or frozen products, for example, not only have to be displayed in dedicated fixtures, but it also makes sense, from a safety and hygiene point of view, to have the products near to the chilled or frozen stockroom storage space. Other products may need protection because they are hazardous or fragile, or simply expensive and attractive to shoplifters. Multi-packs have to be considered in their totality, which makes them larger and therefore more difficult to shelve than single packs. Bottom shelves may be able to be extended slightly in order to accommodate multi- or large-pack items.

Contamination potential is another important consideration for product adjacencies. Products such as washing powder, firelighters and air fresheners have the potential to give off odours, which could seriously affect the quality of any food product placed next to them.

Customer characteristics

Not all space in a retail outlet is accessible by customers. This might be an advantage, for example, for the storage of expensive and fragile goods, but if your target market includes children, then their physical size must be considered in terms of the space allocated to their products. The eye-level space will be lower, and if the product is self-selection (pick and mix confectionery, for example) then the reach must be comfortable for the smaller person. In today's market where 'pester power' is a considerable force, the space allocated to cereals, desserts and soft drinks needs to have the child's viewpoint in mind. Retailers also need to bear in mind the growing number of senior customers, who may have restricted mobility; putting smaller pack sizes on high shelving would not endear the retailer to this customer group.

Fixture limitations

When allocating space to products, retail merchandisers must bear in mind the fixturing that is available for the product. Fragile products, for example, may need fixturing that is attached to a wall to provide additional stability. A large variation in pack size wastes vertical shelf space and looks untidy. Long garments have to be housed on fixtures that prevent the product trailing on the ground, but still enable the customer to see all the product detail. Using flexible fixturing can create additional space, such as dump bins for promoted merchandise, as discussed in Chapter 10.

SPACE ALLOCATION SYSTEMS

Clearly, the factors that contribute to a good or a bad space allocation decision are numerous and often interrelated. Space allocation was therefore an early candidate for computer applications in retailing. Nowadays systems allow retailers to feed in a wealth of relevant data about individual SKUs and, according to objectives of the retailer, the computer system will suggest the space allocation to use.

The most up-to-date systems allow retailers to use both qualitative and quantitative data as inputs. These inputs can be broken down into three types: product information, fixture information and product manager's knowledge.

Product information

- direct product costs, or activity based costs;
- sales data (forecast or actual);
- size of product;
- size variations;
- complementary products;
- bulk delivery restrictions.

Fixture information

- specific display requirements (for example, shelf level);
- size of fixturing;
- number of fixtures available.

Product manager's knowledge (based on experience and expertise)

- space elasticity;
- cross-elasticities;
- stock-holding objectives (e.g. target availability level);
- category lifecycle stage;
- display and fixturing requirements;
- marketing objectives (e.g. to improve own-brand preference).

Along with the increasing sophistication of space allocation systems in terms of the kind of data that can be processed, the outputs of the systems have also improved. Early systems often only gave numerical output, lists of product codes given in the order they were to be placed on the shelves. The use of digital imaging has helped to develop realistic three-dimensional product representations that can be moved around virtual shelving in order to find the most attractive arrangement of product within a space-optimised category. Today's systems, such as those produced by Galleria, JDA, SAS Marketmax and A.C. Nielsen produce illustrations of photographic quality which give store personnel a clear indication of the ideal allocation and appearance of the products on the shelf. These outputs are referred to as planograms and the producer of the planogram, or space planner, provides a link between the buying and merchandising section of the retail organisation and the store network. The planogram helps a retail chain maintain its corporate identity by setting out the arrangement of products within the outlet, whilst maximising space productivity. In fact, for some retailers the focus of space management is moving from productivity and efficiency and towards visual display improvements. Once an optimum level of efficiency is achieved, space planners can move onto the objective of making their products and fixtures look more attractive than their competitors'. Some of the latest space planning systems are able to simulate the entire store environment, so that the product manager can view an assortment plan in virtual reality and make any adjustments they feel are necessary. Recent space optimisation technology applications offer the opportunity to create store-specific planograms.

SPACE ALLOCATION AND CATEGORY MANAGEMENT

Although the performance of individual product lines is important to retailers in terms of the rate of sales which influences availability and the levels of contribution to turnover and profitability, the focus of performance in many retail organisations is at product category, rather than individual SKU level. A retailer is more interested in overall levels of sales and profits generated by their product range, rather than the sales of a single line that might be of interest to its manufacturer. As explained in Chapter 3, the product category has emerged as a manageable classification for most aspects of product management, and certainly applies in the case of space management. In fact, many would argue that space planning and allocation and the systems that drive the process can only be properly implemented in tandem with a category management approach.

Category management seeks to optimise the depth and variety of a product assortment within a specified amount of retail space, and to generate maximum profitability by seeking efficiency in the operations that support the depth and variety. This includes replenishing to guarantee availability and adding new products and running promotions to generate customer interest and increase short-term sales of particular products, without harming the overall profitability of the category.

Space allocation systems allow fine tuning of a category assortment, provide the means by which product and category performance can be monitored and analysed, and by using the planogram output the plans can be easily communicated and successfully implemented within the various retail outlets.

In some categories key brands are dominant, in which case their presence needs to have immediate impact within the space allocation plan. Other categories are very competitive, in which case low price, budget own brand and promotional products would feature strongly on the planogram. Many retailers use the principle that shoppers will 'read' a category from bottom to top, and left to right, and so well-known brands are placed on middle and lower shelves on the left of the category space in order to provide strong cues to the customer. Premium products meanwhile are placed on high level shelves, reflecting their high quality positioning, and the fact that the customer for premium products will seek out the better quality product within the category.

In some categories the customer decision-making processes are quite unique and need to be fully reflected within space allocation plans. For example, the decision sequence for wine is generally as follows:

Colour   ⟶   country of origin   ⟶   price level   ⟶   brand

Whereas the decision sequence for yoghurt might be:

Natural or flavoured   ⟶   type (low fat, standard or luxury)   ⟶

price level   ⟶   brand

These decision processes should determine how products are displayed within the category space.

Aesthetic considerations are becoming more important in space planning. The appearance of products on fixtures makes a considerable contribution to the overall retail outlet's design and as the visual qualities of the space planning systems' output improve, retailers can try different ways of laying out the product category before deciding which one looks the best. Also, space planning systems are increasingly becoming integrated with range planning systems so that visual considerations can be incorporated in the early stages of range planning.

STORE GRADING

The complexity of space planning is taken a level higher when a retailer has a large variation in store size. Most large retail groups apply a system of store grading which is largely dependent on store size and sales level, but can also take into consideration local catchment characteristics such as population profile, shopping centre profile, competition and so on. For each grade of store, a separate planogram will be produced; but even within the grades, physical constraints may make it necessary for store management to use a certain level of interpretation of the general plan to allow a sensible arrangement for their particular store. With the use of virtual systems, however, it is possible to enter individual store information and produce individual planograms for each store in the group. This might be appropriate for a product range that is relatively stable throughout the year, but for a retailer who reacts to season and fashion changes, once again the task becomes so complex that the use of virtual systems may not be cost-effective. An additional consideration for the retailer is that if store planning is so rigidly enforced from a central planning department, local managers may lose the motivation to take initiatives and apply commercial creativity to their stores. The use of a retail manager's commercial acumen and practical application and interpretation may be more efficient than a new systems update.

BOX 8.5 MICRO-MERCHANDISING

When the pressure is on to maximise the contribution from every inch of retail space, the relationship between that space and the customers who use it needs to be highly integrated. A retailer that is experiencing slow selling products, high levels of markdowns and that ends up doing a high number of in-store transfers could be a good candidate for a micro-merchandising strategy. Micro-merchandising concerns the activity of targeting store specific customer audiences with tailored ranges, in order to meet needs more profitably at the local level. Micro-merchandising combines the variable nature of retail space, in terms of how large the store is and where it is located, with the variable nature of customers, in terms of their purchasing behaviours.

Micro-merchandising relies on using customer information, captured and enabled by loyalty schemes and databases. Customer information is then layered over store information, so that the real personality of the store emerges. For example, the size of a retail outlet in Sheffield's busy Meadowhall centre may equate in terms of size and turnover to one located in the elegant and affluent Bath city centre, but the personality of the two stores might be quite different in terms of consumer preference and purchasing habits. In addition, basket analysis can be performed at store level, to inform and influence store ranging decisions. A product that may be a poor seller to a retail chain overall, may be a highly valued line to specific and profitable customer groups in certain stores. If the product is maintained in the offer, long-term customer satisfaction will be retained in spite of the individual poor product performance.

Therefore it is the store's personality traits that determine the core product ranges, and not the size; the size of the outlet determines the width and depth of the merchandise type that would appeal to the local customers. Stores are empowered with the merchandise that allows them to drive local market opportunities and local suppliers can also be involved in the process of providing tailored products for individual store needs.

As retailers offer more formats from which customers may choose to shop, format preferences and product preferences can be matched. For example, Tesco found that its on-line shoppers tended to come from more affluent backgrounds, and so the on-line product offer is tailored accordingly, with a large range of wines and few value lines.

Source: Various, including: Goldsmith, 2003; Scull, 2000; Ziliani, 1999; *Retail Bulletin*

TRIAL AND ERROR

For many small retailers the cost of a computerised space planning system is prohibitive, and so many rely on basic sales and profit margin analysis combined with trial and error in space allocation decision-making. This approach is likely to be sufficient, and the comparisons shown in Figure 8.5 may provide a basic analysis on which to start making space decisions.

SUMMARY

A great deal of space management is carried out in order to achieve relatively short-term retail objectives, such as maximising the benefits of a product or departmental promotion, meeting seasonal sales figures, or improving branch profitability. However, the long-term strategic objectives of the retailer provide the framework within which these decisions are taken. Space allocations must be in line with the overall positioning strategy of the retailer; the variety and depth of assortment and the stock availability service level should not be compromised by the need for short-term productivity gains. In addition, the arrangement of products around the store needs to be considered in the light of the contribution that product items, brands and categories make to the positioning statement. It may be necessary to over-represent new products or to allocate extra space to growing or seasonal categories in order to reinforce an innovative product positioning strategy. The local customer profile may also lead to exceptional space allocations in an effort to meet individuals' requirements more closely. However, the retailer's space is the extent of its empire, and every inch of that space must be used to its maximum effect even if, as we shall see in the next two chapters, some space is designed to be devoid of products. The measurement of that effect, however, must be appropriate in terms of the overall aims for that space.

EXERCISE MALTMANS

Maltmans is a value retailer. Its stores are located on out of town retail parks or stand-alone sites, with an average sales area of 8,000 square metres. They are usually on one floor only. Maltmans sell clothing for all the family and a range of home furnishings. The business is split into a number of departments: ladies' outerwear, childrenswear, menswear, ladies' lingerie/sleepwear; ladies' accessories and shoes; soft furnishings; home accessories (kitchenware, gifts, bathroom accessories).

Maltmans are opening a new stand-alone store located on the ring road of a major city. The store is essentially featureless, with automatic doors at the front of the store, and service space (stock rooms, staff rooms etc.) at the back of the store. The location of the changing room facility has not yet been decided. The dimensions of the store are shown on the store plan shown in Figure 8.6.

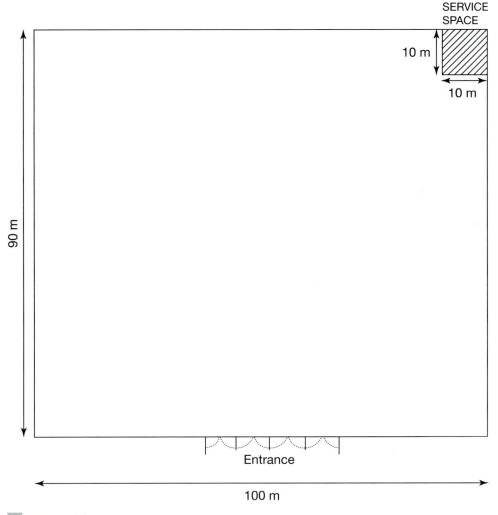

Figure 8.6 Maltman's store plan

Task

To develop a layout plan for the new Maltmans store. You have to decide where the departments should be located within the store, and how much space should be allocated to each department.

The sales figures in Table 8.3 are derived from a store that is similar in size and catchment area characteristics. The figures are from the current (autumn) season's sales.

Table 8.3 *Maltmans' departmental performance*

Department	Weekly sales (£)
Ladies' outerwear	38,000
Childrenswear	29,700
Menswear	28,000
Ladies' lingerie and sleepwear	16,500
Ladies' accessories and shoes	14,800
Soft furnishings	19,800
Home accessories	18,200
Total	165,000

When designing your plan, the following guidelines should be considered:

■ Maltmans usually located a bank of tills at the front of the store, for security reasons. Customers have to walk through the payment area to exit the store.

■ A typical Maltmans store layout takes the form of a 'guided walkway' around the store, with free-flow areas in between.

■ Being a family orientated store, it is important that prams and buggies can be easily moved within the store.

■ Maltmans allocate department space on the basis of estimated sales. For example, if the sales estimate for ladies' outerwear is 30 per cent of the total store's takings, it should be allocated 30 per cent of the selling area.

■ When deciding how to break up the space, remember that each department should be given the opportunity to be seen from the main walkway.

■ Wall space is useful for display purposes. Maltmans make use of moveable partitioning around the store to create more wall space, but it is carefully planned so that visibility between departments is kept at a high level, and additional security problems are not created.

■ Links between merchandise areas should be carefully considered.

To facilitate your task the following information is given:

The total selling area within the store is 8,800 square metres. This does not include the space taken by the till area (25 sq m), the space taken by the proposed changing rooms (25 sq m), the space taken by the walkway (50 sq m) and the service space (100 sq m).

Additional task

Using the historical figures for the previous season's Christmas selling period given in Table 8.4, identify the departments that will need to undergo a seasonal expansion. Create a new plan for the Christmas selling period, which gives the seasonal departments the additional space and impact they warrant.

Table 8.4 *Maltmans' Christmas sales*

Department	Weekly sales (£)
Ladies' outerwear	33,200
Childrenswear	25,000
Menswear	35,000
Ladies' lingerie and sleepwear	24,000
Ladies' accessories and shoes	20,100
Soft furnishings	14,500
Home accessories	50,200
Total	202,000

QUESTIONS

1 Identify the steps that retail product managers need to follow in order to achieve their space allocation objectives.

2 On a matrix, identify the alternative space allocation decisions available to retailers, following an analysis of both sales and profitability of individual items within a range.

3 Review the benefits of computerised space management systems.

4 Identify the practical considerations that retailers should make when drawing up their space allocation plans.

5 To what extent would an independent retailer benefit from a sophisticated space allocation system?

6 Analyse the potential for conflict between allocating space in order to achieve short-term productivity targets and the strategic management of retail space.

7 Discuss the benefits of taking a micro-merchandising approach to space management.

REFERENCES AND FURTHER READING

Corstjens, J. and Corstjens, M. (1995) *Store Wars: The Battle for Mindspace and Shelfspace*, Wiley, Chichester.

Dreze, X., Hoch, S.J. and Purk, M.E. (1994) 'Shelf Management and Space Elasticity', *Journal of Retailing*, 70(4): 301–326.

Goldsmith, J. (2003) 'Off the Shelf', *Retail Week*, 7 November.

Goldsmith, J. (2004) 'Crisp Planning', *Retail Week*, 16 July.

McGoldrick, P.J. (2002) *Retail Marketing*, McGraw Hill, Maidenhead.

Sanghavi, N. (1988) 'Space Management in Shop: A New Initiative', *Retail and Distribution Management*, 16(1): 14–18.

Scull, J. (2000) 'Getting Down to the Nitty Gritty of Range-Planning', *Retail Week*, 12 May.

Ziliani, C. (1999) 'Retail Micromarketing: Strategic Advance or Gimmick?', Proceedings of the 10th International Conference on Research in the Distributive Trades, Institute for Retail Studies, University of Stirling, August.

Web site

JDA Software Group Inc. (US): www.jda.com, accessed 09/05/05

Chapter 9

Retail design

LEARNING OBJECTIVES

The purpose of this chapter is to:

- Explore the scope of retail design and appreciate the extent of choice a retailer has when formulating a design for their outlets.
- Understand the role that retail design plays in reinforcing a retailer's product positioning strategy.
- Acknowledge the importance of an ambience within a retail outlet, and understand how various atmospheric cues are interpreted by customers.
- Become familiar with the terms associated with the design aspects of retail management, including retail brand identity, store image and lifestyle retailing.
- Investigate some applications of technology in the field of retail design and its planning process.

INTRODUCTION

Although the amount of analysis and planning that goes into retail product management might seem vast, a retailer should never lose sight of the fact that each customer has their own personal encounters with a retail outlet and the products within. In retail markets where shoppers have an extended choice of outlet for similar goods, the decision to patronise one retailer over another may be entirely based on the appearance and ambience of the outlet. The use of design in building a visible identity and a positive retail brand image that supports a retailer's product management objectives is the focus of this chapter.

OUTLET DESIGN

The management of the physical product and its relationship with the physical elements within the store, or the designed element within a non-store outlet, is as important as any other part of the product management process. If the product range and the outlet work in harmony, the retailer's positioning strategy is reinforced, but if they work in conflict, the positioning will be unclear to customers, who will become confused and disappointed.

In using the term 'outlet' design all types of retailers are included: large and small stores, electronic retailers and paper-based mail order retailers. It is acknowledged that catalogue and web site design can have an equally vital role to play as store design, but store based retailers are able to maximise the opportunity to use design to create vibrant spaces where consumers can interact with real products. This chapter will therefore concentrate on the principles of retail design and the practicalities of designing a store based outlet, whilst considerations for the design of non-store retail outlets are covered in more depth in Chapter 13.

Design in retailing is a far-reaching concept, and can include many aspects of retail management. Vazquez and Bruce (2001) explored the scope of design management in retailing and found it to extend from product development, through packaging, promotional and display activities to the corporate brand identity. Within the scope of this text we will be concentrating on two main interrelated aspects of retail design. This chapter will consider those aspects of a retail outlet's design that contribute to the general retail environment, such as the materials used in the interior design, the layout of the store, and the atmosphere created within the outlet. Chapter 10 moves on to consider those physical elements, which are certainly part of the overall outlet design itself, but are more closely connected to the actual products within the outlet. This includes fixturing and the various types of product display. The term visual merchandising is used to cover these subjects.

FORMULATING A STORE DESIGN

When a store owner or manager buys or rents a retail outlet, he or she is essentially faced with an empty shell, like a flat that a young person may have just moved into. There may be some interior decoration, but it could be tatty or not appropriate to the new business. There may be some structural work that is necessary to make the store operational, for example the shop windows may need to be enlarged, or if it is a clothing outlet changing rooms may need to be built, or a lift may need to be installed if the store has more than one floor. The architectural features of a store have to be considered very carefully, as they may be subject to planning restrictions, and could be creatively incorporated into a design to provide originality and distinctiveness.

The interior of a building is essentially a collection of materials, colours and space. In a retail store materials have to be sturdy in order to withstand customer traffic, and colours have to be chosen so that they do not detract from the merchandise, but still blend into the overall design. Retail designs, like products, are subject to trends and themes: for example, clean, bright, uncluttered designs have been popular in the early 2000s, with a move towards colour blocking and softer shapes and curves like those used in Selfridges in Birmingham.

BOX 9.1 STORE CEILINGS

Ceilings in stores were ignored for some time. If a customer looked upwards, they would often be met with a very dreary sight comprising faded or grubby tiling interspersed with panels of uninteresting diffused lighting. Thanks to innovative retail designs things are improving, and now this expanse is viewed as an architectural opportunity which may feature a wide range of upward and downward lighting effects, murals, painted skies, sculptures, cornices and even 'flying' mannequins. A variety of materials are being used in a range of imaginative ways, and sometimes features like heating pipes and lighting tracking are left for design effect.

MATERIALS

Retail outlets are public places to a large extent, and therefore they need to send messages out to the general public which will be received and understood by the type of customer a retailer wishes to attract. That section of the public may be large; for example, it may be more important for a superstore not to put off any particular customer group rather than specifically try to attract a particular type. On the other hand, target customers may be more narrowly defined, in which case the interior decoration of the store can go a long way towards making these customers feel that it is a store for them. At one time, for example, Miss Selfridge, the young fashion retailer, incorporated fake animal skin into their store interior, which gave the store a lively and humorous atmosphere; more recently they have used chrome, mirror effects and a sketched heart motif to give a retro feel to the store. Table 9.1 lists a range of materials commonly used in retail outlets.

Table 9.1 *Materials used in retail outlets*

Flooring	Carpet
	Polished wood (dark, light, stained)
	Unpolished wood
	Terracotta tiles
	Linoleum
	Marble or stone tiles
	Textured rubber/plastics
	Coloured and polished concrete
Walls and partitioning	Painted plaster, paint effects
	Opaque or frosted glass,
	Coloured glass
	Wood panelling (dark, light, stained)
	Slatted wood
	Textile
	Textured rubber/plastics
	Ceramic tiles
	Illuminated panelling
Trims	Chrome
	Stainless steel
	Metals – polished, matt, brushed
	Galvanised metal, e.g. aluminium
	Textile
	Coloured acrylic

Decisions regarding the type of material to be used depend on the following.

The type of product being sold

For food retailing the materials should be easy to clean, such as ceramic and marble tiling. In a jewellery store, plush carpet flooring may help to create a luxurious and intimate atmosphere.

The cost involved

Some materials are very expensive and, whilst investing in good quality materials is often worthwhile for mainstream retailing, a discount store would send confused messages if the interior

165

decoration looked too expensive. Something robust and basic, such as textured plastic, is a more suitable choice.

The store traffic

A busy store, such as a supermarket or a DIY superstore where customers are likely to be visiting in their work boots, needs to use material that will withstand wear and tear. Even though a substantial entrance mat is essential in any store, the flooring must not become slippery when damp, and it must be easy to clean. For easy maintenance, department stores incorporate wood block or tiling into the main walkways and restrict the use of carpets to the departmental display area (see guided walkway layouts in Chapter 11). The other advantage of changing the type of flooring is that it can encourage customers to alter their pace around the store: moving faster on hard surfaces and slowing down in carpeted areas.

Fashion

Stores selling fashion-orientated merchandise must keep up with fashions in interior decoration in order to maintain a modern image. The problem is that the more fashion orientated the look of the store, the faster it is likely to look out of date; therefore, fashion retailers have to accept that frequent refurbishments will be part of the retail strategy. That being the case, these retailers are able to be more experimental with materials and not be so concerned with longevity. Miss Selfridge and Top Shop both target the teenage to mid-twenty-year-old consumer, and expect to refurbish their stores every two to four years.

Environmental and safety concerns

Materials should be in keeping with a retailer's desired image. If a retailer professes to be concerned with environmental issues, then natural materials (from sustainable sources) are more likely to be in tune with their overall store design. Retailers also have to conform to health and safety regulations. For example, glass has become very popular in retail architecture, but of course it has to be of a type that will not be dangerous to the public.

ATMOSPHERICS

Retail stores, like homes, have different atmospheres and auras. This formation of a subliminal message is an important part of the store design. There are many things that blend together to create an atmosphere, and atmospherics are cues that act on the subconscious through the senses to create a state of mind in the customer. Table 9.2 gives some examples of atmospheric cues: the more favourable the state of mind, the longer a customer is likely to remain in the store, and thus more likely to make a purchase.

The use of colour in both store and corporate design is an interesting and complex subject. Apart from a colour's ability to be warm (reds, pink, oranges) or cool (blues, greens and white), colours have both cultural and societal meanings and associations which may make them more or less appropriate for use in a retail outlet.

Although some retailers have embraced a colour into their corporate design and carried this through into the store design successfully, many retailers restrict the use of colour in the store to trims and signage, using neutral colours and materials for much of the store interior. Many materials left in their natural state are neutral. Light-coloured wood for example was used extensively in the early 1990s to create a neutral minimalist look in many fashion stores.

Neutral shades (black, white, creams, browns and greys) are useful in store designs because there is little danger of the merchandise clashing or having to compete with the store's decoration, yet they contrast well with a highlight colour used for corporate communications (see Table 9.3). Towards the end of the 1990s many retailers began to use white tiling and opaque glass in large areas of the store in order to create a clean, modern and versatile backdrop for colourful merchandise.

Table 9.2 *Retail atmospherics*

Sense	Cue	Example
Vision	Colour	Red and orange used to create warmth and impact. White and blue/green to create a calm, cool and clean atmosphere
Vision	Material	Galvanised metal to create 'industrial' impression; polished dark wood for a formal atmosphere
Hearing	Music	Mozart piano concertos to create a relaxed atmosphere in which to browse; dance music in a high fashion retailer
Smell	Aroma	Bread in supermarkets or coffee from a retailer's restaurant to create a 'homely' feeling
Touch	Texture	Glass and ceramic to create clean, hygienic impression; baskets and wood to create a 'natural' feel
Touch	Temperature	Constant temperature to relax customers; warm but not stuffy changing rooms
Vision/smell	Colour/aroma	Fresh fruit, vegetables and flowers at the front of a supermarket to give a lively sense of freshness; perfumes and cosmetics at the front of a department store to give a plethora of product interest and a luxurious atmosphere

Table 9.3 *Retailers who have used colour consistently in their corporate and store design*

Body Shop	Green	Store fascia, bags, corporate communications
Boots the Chemists	Blue/white	Fascia, packaging, uniforms, bags, fixturing
Next	Black and cream	Fascia, bags, corporate communications

BOX 9.2   RETAIL AROMATHERAPY

Magnet is a leading kitchen furniture retailer with around 200 stores in the UK. Over the years, customers buying kitchens have become more emotional in their purchasing, with more concerns about the design and 'feel' of the kitchen, rather than functional and technical aspects. In response to this, and competition from other kitchen retailers like Ikea, Magnet has reinvented its kitchen showroom format. A more minimalist, clean lined approach has been taken with the layout, and point of sale clutter has been removed so that customers are encouraged to interact with the kitchen, even cook in it if they wish to. The retailer even organises in-store cooking events to provide additional customer interest.

Piped music, artificial aromas and relaxation areas all add to the relaxed atmosphere, encouraging customers to browse and linger around the displays. Throughout the day, the smells wafting through the showroom change from freshly made coffee and cookies in the morning, through garlic and herbs roasting at lunchtime, to baked apple pie in the afternoon. By working on the subliminal plane, Magnet has achieved an average order value uplift of over 40 per cent.

Source: Retail Week 2003; www.magnet.co.uk

LIGHTING

A great contributor to the general atmosphere in store is the lighting used. The overall level of ambient light needs to be such that customers can see the merchandise clearly and the store looks bright and inviting. However, lighting can be used to create interest in the store design itself, for example, by using banks of up-lighters or down-lighters or pendent lamps, and the space in the store can be moulded by using a combination of wall lights and spot lights. Lighting is an integral part of any feature display, and enormously enhances the dramatic effect, with product areas being accentuated by suspended lighting and pin spots. Modern halogen or metal-halide spots are smaller, more powerful and more able to be controlled and so add precision to lighting designs. In addition, more fixtures are being designed with integral lighting systems, such as supermarket gondolas with incorporated strip lights, or back lit display shelving for shoes.

Lighting can also affect the colour of merchandise. This can be used positively to highlight products; for example a blue light might be used to create a cool and hygienic mood in a toiletries department, whereas orange lighting enhances the colour of bread. However, lighting can create problems when it comes to colour matching, and so buyers should ensure that they use both store lighting and natural lighting when approving colour matches in the product development process.

Although fixtures, fittings, display props and mannequins will be dealt with specifically in the next chapter, their contribution to the overall design of the store must not be overlooked. The materials used in the fixtures should complement those used in the interior decor, and the styling of fixtures should be in keeping with the architectural design of the store, so that all the physical features work in harmony and deliver a consistent message to the customer.

SIGNAGE

Much of the communication process within a store relies on visual cues rather than the written word. However, there may be messages for customers that are so important that they have to be spelt out. Retail signage can be broadly broken down into four different types.

In large stores in particular *signage is required to help customers locate the merchandise they are looking for*. Signage therefore needs to be incorporated in the general store layout to guide customers to the different departments, aisles or service areas and to prevent them getting lost. These signs need to be large, clear and consistent in their appearance so that they make a contribution to the overall store image. Primark, the value orientated variety store, for example, use images rather than bland graphics to steer customers to different departments (Mintel, 2002).

Another type of corporate sign is *that which relays messages about a retailer's overall organisational policy*. An example of this would be the returns policy for clothing or a policy on sourcing of food products. These signs need to be placed in relevant positions such as near to the merchandise in question, near to the till area, or at the customer service desk.

Once customers have located a department or product category of interest, *signage can help to guide shoppers through the merchandise*. Signs indicating different brands, sizes, prices and special product features are useful to help customers in their shopping tasks.

The fourth type of signage is that which is related to promotional activity, and this can extend from banners and window posters, through to shelf-edge price offers.

Different types of signage used in terms of size, lettering, and colours all have to be incorporated into the overall store design. Illuminated signage, either by spot lighting or by using lit-up panels means that smaller signage is not necessarily less noticeable than large. Liquid display screens are being used more frequently in retail outlets as the cost of using them falls. These provide flexibility in the message being relayed and the added benefit of moving imagery or message. More information can be included than on a static sign and a customer's attention can be grabbed more effectively. The signage used in the store, like any other aspect of the design should complement rather than compete with the merchandise. Generally, a retailer has to strive for a balance between giving customers the information they require and preventing the store looking too cluttered.

STORE DESIGN AND THE CORPORATE IMAGE

Retailing is a very visible industry. We are able to become intimate with retail businesses in a way that is not feasible with manufacturing businesses. This interface between the business and the customer is what gives retailers their advantage, as well as many of their problems. Many of the largest retailers around the world have become part of everyday life to people and the relationship between stores and individuals is something that retailers are keen to strengthen in pursuit of customer loyalty. Maintaining a favourable corporate image is therefore vitally important in competitive retail sectors.

Retailers work very hard to keep their image favourable in the mind of the consumer; and although, as we shall see later on in this chapter, the formation of an image incorporates many more components than purely physical ones, the store and its environment play a big part in the formation and maintenance of a corporate image. Retailers that do not update their stores on a regular basis run the risk of appearing out of touch with the customer, and if a refurbishment programme is left for too long, the change required to modernise the store may be so extensive that the retailer runs the risk of alienating the customers who are left.

THE EXTERIOR DESIGN

The exterior of the shop has to communicate to the potential customer what that retailer stands for. The main external features of a retail outlet are the fascia, the window display and the entrance. The fascia is the most visible part of a retail brand. It is the name of the retailer, but it is also the logo, the graphics and the colours that are incorporated into whatever appears over a shop's entrance. The fascia may incorporate exterior lighting to highlight the name, and it may incorporate a company logo or character, such as the children's wear retailer Adams' apple, or Colonel Sanders in the Kentucky Fried Chicken fascia. Whatever the fascia includes, it becomes a key feature of the retail identity, which is then locked into the overall impression that a customer builds up about a store. Table 9.4 compares and contrasts some internationally famous fascia designs.

Table 9.4 *Fascia design components*

Retailer	Graphics	Colours
Ikea	Chunky	Blue and yellow
Toys 'Я' Us	Fun	Multi-primary
Laura Ashley	Classic	Green and cream
Muji	Bold	Silver

The store entrance

The ways in which customers gain access to stores have to satisfy both functional and aesthetic criteria. The opening to a store has to be accessible to all customers, including those using wheelchairs and buggies, and it has to be secured when the shop is closed. A very wide opening may be very welcoming for customers, but this type of entrance is problematic from a store security point of view, it does not offer much protection from the weather, and it does not allow the retailer to construct window displays. A number of alternative store entrance types are illustrated in Figures 9.1 to 9.4.

The open entrance is inviting and accessible, and breaks down the barrier between the store and its exterior. However, open entrances can feel anonymous and do not help to establish a retailer's identity (Din, 2000). One way round this is to use a semi-open entrance, where accessibility is still good, but a window display can be created. Open entrances are often found in enclosed shopping centres, where the shop is protected from the outside elements.

The funnel, recessed or lobby entrance increases the proportion of window display space and invites shoppers into the retail space without the commitment of stepping over the threshold. At the other extreme, a standard doorway gives a more exclusive feel to the retailer, and the window display stands out to communicate the retailer's offer. A problem with the standard entrance is access, which may be overcome by using an automatic door. Awnings or canopies, which originated in order to shade merchandise in store windows, are now often used to give emphasis to a store entrance.

The contribution that window displays make to the external design of the store has traditionally been a very important one. Window displays as part of the visual merchandising function will be explored in Chapter 10; nevertheless, there are some retailers who do not use window displays at all. In this case the retailer relies on their name and reputation (communicated by the fascia) to draw customers into the store, as opposed to the visual product offer. Many retailers who use the superstore or category killer format do not use window displays. It is therefore very important

Figure 9.1 *The open entrance*

Figure 9.2 *Next store with semi-open entrance and closed window displays*
Source: Courtesy of Next

Figure 9.3 *The funnelled or lobby entrance*

Figure 9.4 *Standard door*

for this type of retailer to use a store brand name that gives an indication of the type of product that is on offer. Some retail names leave no doubt: Benson's Beds, Carpetwise, PC World, Toys 'Я' Us, Petworld and so on, whilst others provide a product association, for example, Staples or Homebase. Retailers who do not use brands that are linked to the product offer have to rely on their reputation and other communication tools to interest the customer base. Ikea for example issue a full product catalogue in a wide catchment area around their stores to familiarise consumers with their product offer, and electronic retailers use regular newspaper advertising to remind customers what their product range includes.

LOCATION

The actual location of a store often has a strong bearing on the store design in general, and in particular may impinge on a design strategy quite significantly. Whether it is a greenfield site (building a store from scratch) or whether it is a conversion from a different use, or even if it previously housed a retail business, a retail site will be subject to planning and building regulations. For new stores, it will be necessary to consider the material to be used and whether to incorporate local architectural features, the design may need to be constrained in terms of height, and the surrounding area may need to be landscaped. For conversions, architectural features, both internally as well as externally may need to be preserved, yet the building may also require a programme of modernisation. All these challenges inevitably add to the cost of refurbishment, but compliance may be a small price to pay for a site in the best location. In purpose-built shopping centres there may be certain store design restrictions; therefore, the needs of the centre to create a cohesive look whilst promoting the individual retail identities is a fine balance and subject to negotiation between centre management and tenant.

The location of a store must be appropriate to the retail business: to reach the right kind of customer it is important for a store to be in a street that reflects its image. Oxford Street may be the busiest street in the UK, but for an upmarket clothing retailer like Jigsaw, St Christopher's place, a pedestrianised lane, tucked away just around the corner, offers the kind of environment that attracts a more discerning shopper, with its café bars and outdoor seating, ornate street lamps and flower baskets.

STORE IMAGE

In this chapter, we have alluded several times to the concept that a retail store has an 'image'. Over the years, 'image' has been used as a qualitative, all-encompassing evaluative tool for retailers. The concept was referred to in 1958 by Martineau as 'the way in which the store is defined in the shopper's mind'. In today's retail environment, where consumers have an enormous choice of outlets for products and an extensive range of products within the outlet, where the actual product being offered is generally of comparable standard to many other retailers' products, the image that a store conveys may be a key determining factor in the decision to choose one retailer over another. According to Barr and Field (1997: 11) image is 'multi-sensory, multi-dimensional and subject to fading without reinforcement'; image building, they say, is intended to provide value added benefits to shoppers: a place they feel comfortable, that is in tune with their lifestyle, stocks the items that reflect their taste and requirements in what they wish to eat, wear, give to others and furnish their homes with. The reinforcement of a retail brand, what it stands for and how it is adapted to multi-channel retailing is the focus of many current retail strategies.

Sometimes retailers become aware that their brand image is not as good as it was. This may be because a close competitor has undertaken a change in strategy (for example a store refurbishment, or a change in pricing strategy). It may also be because a retailer has not paid enough attention to its customer's needs. Becoming familiar with retailers is often in the customers' interest: they are able to do their shopping more efficiently, they can go to a store that caters for their taste without having to search around, or they know which retailers will be offering products that are within their price range. However, customers will not be satisfied if that retailer becomes complacent. Customers' tastes change, their lifestyles change and a retailer has a choice of changing with their existing customer or changing to attract new customers to replace the ones that naturally move on. The process of knowing, as a retailer, who your customer is, and what they want from you sounds like a straightforward operation, yet it is probably the hardest thing for retailers to get right. Listening to the customer requires input from all layers of the organisation, as discussed in Chapter 4, and listening to what customers say about a store's image is one of the starting points in this process.

THE RETAIL BRAND

Retail design is an integral part of the branding of a retail company (Mintel, 2002). In a market where retailers are being run more efficiently and the store environment is being used to create interest and tempt the shopper to stay longer and spend more, new designs and refurbishments are a way to maintain competitive advantage. The retail brand, like a product brand, can be extended to offer customers something more than the core product or, in the case of the retailer, the core product range. Understanding what is a core range and what is not, may be a matter for research or judgement, but a number of retailers have been able to successfully introduce more and more product categories without experiencing any detriment to sales of existing product ranges. The superstore grocery retailers have extended product ranges of both manufacturer and own-label merchandise into many non-food areas; many clothing retailers have moved into accessories, toiletries and gifts; and variety stores are moving into coffee shops and restaurants. Din (2000) considers that retail design has an important role to play in this brand-stretching process, because in the long term design adds value to the retailer by increasing brand awareness, confirming brand values and developing new markets.

LIFESTYLE RETAILING

The trend towards offering extended product ranges that are focused onto a particular customer type is called lifestyle retailing, and it has been the basis of many exciting retail developments throughout history. A lifestyle retailer can be either generalist or specialist. A generalist lifestyle retailer would offer a wide variety of product categories, with a shallow but very specific orientation to the products. Muji (see Box 9.3) uses this approach and has gained international appeal. The specialist lifestyle retailer might offer both depth and variety, but targeted to very specific lifestyle needs. Upmarket department stores like Selfridges and Harvey Nichols could be considered lifestyle retailers in this context. The key feature of lifestyle retailing is a real understanding of how far a lifestyle can extend, and formulating a product offer that reflects the approach to life and the likely choices such a consumer would make.

PLANNING RETAIL DESIGNS

Planning a retail design is a risky operation. The interplay between walls, floor, ceilings, lighting, colours, materials and fixtures is a challenging enough process. However, these are the static elements of the retail design. The template must also incorporate two further important, yet changing, elements: the merchandise and the customers. Think of the difference between a store on a quiet morning just a few moments after opening time and a store during its peak selling

BOX 9.3 MUJI

Muji is the shortened form of the original name of a unique Japanese company – Mujirushi Ryohin, which means 'No Brand Goods'. Muji started up in 1980 as a supplier to Seiyu supermarkets. In response to the excessive premiums being charged for branded products, a range of well designed, high quality products was developed to sell as a private label within the supermarket store. The idea was well received, more products were developed and in 1983 Muji opened its own store in Tokyo and expanded its trading in dedicated areas of department stores in addition to the supermarket outlets. Over time, Muji has developed a wider product range, and opened more stores, so that it can now be considered one of the most important international lifestyle retailers, trading as a separate entity from the supermarket that once owned the brand.

Muji's product range is an exemplar of the wide variety lifestyle concept. Very little depth in the product choice is offered, yet the coverage of product items housed in a typical 'high street sized store' is unbelievably extensive: stationery, clothes, furniture, home accessories, toiletries and food products are all on offer. People who like Muji do not need choice; the products are 'the ones the customer wants'. For example, Muji sells two types of bicycle, of similar design, but one is a mountain bike and one is a road bike. They also sell two chairs, both designed specifically for a function: one is a dining chair and one is a casual chair. However, Muji sells a range of stationery as wide as Staples, the category killer, but the Muji approach is one product, one brand and one choice.

The strength of the Muji concept emanates from the principles on which the company operates, stated in their company catalogue:

- good value for money;
- simple and functional design;
- basic and understated colour;
- complete lifestyle range.

These values are translated into a product development strategy that covers the sourcing of low-cost, basic and industrial materials for use in products that aim to enhance the natural properties of the raw materials. They also pay attention to the processes used to create the products, emphasising efficiency, waste elimination, high quality manufacture and minimum environmental impact. Where possible, Muji reduces prices in order to pass on cost and efficiency improvements to customers.

The resulting offer is a range made up of simple, stylish, durable and adaptable products, that evolve with customers' lifestyles and living patterns. The store environment works in harmony with the product range. Bold signage, neutral colours, and industrial materials create a basic functional theme, yet an understated sense of style is added by using the Japanese lettering in the logo and an effective combination of spot and pendent lighting to highlight the products.

Source: Muji product brochure, 1999

175

periods or during an end of season sale, and the impression can be very different. Virtual store plans and computerised visualisations are increasingly becoming an indispensable tool in the pre-installation phase of store refurbishments. Some of the latest models incorporate lighting, fixtures, merchandise stacks, hanging merchandise, colours and even human forms. This allows store designers and visual merchandisers to assess the interplay between the store design elements, the visual merchandising elements and the live elements of a working store. Computer-aided store design systems can provide the following additional benefits to retailers:

- Store designs can be linked to retail productivity and space allocation schemes (discussed in Chapter 9).
- Store designs can link product and the architectural space to create a holistic and consistent image.
- A new store fit can be demonstrated to staff, who can do a virtual walk-through of the store as part of their pre-opening training. This is particularly useful if the new store design is a major departure from previous ones.

FLAGSHIP STORES

Flagship stores are those stores regarded as the pinnacle in the retail chain. They are usually large and located in high footfall, prestigious locations. They offer a full range of merchandise, with an emphasis on the more expensive, high quality and high fashion lines. The role of the flagship store is essentially about retail brand building and reinforcement rather than profitability. The media coverage that flagship stores attract adds to the communications process. When entering new international markets, retailers often begin with a flagship store incorporating the latest store design, to test the reaction to the retail concept. Shops of 'high design' lead the way in retailing, 'along the "avenue" of every major global city' (Glass, in Barr and Field, 1997: 8). Flagship stores are also used by non-retail brands as a way of building and reinforcing a product brand. Famous brands like Nike and Sony use retail outlets to showcase their products in striking shopping environments, so that the customer's perception of the product is enhanced by the surrounding designed retail space. The case study at the end of this chapter illustrates how a flagship store can help to reposition a brand.

As well as the use of stores for long-term brand building purposes, particular stores within a retail organisation can be selected for operational trials. Very often a retailer will have one or a small number of stores that are used for new layout trials. These stores will receive shipments of new product ranges earlier than others, so that the store and product layout can be trialled before being rolled out to the rest of the company. Stores can also be used for trials of new technologies and systems, which can then be evaluated before full-scale investment occurs (see Box 9.4).

BOX 9.4 THE RETAIL DESIGN/TECHNOLOGY INTERFACE IN STORE

For many UK shoppers, promotional kiosks, self-scanning devices and digital display screens are becoming as familiar features in a retail store as trolleys and sales assistants. So what is the next technological wizardry that we can expect to encounter when shopping? Two stores that have received considerable trade press interest are perhaps able to point to the next stages in the shopping evolution process.

German retailer Metro's 'Extra Future Store' in Rheinberg, Germany was launched in 2003, with the intention of piloting some new technologies. These include:

- an intelligent fresh produce scale, whose camera can identify each item and then issue a price ticket without any requirement from the customer to enter a code;
- the PSA (personal shopping assistant) that can convert a shopping list file from a PC into the most logical route around the store;
- an information terminal (kiosk) which screen-reads product bar codes and then suggests recipes and related products;
- self-checkouts;
- electronic shelf-edge labelling;
- RFID deactivator.[*]

Another example of a 'store of the future' is Sainsbury's Hazel Grove store in south Manchester, UK, where the following technological design features can be seen:

- Car parking spaces for disabled customers and those with young children are fitted with sensors to alert staff so that they are ready to offer assistance.
- Dedicated parking spaces are available for internet shoppers who prefer to pick up their orders. Like a drive-in take-away food outlet, shoppers give their order numbers through an intercom and their shopping is brought to their car.
- One corner of the store is devoted to top-up items. Parking spaces near to the area are restricted to 20 minutes, enforced by a digital clock. No penalty, other than the embarrassment of staying beyond your allocation is enforced.
- An enormous vending machine, stocking 150 products can be found near to the store entrance. The selection of both chilled and ambient products can be accessed when the store is closed.
- A wall of plasma screens at the front of the store show information about products and offers. Additional screens are to be found scattered around the store, including ones close to the checkouts that feature local news and weather.
- A café close to the central entrance of the store, with two plasma screen TVs, X-box consoles, and internet access.

Like the Metro Extra Future Store, Sainsbury's Hazel Grove store has self-scanning devices, self-checkout tills and touch sensitive, product code reading screens that provide recipe suggestions, related products and further information on the product itself.

As an extension to the in-store technology, Sainsbury's are trialling what is known as the 'Pocket Shopper', a key-fob sized scanner that allows customers to build up a shopping list away from the store, for example, if a particular product was seen at a friend's house, this could be scanned for future reference, or a complete shopping list can be built up by scanning the packaging of products used at home. By connecting the pocket shopper to a PC, this data can be transmitted to Sainsbury's web site and used either for home delivery ordering or as transportable electronic shopping list.

> The integration of new technology into a store's design to provide customer focused services in a modern shopping environment is sure to enhance the retailer's image as a store of the future.
>
> Source: *Retail Week Store of the Future Supplement*, March 2004
>
> *Note*:
> *RFID stands for radio frequency identification device. This is a new type of product identification which incorporates a live coded 'tag' on a single product, which has allowed retailers increased opportunities to track products in the supply chain and around large stores. The ethical dilemma that this new technology presents to retailers is that unless the tag is deactivated at the point of sale, the product can continue to be traced whilst in ownership of a customer. This is seen by customers as an invasion of privacy, and so by incorporating a device that changes the tag's code sequence to a row of zeros before a shopper's eyes, the customer is reassured that the tag is no longer transmitting data to the retailer's information system.

THE STRATEGIC ROLE OF STORE DESIGN

There are many aspects of the retailing world that are threatening store-based retailers. Many consumers feel time pressurised; therefore, if they do go out to shop, they want and expect a highly favourable experience. Shopping centres are increasingly filled with an international collection of retail businesses, and whilst many UK retailers are searching for opportunities for overseas expansion, the domestic retail market becomes ever more competitive. Shoppers are being offered products from a diversity of marketing channels, giving the consumer the opportunity to shop in all kinds of locations, at all times in the day. The shop-based retailer must therefore work extremely hard to make sure that consumers remain interested in visiting the store. The store, the service received and the product selection must be 'right'. Customers have so much choice: they will not give a retailer a second chance.

In order to keep the consumer of the new millennium feeling interested in store based shopping, retailers have to make 'functional service spaces into places that feed the popular spirit' (Williamson, 1999). By creating a store environment that delights and enthuses the customer, retailers are able to transcend the pulling power of manufacturers' brands and the store space provides them with an enormous advantage over the non-store channels. Consumers play out rituals when they shop, such as making lists, searching out and trying on, making choices and carrying the bag. Store based retailers need to continue to raise the enjoyment of store based shopping, so that customers do not desert them for other forms of shopping or other leisure pursuits. The shopping trip must be worthy of recall and repetition. When the Bluewater shopping centre opened in east London in March 1999, 200 of the 300 stores opened with a new store-branding concept. This highlights the importance that retailers are putting on fresh approaches to store environments as part of their strategic direction. The celebrated Bullring shopping development in Birmingham, opened in 2003, gave retailers like Selfridges department store and Orange communications retailer, the perfect showcase for ground-breaking interior designs in their stores, working within the constraint of the design guidelines of the centre.

Levy and Weitz (1998) compared the store environment to a theatre where the walls and floor represent the stage; the lighting, fixtures and signage represent the set and the merchandise is the show. But Williamson (1999) went one step further, suggesting that shopping is the living act in an event, and the customer is the star in their own 'self-created, brand assisted drama'. As good retail design becomes more widespread and consumers respond positively, the pressure to introduce new designs increases resulting in an accelerated design cycle and more investment (Mintel, 2002).

SUMMARY

Retail environments have to satisfy the operational objectives of minimising costs, allowing flexibility and providing the right kind of space for merchandise. In this respect the practical aspects of store design, such as the materials used, the lighting, and the signage, as well as the size and location of the store, all have to be blended into a spatial totality. However, retail design is also very much concerned about communicating the right messages to the target customer, reinforcing the retail brand values and encouraging consumers to experience the retail outlet and the products within. A store atmosphere adds emotional feelings, heightening the shopping experience, to create the enthusiasm and loyalty. Retail design is becoming increasingly concerned with supporting a multi-channel approach to retailing, and so design elements should be integrated across retail formats and regularly updated to remain relevant to the increasingly design conscious shopper.

CASE STUDY   BEN SHERMAN

Ben Sherman is a well-established clothing brand, made famous in the 1960s as a preferred label of the 'mods'.[*] The company was originally a formal shirt-making concern, but moved into casual shirts and then supplemented these with a full range of casual items, including jeans, jackets and T-shirts. Although Ben Sherman is a well-known brand in the UK, distributing through a network of department store and speciality clothing retailers, the brand image held outside of the UK is generally more aspirational; a 'cool London look' (Firth, 2002).

In autumn 2002, Ben Sherman decided it was time to open a flagship store to help to create a more favourable image with its domestic customers. The location was the first decision, and when an outlet in London's Carnaby Street became available it was a natural choice; not only has Carnaby Street a history and a heritage in terms of popular culture and fashion, it has previously been the site of Ben Sherman's company headquarters and has more recently become a popular location for casual clothing brands including Puma, Mambo, Diesel, Base and Miss Sixty.

When designing the flagship store, the retailer and design company (Caulder Moore) wanted to make reference to the company's history, but in a way that gave a forward looking approach, rather than a nostalgic, museum-like feel. The design elements in the store therefore, subtly reflect company heritage. One of the walls in the store is pebbled, making reference to the beach in Brighton where the first Ben Sherman shirt factory began. On another wall a glass brick wall in red, white and blue makes reference to the 'Britishness' of the brand, but without being obvious; the shades picked for the red, and blue are darkened, rather than the bright colours of the Union Jack (the British flag). Red, white and blue is also used subtly in the overhead lighting system, and structural pillars are covered in white vinyl picked out in blue and red stitching. The white vinyl theme is continued into the interior of the fitting rooms, which are themselves unique in design; semi-circular cylinders, which revolve by hand to conceal the changing customer.

The store also has a PR room upstairs where celebrity customers like DJ Norman Cook and footballer George Best can be fitted out away from the gaze of the general public. The London flagship is treated more like an international store, with the best taken from the product ranges sold through UK distributors, and other styles that are exclusive to overseas stores. In this way the company is attempting to shift the perception of the Ben Sherman brand in a more 'cool and groovy' direction.

Source: Based on Firth, 2002

Note:
*The 'mods' was the name attached to a cult youth movement in the 1960s. The groups had a particular style; the look was 'smart casual', with preferred clothing items being the straight-leg Levi jeans, Doc Marten boots and a Ben Sherman shirt. Their favoured transportation mode was the scooter, and lifestyle references included going to dances in Brighton on the south coast of England.

QUESTIONS

1   Review the physical elements that contribute to a designed retail environment, indicating the variety of materials that can be used and the messages these elements send out about the retailer and its product assortment.

2   Examine the contribution that the following make to a store's design, and suggest ways in which they interact with products.

- lighting;
- signage;
- architectural base;
- exterior.

3   Outline the benefits of using technology in the planning and implementation of store designs.

4   The store environment blends tangible features with intangible auras, in order to create an appeal to customers and support the product range. Discuss.

5   Make a critical analysis of a store design of your choice, with an emphasis on the relationship between design elements and the products.

6   Discuss the notion that the role of store design in a retail brand reinforcement strategy increases as more people turn to alternative shopping methods.

REFERENCES AND FURTHER READING

Barker, J., Levy, M. and Grewel, D. (1992) 'An Experimental Approach to Making Retail Store Environmental Decisions', *Journal of Retailing*, 68(4): 445–460.

Barr, V. and Field, K. (1997) *Stores: Retail Display and Design*, PBC International, New York.

Bellizzi, J.A., Crowley, A.E. and Hasty, R.W. (1993) 'The Effects of Color in Store Design', *Journal of Retailing*, 50(1): 21–45.

Din, R. (2000) *New Retail*, Conran Octopus, London.

Doyle, S. and Broadbridge, A. (1999) 'Differentiation by Design: The Importance of Design in Retailers' Repositioning and Differentiation', *International Journal of Retail and Distribution Management*, 27(2): 72–82.

Firth, D. (2002) 'All Mod Cons', *Retail Interiors*, December.

Levy, M. and Weitz, B.A. (1998) *Retailing Management*, McGraw Hill, Maidenhead.

Kotler, P. (1973) 'Atmospherics as a Marketing Tool', *Journal of Retailing*, 49(4): 48–64.

McGoldrick, P.J. and Pieros, C.P. (1998) 'Atmospherics, Pleasure and Arousal: The Influence of Response Moderators', *Journal of Marketing Management*, 14: 173–197.

Mintel (2002) *Retail Store Design UK*, Mintel International Group, London, December.

Retail Week (2003) 'Magnet Uses Coffee to Woo its Customers', editorial, 14 March.

Sullivan, M. (2002) 'The Impact of Pitch, Volume and Tempo on the Atmospheric Effects of Music', *International Journal of Retail and Distribution Management*, 30(6): 323–330.

Vazquez, D. and Bruce, M. (2001) 'Design Management: The Unexplored Retail Marketing Competence', *International Journal of Retail and Distribution Management*, 30(4): 202–210.

Web site

http://www.bensherman.co.uk accessed 25/10/04.

Chapter 10

Visual merchandising

LEARNING OBJECTIVES

The purpose of this chapter is to:

■ Gain an appreciation of the contribution that visual merchandising makes to the product management process and understand how it helps to achieve both short-term and long-term product management objectives.

■ Explore the scope of visual merchandising and discover how elements of visual merchandising vary according to different retail contexts.

■ Understand the supporting role that visual merchandising plays within a retailer's positioning strategy.

■ Appreciate the extent to which visual merchandising and store design can work together to create a stimulating retail environment.

■ Provide an insight into how creativity in visual merchandising and display can be used to enhance the appeal of products.

INTRODUCTION

Visual merchandising is a commonly used term for the aspect of product management that is concerned with presenting the product within a retail outlet to its best advantage. After all the product management work that has gone into planning the ranges, selecting the products, liaising with suppliers, and getting the physical product through the supply chain, the product now makes its entrance into customer space. The aim of this chapter is to show how visual merchandising combines a commercial approach with a design approach within the store environment. It helps to achieve operational product management objectives; maximising the efforts of the buying teams by giving the product the best opportunity to sell. Visual merchandising blends with the store design to create an environment that sends out strategic messages to consumers in order to reinforce the retailer's brand values.

THE SCOPE OF VISUAL MERCHANDISING

Visual merchandising has often been used as a synonym for display in retailing, but in today's retail industry the term incorporates a much wider brief. According to Corsie (2003: 1), visual merchandising allows retailers to 'make the market place innovative, exciting and stimulating by creating product-led stories supported by merchandising solutions'.

Visual merchandising encompasses a wide range of activities; across all retail sectors; visual merchandising may include all or some of the elements outlined in Box 10.1. Visual merchandising plays a much greater part in the product management process in some retail sectors than others. Fashion and home furnishings have always devoted considerable resources to display, but even in a grocery superstore elements of visual merchandising can be found, and indeed some grocery retailers have used visual merchandising as a way of providing interest to the customer and as a way of differentiating themselves from their competitors (see Box 10.2). As discussed in Chapter 8, new generations of computerised planning systems allow space management to combine visual display objectives with space productivity objectives. Corsie (2003) suggests that some of the most effective in-store visuals are the result of simple creative ideas using everyday objects. Retail outlets have to look good if they are to retain an increasingly style conscious customer base.

BOX 10.1 THE SCOPE OF VISUAL MERCHANDISING

- Choice of fixtures and fittings to be used
- Method of product presentation
- Construction of 'off-shelf' displays
- Choice of store layout (to encourage complementary purchases)
- Use of point of sale material (to encourage impulse purchases)
- Construction of window displays

VISUAL MERCHANDISING PLANNING SYSTEMS

Like most other areas of retail management, information technology applications are helping to improve the visual merchandising process. In particular they are helping to forge stronger links between product range planning, space allocation and product presentation. A fully integrated visual merchandising system such as Compass Software's SmartVM can provide store personnel access to space planning visualisations via a corporate internet. This system can be used by buyers and merchandisers as they build ranges for the next season, and then when finalised and ready for delivery photographic quality visual guidelines can be effectively and quickly communicated throughout the retail business. The improved quality of the output of this type of system will be particularly helpful for fashion buyers when presenting their ranges within a floor plan context, helping store personnel to understand product linkages (Ody, 2003).

BOX 10.2 REGIONAL SUPERMARKETS WITH A DIFFERENCE

The grocery supermarket sectors of most European retail markets are highly concentrated. In the UK, the grocery sector is dominated by retail giants Tesco, Asda and J. Sainsbury. Below this 'premier league' of operators, a number of smaller, regional chains are managing to survive.

One such retailer is Morrisons. Founded in 1899 by William Morrison, the father of the current chairman, the company has survived up until recently as a regional grocery supermarket chain, with the majority of its stores covering the North of England. Morrisons' stores offer a wide product range in both foods and non-food items, half of which are sold under the Morrisons brand. The stores are supported by modern retail operations, and a central buying organisation.

In fast moving consumer goods retailing, differentiation is not easily achieved; however, Morrisons have chosen to use store design and visual merchandising as a route to making their outlets a little different to the other grocery stores that they compete with. The careful attention to store design begins with the architectural detail of the stores; many of the stores being visually different, and complementary to local architectural styles and materials. For example, the Sheffield store is housed in disused Yorkshire stone army barracks, which make for a sturdy and impressive backdrop to the store. Inside, Morrisons have adopted a 'market street' concept, where a number of stall-type service counters, complete with striped awnings and street signs, hark back to the time of the traditional specialist shops, and include a butcher, a fishmonger, a pie shop, a delicatessen and a baker. The signage and canopies help to create the atmosphere in this part of the store, where customers are encouraged to interact with store personnel, and gain the individual attention often lacking in the supermarket shopping experience. Other themed areas include modern food combinations such as pizza and curry selections and salad bars, whilst the fresh produce area returns to the traditional theme, with fruit and vegetables displayed on old-fashioned wooden carts. In 2004 Morrisons took over Safeways, the fourth largest grocery chain in the UK. Safeways had a more widespread geographical coverage and so the combined force gives Morrisons the opportunity to compete with the other 'big 3' on a national level.

RESPONSIBILITY FOR VISUAL MERCHANDISING WITHIN THE RETAIL STRUCTURE

Responsibility for this part of product management varies between retail organisations. Lea Greenwood (1998) found that visual merchandising was under the remit of directors of visual merchandising, corporate communications, or promotions. In some retail organisations a team of brand managers co-ordinates the visual merchandising effort with other promotional activities, so that it becomes part of the marketing activities. In fact elements of visual merchandising (particularly the use of point of sale material and photographic imagery) is sometimes referred to as 'in store advertising'. Advertising, by traditional definition refers to communications that are transmitted via paid media, such as magazines or television; therefore, a retailer using their own imagery within the store cannot strictly be counted as advertising. However, the retail environment is a place where manufacturers display various types of branded materials, which again appear to be advertisements. The extent to which a manufacturer will have paid the retailer for this privilege can vary from nothing to a considerable, but probably undisclosed, sum. The term 'ambient media' is a useful one in this context and refers to the various ways in which messages about products and services can appear in a selling environment, but do not fall into the traditional definition of advertising. Chapter 11 considers the contribution that promotional communications can make to the product management process.

The structure beneath the director is sometimes unclear, but a visual merchandise manager, supported by area teams, is a format frequently used in multiple retailers. In smaller retail companies, somebody based in the store may be partly or wholly responsible for visual merchandising. Visual merchandising at the implementation level is a creative activity and usually attracts people with a design training or background, although specific training for this aspect of retailing is available.

VISUAL MERCHANDISING AS A SUPPORT FOR A POSITIONING STRATEGY

In a retail environment that is increasingly saturated, competitive and subject to international competition, visual merchandising is a way of communicating and differentiating the retail offer. It must be an integral part of any strategy in which a retailer attempts to position or re-position the retail offer in the mind of the consumer. It is apparent, then, that visual merchandising is frequently used by multiple retailers to strengthen the retail brand, but a highly centralised and inflexible approach to visual merchandising may not be appropriate in all circumstances. Table 10.1 considers centralised and decentralised approaches to visual merchandising.

Table 10.1 *Visual merchandising: local and centralised approaches*

Local approach	Can adapt to local market product preferences
	Can incorporate local themes into displays
	Can adapt to local competition
Centralised approach	Controls retail brand communication
	Promotes a stronger identity nationally and internationally
	Can integrate corporate communication themes and messages with the visual merchandising effort (for example by using images from media advertising in displays)

FIXTURES AND FITTINGS

The way products need to be presented and displayed within the store will largely determine the choice of fixturing. The principal types of fixtures are illustrated in Figures 10.1 to 10.4.

Gondolas

The term gondola refers to a system of shelving which offers stacked merchandise to the customer in a longitudinal presentation (Figure 10.1). The gondola is used in the 'grid format' where consumers move along aisles between gondolas, which offer merchandise on both sides. The end of the gondola is particularly effective in attracting customers to products as they slow down to turn the corner to view merchandise on the other side. Some gondolas are made up of a number of fixture modules that give flexibility in terms of fixture sizing, and the opportunity to alter the configuration of shelving.

185

Figure 10.1
The gondola

Source: Courtesy of
J. Sainsbury

Round fixtures

As the name suggests the round fixture offers merchandise in a circular presentation. The merchandise might be hung on a series of prongs, as in the case of belts or bubble packed products, or the fixture may be a more solid structure, showing the variety available in a merchandise type. Gap use this type of fixturing to show all the colours available in basic tops or sweaters. Round fixtures are useful for showing a variety of merchandise within one category, but they are not very space efficient because customer access is needed from all sides.

Four-ways

Four-way fixtures offer the retailer flexibility when a degree of co-ordination is needed. The fixture offers a combination of front facing merchandise presentation, with the space efficiency of side hanging (Figure 10.2). The four-way provides the opportunity to present a wide variety of merchandise and is more space efficient than a round fixture.

Figure 10.2
A four-way fixture

Source: Courtesy of
Marks & Spencer

Shelving

Wall space is useful for incorporating the general display of merchandise within the overall interior design of the store. Casual clothing retailers, for example, often use wall shelving to house large quantities of merchandise, stacked from floor to ceiling, whilst offering interest by showing all the alternative colours and shades of denim. Gondolas in various shapes and sizes incorporate shelving to accommodate different types of product (see Figure 10.1)

Rails

Rails can be mounted onto walls, or incorporated into a free standing fixture. Height flexibility can be introduced using adjustable rails and modular rail fixtures provide longitudinal variations. Cascading rails improve the appearance of forward-facing hanging garments, and allow the customer better access to the product.

Bins, baskets and tables

Bins and baskets are normally used to house large quantities of merchandise. They are effective for small items and for heaps of promotional merchandise (see Figure 10.3). They may be filled with one type of product, or the customer may be invited to rummage through a variety of products retailing at a particular price point. Promotional merchandise can also be stacked on tables, which provide flexibility in terms of space allocation and display area. However, tables can also be used in a more elegant display of product.

Figure 10.3 *Displays using tables and baskets*

Source: Courtesy of J. Sainsbury

The increased use of self-service in retailing has meant that the use of drawers and cabinets has decreased, but they may still be used for very functional merchandise that does not really need displaying, or in instances where merchandise needs protection. For example, traditional hardware stores that sell loose items rather than pre-packaged keep this type of merchandise in drawers. Watches and jewellery are often housed in glass cabinets in order to prevent damage and theft.

Many retailers have their own customised fixturing and their own customised terminology for it. Fixturing should have a degree of co-ordination through the store, so that they can be considered in 'families', using the same type of materials, whether it is chrome, wood, acrylic or glass, and the same set of design features. New designs for fixtures often incorporate lighting within the structure so that merchandise on display can be highlighted without the need for spot lighting from walls or ceilings (see Figure 10.4).

Figure 10.4 *Fixture with integral lighting*

Source: Courtesy of Next

In all retail circumstances fixturing should complement and not compete with the merchandise, although the fixturing may be used to reinforce a particular retail brand image. Fixturing also needs to be flexible, so that an ever-evolving product range can be successfully accommodated. Many modern systems are modular which enables a great number of alternative combinations to be built.

PRODUCT PRESENTATION

The way in which products are presented as routine will depend on the type of fixture available (see above) but essentially can include:

- *vertical stacking*, for example, for magazines or CDs;
- *horizontal stacking*, for example tinned foods or folded garments;
- *hanging – on hangers or hooks*;
- *hanging – mounted on card or bubble packed*.

Merchandise presentation is largely determined by product category or end use of product, but in some instances, other product characteristics may bear a relation to the presentation method. Colour, for example, is often used effectively, and many clothing and home furnishings retailers incorporate a corporate colour palette into the buying plan so that different product categories can be presented together.

Retailers may group merchandise together according to price levels or even sizes. Price lining can be used both to plan merchandise assortments and provide guidelines for display. For example, men's ties might be grouped at £9.99, £15.99 and £19.99 and over £19.99. Women's clothing retailers may use sizing groups such as petites, regular and 'plus', and charity shops generally use product, size, and then colour to provide some logic in their disparate merchandise offer. There may also be a case for grouping products according to levels of technical involvement, for example, PC World houses software and accessories at the front of the store and the full PC systems are positioned at the back. The customer is faced with gradually increasing product complexity as he or she moves through the store.

Product presentation can instigate a number of issues for other members of the product management team. Fixturing may determine the size variation a retailer offers, for example a small convenience store may not find it practical to stock family-size cereal packets as they require such tall shelves; it would be preferable in this type of retailer to offer a smaller pack size and another product item in the same available space. The method of presentation may also determine the packaging or 'get up' of the product; for example, a folded shirt is likely to need board and pins, or a paper sash around it to keep it looking neat, but all these add to the cost of the item. Small items, such as stationery products, are much more manageable when bubble packed or mounted on card and hung on a wall fixture. It may be necessary to attach an illustration of the product in use if it has little 'hanger appeal'; for example a swimsuit tends to look like a crumpled rag on the hanger, and most uncooked pre-prepared meals look unappetising, and rely on the photograph on the package to encourage purchase.

New approaches to point of purchase presentation methods have been part of the orientation towards category management in the management of customer demand. Dedicated product fixturing can provide clarity and logic to the product presentation, whilst incorporating suggested complementary and impulse purchases in the arrangement. The relationship between product presentation and the communication process is expanded further in Chapter 11.

STORE LAYOUT

Visual merchandising also encompasses the design of a store layout. A store layout will be heavily influenced by the assortment and variety on offer (see Chapter 1) and will be constrained by the size and structure of the shop itself. The layout used will also determine or be dependent on the type of fixturing used. There are a number of different approaches to store layout, although they are all designed with the intention of moving customers to every area in the store in order to expose them to the full range of products.

A common store layout has fixtures positioned in the form of a grid (Figure 10.5). This method maximises the use that can be made of the available space and provides a logical organisation of the products on offer. However, it is rather mechanical in its approach, and rows of gondola-type fixtures with aisles between them can lack interest.

An alternative approach is to place the fixtures in a more random pattern. This type of layout is appropriate when variety in the fixturing is needed and when the shopping process involves browsing rather than a more systematic product selection process. Referred to as a free form or a free flow layout, this kind of arrangement can successfully incorporate a mix of small gondolas,

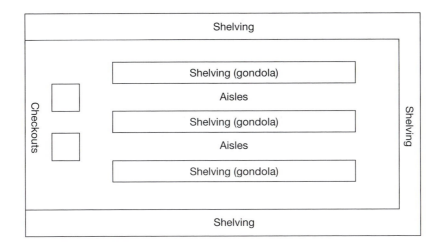

Figure 10.5 *A grid layout*

hanging rails and shelving units. Although the free-form layout generally offers more opportunity to create interest than the grid layout, a unending mass of fixtures set out in a random fashion can look chaotic and for large expanses of retail space, such as in a department store, some attempt must be made to break up the space and create pockets of interest for the customer. According to Din (2000), the product areas in a free-form layout should not be too large or too deep, to prevent customers from feeling trapped (see Figure 10.6).

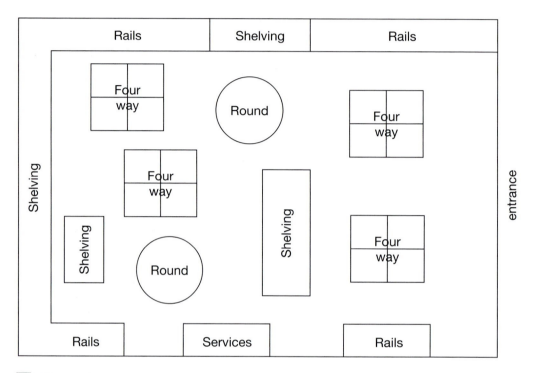

Figure 10.6 *Free-form layout*

Where the merchandise range is limited, or in situations where a high level of personal selling is desirable or necessary, a 'boutique' layout could be used. This layout surrounds the customer with merchandise, most of which is displayed in or on wall fixturing, with one or two other central fixtures offering interest or, perhaps, to house the till. In larger stores a definite guided walkway or 'racetrack' is incorporated into the layout, which guides the customer between the main classifications of merchandise, which are often set out in free-form or short grid fixturing.

Modern layouts are generally more airy, with voids replacing walls and glass replacing solid partitioning. 'Decompression zones' are used to give shoppers time to relax and refocus their attention, for example at the front of the store, or near escalators. Vertical access and visibility is becoming increasingly important as a means of encouraging customers to multi-level retail space, as the amount of available ground floor space decreases in prime shopping centre locations.

Complementary products

Within the overall store layout, decisions concerning which categories of merchandise should be placed next to one another need to be made. This is where the principles of space allocation and store layout are intertwined. A store layout must provide logic to the customer, whilst helping the retailer to achieve its own objectives in terms of exposing the store visitor to as much of the product range as possible and to increase the value of the transaction of each customer. As we saw in Chapter 9, product adjacencies are an important part of the space planning process within a retail outlet, so that related product purchasing opportunities can be maximised to full potential. Visual merchandising may not only encourage complementary purchases, but it can also be used to encourage customers to 'trade up' by highlighting premium brands within a display. Customers may switch brands at the point of purchasing decision, or they may buy something on impulse because a display attracted their attention and created interest in the product. The use of 'clip strips' to increase impulse purchasing is shown in Box 8.4.

Although the achievement of this kind of retailer objective might be viewed as a manipulation of customers, more and more shopping trips are made with only a vague plan or 'list'. Introducing product suggestions on the shelf, or by virtue of the outlet layout, could be viewed as a provision of retail service – making the shopping experience easier and more convenient for the time-pressured customer. In supermarkets customers find dips displayed alongside nacho chips and salad dressings alongside pre-prepared salads. In a department store accessories will be located in their own department for customers who have a specific purchase in mind, and alongside larger items like suits or coats in order to encourage impulse buying of related products.

DISPLAYS

Displays can normally be broken down into three different types: on-shelf displays, feature (or off-shelf displays) and window displays. On-shelf displays are the 'normal' displays around the store that show all the different variations of product on offer in some kind of logical sequence. The various presentation methods used in on-shelf display are discussed in the section concerning product presentation above. The customer is normally free to interact with the product and make a self-service selection from the on-shelf display.

Feature (off-shelf) displays

These displays are designed to have additional impact, by showing the product as it might be used, or perhaps alongside other products to suggest complementary purchases. This type of display can also be considered to be a visual feature that creates interest or excitement within the retail outlet. They might be placed on walls, within alcoves or at the end of a fixture such as a gondola. Whilst on-shelf displays have to combine functionality with aesthetic sensibility, many off-shelf displays are not used in the routine selling process and therefore can be constructed to make a significant visual impact. They are often very carefully designed and artistically arranged and only changed by the visual merchandising team. They may incorporate 'props', which are not part of the product range for sale, or they might be based on a body form or mannequin (see Box 10.3).

BOX 10.3   BODY FORMS

Products that we wear can look entirely different, with or without a body in them. Retailers use a wide range of body forms in clothing displays, from headless torsos for tops, bum-forms for jeans, to stylised figures and lifelike mannequins for full outfits. Body forms can be a much more important part of a store design than a glorified coat hanger. Customers relate strongly to body forms because of their human imagery and so the choice of mannequin is a crucial decision in order to send the right kind of messages to the target customer. Body forms are an expensive part of the visual merchandising tool kit, and so ideally should have lasting appeal. Using the features of role models, such as supermodels, pop celebrities or sporting heroes is an effective way of communicating with potential customers, but they may have a limited life. Posters can provide a more flexible and contextual way of displaying products on real-life models, and may be used in conjunction with the body form.

In contrast, off-shelf displays are also used for promotional purposes and may well incorporate a fixture such as a dump bin, which offers the functional purpose of housing an increased quantity of the promotional item with the visual impact of a high volume display.

In 1981, Rosenbloom described a number of different display types, including open, theme, lifestyle, co-ordinated and classification dominance displays. Nowadays, most on-shelf displays can be regarded as open displays as the customer is encouraged to inspect, and handle products unaided in most retail situations. However, many of the other display classifications are still seen regularly in retailing, most commonly for off-shelf, artistic displays.

The themed display can be used for a local event, like a theatre production or a film release, and is commonly used for seasonal purchases. Display props can be worked into the product theme, as shown in Figure 10.7.

Lifestyle displays offer the opportunity to incorporate a wide variety of products. For example, a display based on the theme of a barbecue could involve garden furniture – the barbecue itself, outdoor tables and loungers; kitchenware products – utensils, plastic crockery and tumblers, informal cutlery; essentials such as charcoal and matches; food produce such as marinades and

Figure 10.7 A themed display

Figure 10.8 *A classification dominance display*

sauces; accessories such as outdoor lighting and candles; and books on the subject of barbecue building or barbecue cookery.

The 'classification dominance' display allows a retailer to show that it has a very deep assortment of merchandise within a classification, or category. The photograph in Figure 10.8 shows how salami sausages are displayed to show the extensive range on offer.

At the opposite end of the scale a display can be very eye-catching if the same product is used in a quantity that is much larger than normal. Referred to by Levy and Weitz (2004: 607) as tonnage merchandising, this type of display is often used for in-store promotions (Figure 10.9).

Figure 10.9 *Tonnage merchandising*

193

BOX 10.4 VISUAL MERCHANDISING FOR SEASONAL SALES

Although less relevant for many retailers these days, as knowledge of sales patterns improves and responsive product replenishment systems are implemented, the end-of-season sale still attracts increases in shopper footfall and gives an opportunity to clear out redundant stock to make way for new arrivals. Not only do sales attract a different set of customers for many retailers, but customers shop the store in a different way, and so it makes sense to change the product presentation to reflect the needs of the bargain hunters. McKeever (2003) suggests the following guidelines for visual merchandising during sales periods:

- Ensure that reduced products stand out visibly in the layout. Separate out reduced lines from regular stock and display boldly in a dedicated space.
- Segment the same product types together. Bargains tend to be shopped on a one-time basis; this way, shoppers can easily compare items without being distracted by attempts at co-ordination. Merchandising by size within the product category might help the shopper further.
- Simplify fixtures. Fixtures that are easy to shop, like hanging rails, and dump bins which allow shoppers to rummage, should be used to encourage shoppers to get through the merchandise efficiently, whilst keeping the environment as tidy as possible.
- Make it easy to shop. Simplified presentation methods using floor and shelving to stack merchandise encourage shoppers to help themselves and help to make the promotional message clear.
- Keep point of sale material bold and accurate. Focus on the messages that make the offer clear, such as prices, sizes and key product information.

Source: McKeever, 2003

The co-ordinated display often uses a colour theme to connect the products being grouped together. It is quite common for lifestyle displays to be colour co-ordinated in order to create additional impact. Home furnishings retailers for example, often use colour themes in both on-shelf and off-shelf displays to arrange their merchandise, rather than by grouping by product category. Other co-ordinating themes could be texture, style, or brand. Co-ordination can also be based around the end use of product, sometimes referred to as idea orientated displays. DIY retailers like B&Q use 'projects' to co-ordinate a seemingly diverse range of products that will be used during a specific DIY task, and even have demonstrations of projects in store to get customers started. Similarly, grouping products into meal ideas can stimulate unplanned purchases of components for a new menu. Figure 10.10 shows a colour co-ordinated window display.

Product focus displays reflect the trend for spacious retail interiors. A single product, or a small group of products are displayed in isolation, leaving the product and its juxtaposition with the space around it to create a visual impact. This type of display is most frequently used for products with prestige and high monetary value, because of the resource implication associated with a higher customer space to merchandise space ratio.

Figure 10.10 *A colour-coordinated window display*

The principles of design

Although the principles of design relate as much to the overall design of the store as a display within, it is perhaps appropriate to consider them in relation to product displays. According to Diamond and Diamond (1999) a visual merchandiser generally employs more than one of the following principles in a display:

- balance, whether symmetrical or asymmetrical;
- emphasis, including the use of size, repetition or contrast;
- proportion and scale;

195

- rhythm, including continuity, progression and alternation;
- harmony.

WINDOW DISPLAYS

Window displays have a particularly important role to play in communicating to the potential customer what the retailer stands for in terms of product and shopping environment. Window displays make customers aware of the type of merchandise being sold, and hopefully will attract the interest of target customers. In fact the window displays of retailers such as Selfridges, Harvey Nichols, and Bloomingdale's are so novel and exciting, that they have become visitor attractions in themselves. Window displays can be open, which allows the customer to see past the merchandise and into the shop. Alternatively, windows may be backed by partial or complete boarding, which allows the retailer to build promotional photography into the display or to create dramatic effects. Some window displays have even incorporated moving features, for example Top Shop's flagship store at Oxford Circus in London had animated legs and arms in its Christmas 1999 party season window display, and Levi's London flagship store has interactive touch screens (see Box 10.5). High-fashion footwear retailer KoKo of Carnaby Street (London) incorporated ceiling mounted revolving fixtures to show a wide range of boots and shoes in their window. Material and design elements from the store's interior were replicated in the fixtures, which are constructed from aluminium tubes coated in an epoxy powder, with glass-effect acrylic shelves. The look is fully integrated, sleek and contemporary, and supports the retailer's trendy brand identity (*Retail Bulletin*, 6 May 2004).

BOX 10.5 INTERACTIVE WINDOWS

When the bustle of the busy shopping day has died down, retailers can provide more than passive window shopping when the doors are closed, and when the doors are open, interactive windows can be the start of a great shopping experience for customers.

In 2002, Levi's turned a shop window into a film scene showing footage of a male model dressed in the latest Levi's collection, who beckons shoppers to come closer and then shouts 'Hey, look at me', followed by an invitation to call a phone number which lists options to determine what he does next, which includes the option of him doing a striptease. Another option is for a girl model to join him wearing the female collection.

In a more subtle approach perhaps, Lunn Poly, John Lewis and Marks & Spencer have used 'whispering windows' to grab shopper attention. Lunn Poly, the travel agents used music, spoken messages, 'sunshine' and aromas projected at shoppers as they passed on the street to encourage holiday bookings in a three week promotional campaign in January 2004. Marks & Spencer used sound projected from plasma screens in store windows to promote its new '& More' combined credit and loyalty card in autumn 2003. Department store group John Lewis used the device to project the sound of music playing on DVD players and high-end plasma television sets in its store window. The window is able to monitor the level of external street noise and set its sound output just above the ambient level.

Source: *Retail Interiors*, December 2002; *Retail Bulletin*, February 2002

Some retailers do not use window displays at all. This is commonly the case in superstores and retail warehouses, where the retailer's name either must be so well known that the general public will know what that retailer represents, for example J. Sainsbury (grocery) or Curry's (electrical) or the name of the retailer leaves little doubt to the customer what the retailer is selling (Toys 'Я' Us, PC World, Shoe Express).

VISUAL MERCHANDISING IN NON-STORE RETAILING

Although the objectives of retail design and visual merchandising are the same in both store and non-store retailing, and revolve around presenting products attractively, whilst reflecting customer needs, non-store retailing presents some additional challenges for visual merchandising, whilst offering some unique opportunities. The fact that non-store retailing relies on product representations rather than the 'real thing' means that some visual merchandising techniques, like tonnage merchandising and classification dominance displays are less effective. The store environment offers more scope to use the physical presence of the products for impact while restrictions associated with the non-store medium can be significant. Catalogues are only able to show a product in two dimensions, and retailer's web sites have a tendency to be very similar in style and operation, negating many of the efforts that are made by store retailers to achieve differentiation. Nevertheless, novel ways of presenting products in a lifestyle context, the use of corporate colours and high quality photography combined with creativity have all contributed to the success of strong non-store retail branding. These aspects of product management are considered further along with others that are unique to non-store retailing in Chapter 13.

SUMMARY

Although a perfectly merchandised supermarket has been a main exhibit in an art exhibition (Liverpooltate.co.uk), the role of visual merchandising within retail product management cannot be separated from any of the more 'scientific' aspects of retail product management. Getting the product right in all its attributes, ensuring it arrives in the store at the right time and in quantities that are appropriate to customer demand, are only worthwhile objectives if customers notice the product when they walk into the store. Visual merchandising highlights and draws attention to merchandise and has the ability to set the 'tone' of the retail brand (Din, 2000). Visual merchandising therefore plays a crucial role in the creation and support of a retail brand's proposition. Consumers are using an increasing variety of distribution channels for shopping including the specialist catalogue, the internet, and even the vending machine. Only stores can offer customers a social experience with actual products in real space, and if they do not use this key asset to their competitive advantage, the drift of customers away to alternative shopping formats will continue. Effective product management brings the buying arena and the selling arena together in a seamless product strategy.

QUESTIONS

1   Outline the various aspects of retailing management that would fall under the heading 'visual merchandising'.

2   Compare a centralised approach to visual merchandising with a local approach.

3   Review the different methods of product presentation, and discuss how they impact upon the choice of fixturing, and store layout.

4   Make a distinction between on- and off-shelf displays, indicating how the latter provides more opportunity for artistic creativity.

5   For a retailer of your choice, make a critical appraisal of the fixtures that are used in the store. In particular, comment on the variety and flexibility in the fixturing and the extent to which the fixtures are complementary in terms of design and material.

6   Analyse the use of different store layouts in the following retail sectors:

   ■ beauty and healthcare;
   ■ electrical/electronic;
   ■ grocery.

7   Explore the relationship between visual merchandising and the reinforcement of a retail brand.

8   Use your local shopping centre to find examples of displays that illustrate the various types of display described in this chapter. Also, indicate how the principles of design have been used in the display.

REFERENCES AND FURTHER READING

Barr, V. and Field, K. (1997) *Stores: Retail Display and Design*, PBC International, New York.

Blyth, A. (2004) 'A Window on the Web', *Retail Week*, 1 October.

Corsie, K. (2003) 'Making the Ordinary Extraordinary', *VM World*, February, p. 1.

Diamond, J. and Diamond, E. (1999) *Contemporary Visual Merchandising*, Prentice Hall, Englewood Cliffs, NJ.

Din, R. (2000) *New Retail*, Conran Octopus, London.

Lea-Greenwood, G. (1998) 'Visual Merchandising: A Neglected Area in UK Fashion Marketing?', *International Journal of Retail and Distribution Management*, 26(8): 324–329.

Levy, M. and Weitz, B.A. (2004) *Retailing Management*, McGraw Hill, New York.

McKeever, K. (2003) 'Sales Pitch', *Retail Week*, 10 January.

Ody, P. (2003) 'HoF In-store Planning System Revamped by Compass Software', *Retail Week*, 7 March.

Rosenbloom, B. (1981) *Retail Marketing*, Random House, New York.

Web site

Retail Bulletin (2004) 'Carnaby Street Showcase for British Turntable', editorial, http://www.theretailbulletin.co.uk?index.php?u=11407&page=61, accessed 06/05/04

Chapter 11

Communicating the product offer

LEARNING OBJECTIVES

The purpose of this chapter is to:

■ Introduce the idea that whilst most product related communications are focused on short-term objectives, product based events can also be valuable tools in strategic communications.

■ Explore the relationship between the various types of communication channel and the different product management objectives that retailers might have.

■ Identify the challenges that are associated with the communication of the benefits of a diverse product range.

■ Understand the need for stock management support when implementing promotional activity.

■ Introduce the concept of integrated retail communications and explore the role internal communications play in preparing for an integrated campaign.

■ Develop an appreciation that retailers and their suppliers often have conflicting promotional objectives, but by working together effectively, they can achieve promotional efficiency and improve category performance.

INTRODUCTION

Providing information about products that a retailer sells is a very effective way of enticing customers into an outlet. Having said that, a challenge that most retailers face is how to represent the complete product offer in communications to potential customers outside the outlet. This is a familiar problem for internet retailers who have the advantage of almost unlimited virtual space, but severe limitations when it comes to portraying the extent of this range to the web site visitor when they first arrive. Large retailers may have a product range comprising thousands of product items spread over hundreds of product categories, and incorporating myriad brands. The advancement of information and communication technology further extends the complexity of retail to consumer communications by offering numerous media through which to communicate. The purpose of this chapter is to explore the relationship between product management and retailer to consumer communications, focusing on the use of promotional communications to draw a shopper's attention to specific products, with the view to maximising sales opportunities and optimising category profits.

RETAILER TO CUSTOMER COMMUNICATIONS

Whilst the retail environment itself is an extremely effective tool for communicating a retailer's brand values, and visual merchandising allows retailers to present visual cues to the customer concerning products, these methods of sending messages to potential customers rely on people actually being in the outlet. In order to maximise footfall and sales it may be necessary to send messages further afield in order to encourage people to visit.

Marketing communications objectives are usually broken down into two broad types. Some objectives have non-specific, long-term aims, whilst others concern themselves with more specific targets, focused perhaps on product, category or store performance or gaining new customers. Table 11.1 explores these different types of objectives. Of course, retailers may have messages that they wish to send to potential customers that are not specifically related to the product range, for example a new customer service initiative, the launch of a loyalty scheme or the opening of a new store; however, for the purpose of this chapter, the discussion will concentrate on retailer communications that are linked to product management, whether they are strategic or tactical in nature.

Table 11.1 *Marketing communications' objectives*

Strategic Long term (examples)	Operational and promotional Short term (examples)
Establishing a clear market position for a retailer	Increasing customer awareness of category X
Changing consumers' attitudes towards a retailer	Increasing sales of brand Y
Improving a retailer's image	Increasing transaction levels per customer
Portraying a retailer as a customer focused organisation	Informing customer that prices have been reduced
Enhancing a retailer's reputation as a responsible corporation	Encouraging customers to buy product A with product B

It is not within the scope of this text to explore all the different media alternatives and the decision stages retailers go through when devising a communications strategy; these are adequately covered in marketing communications and retail marketing textbooks elsewhere. However, what this chapter seeks to illustrate is the appropriateness of using various communications methods in order to support retail product management objectives, and to consider some specific issues concerning the product management process. After all, having decided on the right type and brand of products within the assortment, and made arrangements to get supplies into the retail outlet, it makes sense to draw customers' attention to the availability of products at attractive prices. Communications also play a vital role in reinforcing the market position that the retailer is aiming for in terms of the variety, depth and price level of the product assortment.

RETAIL COMMUNICATION CHANNELS

In Chapter 1, product range extension and development were identified as one direction in which a retailer might grow their business. Adding new products or categories may help a retailer to increase customer transaction values or add to their customer base. Constant refinement of the product range allows a retailer to remain relevant to customers and so changes made to the product range need to be communicated to customers to give the launch of any new product the best possible chance of success. The retailer has the opportunity to integrate communications both outside of and inside the retail selling environment to draw attention to their new initiative. For example, a TV advertising campaign might be used to inform consumers about the availability of the new product at the retailer, and at the point of purchase dedicated fixturing and banners might be used to attract attention to it. Information leaflets and informed sales personnel might provide additional information about the product, and information may be sent to a retailer's customer database (for example generated by a loyalty scheme) with a voucher to encourage trial.

ADVERTISING

National advertising, using TV, radio, magazines or newspapers is a very effective way of communicating product offers to consumers as it has a large 'reach'; the communication is received by a large number of consumers, in all areas of the country. However, this advantage can cause a retailer problems because, as a business they may not have national coverage and even if they do, a product or product category may not be suitable for all-store distribution and therefore the product advertised may not be readily available.

As well as a wide reach, media advertising has the advantage of having a relatively high impact. The message can be accompanied by colourful images, emotion-arousing atmospherics and the message output is carefully controlled. In addition to national advertising media, a plethora of media vehicles are targeted at specific audiences (defined by for example age group or personal interests and lifestyles). These vehicles may be particularly useful for specialist retailers. For example, a magazine like *Practical Parenting* may be a particularly relevant media vehicle for a retailer like Mothercare who aims to provide all the necessary requisites for new families.

One of the key difficulties concerning advertising of any sort is how a retailer gets across information about all the products they sell in a restricted space (for example, in a newspaper or magazine) or time (for example, TV or radio). This restriction led retailers in the past down the route of cramming pictures of products together with a small amount of information (very often the brand and the reduced price) onto one page of a newspaper or into a TV advert. This type of approach can be effective for price orientated messages, focusing on a small selection of product items as a way of illustrating the availability of low prices for these products, and then hoping for a transfer of this positive price image to all products within the outlet. In order to avoid the problem of only focusing on a very small part of a retailer's product offering, retailers have used creativity and innovative approaches to get across to customers that their product range is relevant to their needs. A good example of an advertising campaign that supported a major repositioning of a product range was one used by Tesco in the early 1990s. The advertisement featured the late comic actor Sir Dudley Moore who played the role of a Tesco buyer who scoured the globe for high quality suppliers of unique products for the business. This TV campaign reinforced a strategy to move the perception of Tesco's product range from a 'low price basics' appeal to one that included high quality, specialist 'gourmet' products. More recently Tesco have used the mother and daughter duo (played by comedy actors Prunella Scales and Jane Horrocks) to extol the various virtues of product ranges including the Value products and the Finest range of ready meals.

The use of well known characters or 'celebrities' in retailer advertising is a popular theme amongst the UK retail industry; the advantages and disadvantages of this type of approach are summarised in Box 11.1.

Some retailers use direct celebrity endorsement as the basis for the advertisement, such as the famous TV chef Jamie Oliver's endorsement of the food range of UK grocery retailer, J. Sainsbury plc. Other retailers use actors to play roles in scenarios in which some aspect of a retailer's offer is reinforced. Argos, the UK based multi-channel home furnishing and appliances retailer used actor Richard E. Grant as an upwardly mobile father who has been converted to the contemporary styling of Argos home furnishings. Both of these campaigns are concerned with communicating product benefits to potential customers. In the case of Jamie Oliver and Sainsbury, high quality, speciality, variety and convenience in the food ranges is emphasised and reinforced as part of a strategy for Sainsbury to return to core product values rather than compete on price in the very competitive grocery sector. For Argos, the objective of the advertising campaign was to reposition a rather traditional catalogue showroom retailer as a modern, stylish retailer whose products would appeal to image conscious consumers, portrayed humorously by the pompous character played by Richard E. Grant. The advantage of the non-specific product/price advertisement is that the virtues of the product assortment can be communicated without the need to specify individual products and their prices, although some examples are usually 'thrown into' the sketch.

BOX 11.1   THE ADVANTAGES AND DISADVANTAGES OF USING CELEBRITIES IN RETAIL ADVERTISING

Advantages	Disadvantages
Recall – consumers will tend to remember the advertisement	High cost
Recognition – recognising the well known person draws attention to the retailer advertisement	Incorrect association – consumers remember the celebrity but not the retailer or their products
The positive feelings consumers have about the celebrity are transferred to the retailer	Celebrity may fall from grace, or suffer from over-exposure, resulting in negative feelings being transferred from celebrity to retailer
The celebrity adds credibility if they have a strong association with the retailer's product (valid endorsement)	Consumers may conclude celebrity is only 'doing it for the money', especially if they have little association with the retailer's offer
Actors can be used to play roles, which can be used in scenarios to draw attention to particular aspects of a retailer's offer	Consumers may tire of the same people being used in every advertisement for the retailer
Celebrity advertisements are often humorous, which aids recall and generates positive feelings	Some celebrities may not be known to some consumers, therefore, the 'point' or humorous aspect of the advertisement may be lost
	Use of celebrities in retailer advertising becomes too frequent and loses novelty

Ambient advertising

With the costs of media advertising increasing, while the effectiveness due to media fragmentation and message clutter are being brought into question, retail and product marketers are exploring alternative ways of transmitting brand messages. Ambient advertising is a term that refers to the placement of advertising in unexpected locations, such as on a petrol pump nozzle, on the floor of a public place or on a screen in a retail outlet. Tesco, for example, have an in-store digital media network, which allows corporate or product related communication to be transmitted onto neat plasma screens located at strategic locations within stores. Spar has also trialled digital promotion successfully, with significant sales uplifts on products promoted on screens located close to the product in the store. Digital media networks combine flexibility and the benefits of high quality, moving imagery, with the message being relayed as close as possible to the point of purchase (Larner, 2004).

PRODUCT SPECIFIC PROMOTIONAL COMMUNICATIONS

Although the variety of products on offer presents a real challenge for retail communications using conventional media, the product range itself provides an arena in which many product-related communications can be made very effectively. Once a customer has found a product or category of interest, a number of methods can be used to draw a shopper's attention to specific products. The type of objective that a retailer might be trying to achieve with this type of communication is

- increase sales of this brand (retailer's own brand or manufacturer brand);
- encourage customer to try the product;
- encourage the customer to trade up within category (increase transaction value);
- encourage multiple purchases of brand or linked products;
- to counteract promotional activity of a competitor;
- to capitalise on seasonal sales.

The methods that can be used to draw customers' attention to particular products or brands are generally included under the broad term 'Sales Promotion'. Given the variety of activities used, it is difficult to define a sales promotion; however, it generally refers to initiatives that act as an incentive for customers to trial or purchase a particular product (see Figure 11.1).

In order to maximise the effectiveness of the sales promotion activity, promotional material usually supplements the sales promotion. So for example, if a retailer is offering a buy-one-get-one-free (BOGOF) deal, they will normally provide some kind of sign or fixture that draws attention to the offer. This type of material, often referred to as point of sale (POS) or point of purchase (POP) can vary from a simple shelf edge ticket, to special displays and fixtures dedicated to the product on offer.

The use of displays to communicate a product range was considered in Chapter 10. Some types of product display are used to draw attention to merchandise that is being promoted within the retail outlet, usually because of a price reduction/offer or because there is an opportunity to maximise sales due to seasonal demand, or as part of an all-store promotional activity. Certain display techniques are particularly effective for promotional activity; for example, volume displays, dump bins and tables. The key to effective promotional communications is making an impact at the point where the purchase decision is made, focusing the shopper's attention on a particular product category, product item or brand.

Sales promotion activity is very important for a retailer when introducing a new product or product category. The promotional activity will make customers aware of the new range, or

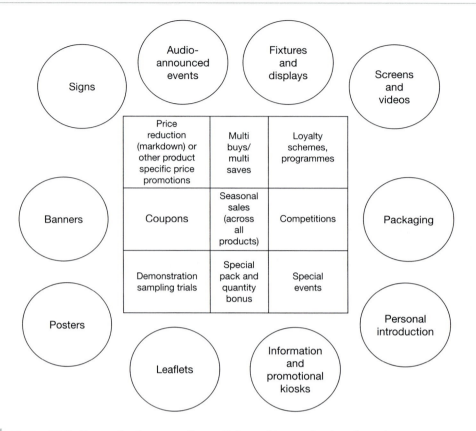

Figure 11.1 *Types of sales promotion activity and types of point of purchase support*

remind them of some other communication that they may have received, such as an advertisement or a direct mailing informing them about the new initiative. Information provided by leaflets, or sales personnel will help to move the customer from awareness to purchase intention. Given the high numbers of product introductions that fail, and the subsequent costs incurred with introduction activities, it is very important to give them the best possible chance of success.

PROMOTIONAL PRODUCT PLANNING

Many retailers rely on promotional activity to increase sales. A promotion may be part of an offensive strategy in which advance planning, budgeting and forecasting will take place in order to maximise a specific selling opportunity, for example, a cosmetics promotion for Mother's Day in a department store. Other promotions, however, may be part of a defensive move to get a retailer out of trouble. If, for example a retailer finds that an exceptionally warm autumn has reduced demand for coats and heavier-weight outerwear, it may decide to run a promotion on those particular merchandise categories to stimulate sales to the forecast level. By reducing prices, demand is restored to the planned level, and whilst the short-term profitability is hampered, the retailer is not faced by an overstock situation, which may cause even more serious logistical problems in the very important pre-Christmas selling period.

Planning a promotional campaign may involve a host of in-store and out-of-store activity. A campaign may include the co-ordination of TV and print based media advertisements, coupled with additional space allocation and point of purchase material within the store. In a successful promotion the increase in gross profit (an increased turnover with reduced profit margin being the likely formula) should ideally outweigh the costs involved with the promotion, but a retailer may be content with a break-even result on a direct profit/promotional cost basis because of the increased footfall and therefore sales in other departments.

The retailer must be sure then that the increased sales turnover is possible. If there is not enough stock, then the money invested in promotional activity will have been wasted. Long-term, well-supported promotions will strengthen the image of the store in terms of product assortment, but too many minor promotions, where the benefit to the customer is not very credible, can be damaging to the store's reputation, and a communicated 'offer' which cannot be found in the store is likely to cause high levels of customer dissatisfaction.

Collaborative promotional planning allows retailers and their suppliers to co-ordinate each other's promotional activities for mutual gain; a calendar of events can be drawn up which highlights for example national advertising campaigns that the supplier undertakes and any cross-store events the retailer is running. In this way, the retailer can be prepared to support and gain from supplier instigated promotions and the supplier can help the retailer during their own promotional events by making sure products are available and replenished quickly. Collaborative planning, forecasting and replenishment, discussed in Chapter 7, is particularly relevant in the context of promotional activity.

STRATEGIC PRODUCT COMMUNICATIONS

Some products and product ranges provide retailers with an opportunity to do more than sell. For example, the introduction of ethically sourced products allow a retailer to link the product to their overall sourcing strategy and enhance their image as a socially responsible retailer. Stocking a range of products designed or endorsed by a well known person, or linked to a new movie allow the style, trend and general interest association to be transferred from the products themselves to the retailer's more general brand image. In addition, this type of activity gives retailers an opportunity to gain publicity, capitalise on public relations activities, and benefit from word of mouth recommendation. It is also possible for a retailer to highlight products that are of strategic importance in corporate communications such as in company reports or on educational web sites. The following examples of strategic retail communications illustrate the relationship between the retailer's long-term, image based objectives and related product opportunities.

Cultural events

Selfridges, the London based department store, are well known for their themed extravaganzas. These have been based on Brazil (2004), Tokyo (2003) and Bollywood (2002). Every department within the store is involved and features merchandise that has a connection to the theme. The window displays are particularly lavish, incorporating interactive peepholes and moving imagery. In the Tokyo promotion, one of the window displays was completely converted to a Japanese style convenience store, and for the Brazil 40 event a cinema was built in the store to reflect its important place in Brazilian culture (retailbulletin). Not only does this type of event attract large amounts of publicity, it reinforces Selfridges' image as a retailer with its finger on the pulse of not only fashionable products, but also 'happening' destinations. The special merchandise brought in for the promotion may find a place in the product assortment permanently if it proves to have lasting popularity.

Film releases

The launch of a new fantasy film, such as *Harry Potter* or the *Lord of the Rings* provides toy retailers like Toys 'Я' Us with the opportunity to build themed displays that incorporate a selection of toys from a number of different product categories. Models, costumes, interactive computer games and even confectionery are examples of the licensed merchandise that can be brought together to maximize sales at the time of a new release, as well as providing the opportunity to create an exciting and interesting store environment.

Ethical issues

The Co-op have become heavily involved in the development of Fair-traded own-brand products. In the mailings sent to holders of the 'Dividend' loyalty card, information about these products has been included. Not only will this direct mailing attract customer attention to the products in this range, this product communication contributes to the Co-op's overall socially responsible image.

B&Q produce leaflets, which are available in store, concerning the environmental impact of their products, the sourcing of raw materials for products and supply chain activities. Products that were highlighted in a brochure produced in 2000 were: timber products made from wood from 'well managed forests'; peat free compost; garden furniture from sources with improved working conditions and paint with clear labeling regarding the content of VOCs (volatile organic compounds that contribute to atmospheric pollution).

PUBLICITY

Strategic communications are often carefully controlled, for example in the case of the Co-op's direct mailing cited above, as part of a customer relations exercise. Publicity, on the other hand can be either positive or negative, and however closely it is managed the retailer does not pay directly for it and so they have little control over the content and coverage. An advantage of this type of communication, however, is that it is generally more credible than advertising, which today's marketing literate consumer knows is paid-for space in the media. Retailers, like other organisations, can attempt to manage public relations so that positive publicity is maximised and negative releases are minimised or counteracted. This involves being prepared with good quality positive information about a retailer and its products, which can be used by the media in their independent editorial features. Retailers can often generate publicity by emphasising store related promotional activities in press releases. The opening or refurbishment of a flagship store (see Chapter 9, a themed event or a birthday celebration (see Box 11.2) are all good opportunities for publicity.

BOX 11.2   BIRTHDAY PROMOTIONS

A celebration to mark the anniversary of a number of years' trading provides retailers with a flexible marketing opportunity. It gives retailers an opportunity to remind customers of their existence, send out special vouchers, undertake a discounting campaign or even launch a special range of products. Burton, for example, launched a limited edition 'Centenary' menswear collection to mark its 100th birthday in 2004.

Retailer's birthdays are also used for internal marketing; providing the opportunity to boost staff moral and give them recognition for their part in the organisation's success. Retailers may use bonuses, parties or in-store events as a way of celebrating and saying thank you to staff and customers. Gap reached its 35th Birthday in 2004 and celebrated by launching a limited capsule collection of clothes featuring retro logos harking back to an era when the store only sold jeans and records. This was accompanied by competitions and party packs for staff.

Some retailers take a short, sharp burst of promotional activity, with a focus on impact and short-term sales. Others have extended the event over most of the anniversary year; which allows more product related promotions and the opportunity to maintain the momentum of increased awareness and in-store interest over a longer period of time.

Source: Morrell, 2004

PERSONAL COMMUNICATIONS

As well as using various media through which messages are related to customers, retailers have the advantage of being able to use both their outlet space and their sales personnel (in-store formats) to communicate with customers. As we saw in Chapters 9 and 10 outlet design and visual merchandising are concerned with sending customers strong messages about the retailer's products and their positioning in the market. Displays and point of sale materials in particular link the area of customer communications with operational aspects of product presentation and space allocation. Dedicated fixturing at the point of purchase, for example, can help a retailer to achieve strong category representation as well as communicating key brands within the category to the customer, whilst at the same time providing a tidy and attractive display.

For some products, however, dedicated fixturing is not enough to move a potential customer from the stage of searching for information about a product to a sale. In Chapter 2 the idea of product complexity was introduced, and earlier on in this chapter the role people can play in communicating information about specific products has been mentioned. The higher the complexity of the product, the more important this role becomes. In fact in some retail situations, the communication between a person representing the retailer and the customer is the most effective method of communicating. This area of communications is often referred to as personal selling, and indeed the retailer's objective is ultimately to close the communications process with a sale. However, with consumers increasingly using different channels within the shopping process (Dennis *et al.*, 2004) the actual moment of purchase transaction may not coincide exactly with the moment of purchase decision. Customers may spend considerable time building up information on a purchase using the internet or catalogues, but leave the final purchase decision until they are in a store to see the product in 'the flesh'. A customer may just as easily browse around shops but then go home and order the item they have chosen from a retailer's web site. It is wise, therefore, for retailers not to simply have 'close sale' as the retailer–customer interface objective. Sales personnel need to provide the customer with enough information to make a satisfactory purchase decision, whichever outlet from a retailer's portfolio a customer chooses for the final stages of their shopping process.

Within this communication process, the main objective is to match a potential customer's needs, wants and aspirations, to product benefits. In order to do this effectively, the retailer's sales personnel need a high level of product knowledge. This knowledge can be built using specific product training, but the unearthing of customer needs and wants in order to match up with product features very often requires experience with a variety of customers. Formal sales training can help a retailer's representative to use techniques that will help the process along; some of these are listed below:

- Engage the customer in conversation to find out why they might want to buy the product. Are they replacing, or upgrading or buying as a gift?
- Establish what product features are important; try to sort important features into categories of 'must haves' and 'would likes'.
- Establish the price threshold(s) that might be applicable to the customer, including ability and willingness to pay.
- Do certain brands have resonance for the customer, would they be receptive to a retailer brand alternative?
- Give the customer space to think about purchase and/or discuss with peers (friends, partner, family) who may influence the decision. Try to establish what benefits are important to these 'influencers' and match these too (they may have entirely different features as must haves and would likes).
- Try to help the customer imagine themselves using the product.
- Empathise with any problems or objections that customer may have, and try to offer solutions to overcome these.

Readers may wish to consult Chapter 4 to remind themselves of the different categories of product selection criteria. A retail buyer needs to try to cover all the needs and wants of the potential customer base in those criteria. The retailer's sales person needs to be able to interpret those selection criteria as benefits for the consumer within the constraints of the product range on offer.

COMMUNICATIONS THROUGH PACKAGING

Within the retail environment packaging can play a very important communications role. For example, consider the way in which a few grocery items bought from a convenience store are simply placed in a thin plastic carrier bag and compare that to the way a dress bought in a designer boutique is packaged. The dress will be carefully folded into tissue, which may feature a subtle imprint of the shop's logo. The item will then be carefully placed into a substantial bag made of good quality card, with ribbon handles. The bag will have a distinctive design with the retailer's name emblazoned across it. These different approaches to the packing of the products purchased reflect the involvement level of the customer in the purchase and clearly communicate the price positioning of the retailer (see Boden case study in Chapter 13).

Packaging not only refers to the way a product is transported out of the retail outlet and into a customer's home, but also how the product itself is presented on the shelf. Most food products have some sort of packaging in order to transport and protect its quality (see Chapter 4 for a detailed discussion on the role of packaging in a product's specification) and the packaging acts as a vehicle for information about the product, including in many cases a representation of the product in use. The design of the packaging therefore communicates with the customer about the product's physical and tangible aspects, but it can also send out subtle messages concerning price, style and quality positioning. The colours used, the typeface and the graphics will vary according to the type of product and the customer being targeted. Figure 4.3 illustrates this point clearly within the context of Sainsbury's biscuit category.

INTEGRATING PRODUCT RELATED COMMUNICATIONS

As we have seen in this chapter, a retailer can communicate its product offer to its customers and potential customers in very many different ways. However, a customer will be confused if the messages it receives from a retailer are all saying different things, so it is extremely important to ensure that all communication activity is coordinated and integrated. A clear and consistent message delivered across all outlets and at all levels within a retailer's organisation will help a retailer to achieve long-term product management objectives, while carefully orchestrated promotional activity will help a product manager to maximise sales opportunities and improve category performance.

Loyalty schemes are a type of promotional activity that, by their nature, has to be integrated. Most loyalty schemes offer a customer the opportunity to accumulate points that can be redeemed against future purchases, or saved up for a special purchase. The additional benefit for the retailer and the customer is that customised promotional incentives can be generated based on the type of personal and purchasing profile of the customer. These offers need to be recognized at store level. In addition, other offers can be introduced within the store, such as extra points for particular products, or for multiple purchases of an item. It has been suggested that there has been a shift in expenditure from conventional advertising to sales promotions, which includes loyalty schemes (McGoldrick, 2002, Mintel, 2000). Loyalty schemes are costly to set up and run, but are less wasteful in terms of reach and the ability to customise communications and facilitate micro marketing initiatives (see Box 8.5).

Another important example of integrated communications is using paid-for media to advertise a promotional activity. Whether the promotion involves a simple price reduction on a selection of products from the total assortment, or it extends to the reaches of a Selfridges type of 'event', additional customer footfall generated by media advertising can help a promotional activity to be successful. Specific price offers can generate interest in particular products, but a retailer must ensure they have enough stock to avoid disappointing customers should the promotion be so successful that the item sells out. A more general communication can generate a more widespread interest in offers across a number of categories. Advertising for a themed event should convey the same level of excitement and interest that customers experience within the store. Boots, for example, used a high profile billboard advertising campaign to support the launch of 5,000 new product variations in 2003. The objective of the advertisements was to generate customer traffic and entice customers to try the new products. In Boots stores attention was drawn to them with mirrored hoardings and point of sale material encouraging customers to try different make-up looks that could be created with the new products (Wood, 2003).

Not only should a retailer co-ordinate the messages in a communications strategy; given that most of the communication is delivered through non-personal channels, the 'look' or visual strategy should also be consistent in order to reinforce the retail brand. This means that corporate colours, typefaces, logos and images should be used consistently across media advertising, direct mailings, point-of-purchase material, even down to store signage and carrier bags (Harrington, 2002).

INTERNAL COMMUNICATIONS

In centralised retail organisations, where many decisions concerning a retailer's product offer are made by product teams working on behalf of the whole organisation, there is a need for a considerable amount of internal communications to implement product plans at the outlet level. There are a number of key areas where product managers need to relay their plans to the various outlets:

- *Product information*: Sales personnel need to have as much information as possible about new and improved products so that they can then inform customers of their benefits in the selling process.
- *Product display*: The way products are intended to be displayed on fixtures should be communicated. This can either be done in the form of written and visual guidelines, or via the output of a space planning system (planogram) – see Chapter 8.
- *Promotional activity*: Retail outlets need to be informed about any price changes, or other promotions, so that the initiative can be properly co-ordinated and supported. Details about the POS material to be used, how to construct special displays, and changes to store layout and space allocation need to be included. All colleagues should be aware of any out-of-store promotional activity, such as advertising, so that they can give informed responses to any customer's questions or comments prompted by the campaign.

Internal communications should not be a one-way route; store personnel will need a formalised and open communication network to encourage valuable feedback to the head office teams (see Chapter 2). For example, if problems with products (such as safety or quality concerns, fit, instructions for use or maintenance) go unreported, mistakes can be repeated.

RETAILER–SUPPLIER RELATED ISSUES

Whatever method of communications a retailer uses to inform customers about products, there is one golden rule regarding products that retailers surprisingly often overlook, and that is if your objective is to sell more of a product, then you must have plenty of stock to sell. The fact that it is necessary to state the obvious in this respect can be borne out by a trip to almost any store. Somewhere within the outlet there will be an empty or virtually empty shelf with a promotional communication attached to it. Keeping promoted products in stock would therefore seem to be one of the biggest challenges to retailers.

Promotional communications that manufacturers send to consumers are out of a retailer's direct control, yet in theory retailers should be able to benefit from the additional sales the promotional activity stimulates. Supporting a supplier's promotion however poses some difficulties for retailers, as follows.

Different promotional objectives

Retailers and suppliers have different promotional objectives. Suppliers undertake marketing communications to promote their brand, to increase awareness and loyalty for it. Retailers on the other hand are not generally as concerned about the performance of a single brand, as they are likely to be offering alternative brands within a product category. They are interested in the performance of the category, and if they are interested in product items at all, they are more likely to be interested in the retailer's own-branded products.

Attitude to POS materials

A supplier may wish to undertake in-store promotional activity to promote their brand; they may supply point of sale material; they may want to send representatives to demonstrate the product in stores, and they would like to have extra selling space. A retailer may consider the POS material and initiatives to be extraneous clutter, and they may not be willing or have room to devote extra selling space. The presence of supplier orientated POP may be considered to be out of place in a corporate retail branded environment (Dowding, 2002).

Conflicting images

A supplier may be interested in promoting a product that a retailer does not consider to be their best example in terms of their long-term product positioning. For example, the product may be at the lower end of the quality scale, or be relatively unhealthy. A retailer will be more interested in supporting promotions of products that have very positive consumer associations, and can reinforce a retailer's good reputation. A good example of this is cause-related promotions (see Box 11.3).

BOX 11.3 CAUSE-RELATED PROMOTIONS

Cause-related marketing is attractive to retailers for two very good reasons. First, getting involved in activities that are charity related will improve their public image and reputation for corporate social responsibility. Second, doing so makes good business sense. Research has indicated that sales uplifts of more than 10 per cent can apply when retailers, manufacturers and charities combine forces. In 2003 Tesco got involved with two promotions linked to the Comic Relief charity. The products involved were Persil's Charity Begins at Foam washing powder and Mr Kipling Cherry Bakewell 'Red Nose' cakes. The manufacturers agreed to donate a small sum of money for every product item sold. Not only was the campaign successful for the amount of money raised for Comic Relief, Persil, for example, raised over £400,000, but sales uplifts continued to apply to the brands after the promotional period had ended. However, cause related promotions need careful planning and execution; ensuring that brands, retailers and the causes have resonance with their own objectives and image. Cadbury (chocolate manufacturers), for example, undertook a Get Active campaign in partnership with the Youth Sport Trust, which in today's health conscious (if not actually healthy) society was found to be contradictory.

Another benefit retailers can accrue from this type of campaign is the interest that a cause-related product promotion can bring to a mature and unexciting product category. In the previous year, Walkers promoted a Comic Relief baked bean flavour crisp, with all the humorous connotations that went with it. This was a rare opportunity to introduce a new product temporarily into the crisp category, encouraging customers to take a fresh look at the products available.

Source: Davis, 2004

Non-compliance at store level

Promotional activity in a multiple retailer is generally centrally controlled; a buyer, merchandiser or a category manager will negotiate with suppliers on a range of promotional activities, as discussed above. Their discussions, which may have been within the framework of CPFR (collaborative planning, forecasting and replenishment – see Chapter 6) will have resulted in an agreement concerning product price and promotional collaboration. However, the agreed action concerning stock intake, space allocation and POP activity does not always materialise in the store. This can be frustrating for both suppliers and product managers, and could be seen as unfair practice by the retail company. The IGD (Institute of Grocery Distribution) has played a mediating role by surveying supermarkets in order to find out the extent of the non-compliance problem, by checking whether agreed promotional support is being implemented at store level (Hemsley, 2004).

CO-OPERATIVE PROMOTIONAL CAMPAIGNS

Co-operative promotional campaigns, however, can bring retailers significant benefits and are particularly valuable to smaller retailers who may not have the resources to undertake customer communications activity on their own. The main benefits of co-operative promotions are:

- a pooling of financial resources should result in better campaigns, access to better advertising or marketing agencies, and a wider choice of media could be available;
- the promotional activity can give a smaller retailer access to professionally produced advertising copy and POS material and an opportunity to create in-store interest;
- the retailer and supplier both benefit from good image associations from each other;
- better co-ordination of timing of promotional activity;
- the cost of a supplier's promotional activity may already be built into product cost prices, therefore the retailer is 'entitled' to benefit from their communications (McGoldrick, 2002).

EVALUATION OF PRODUCT RELATED COMMUNICATIONS

For product specific promotional activity, evaluation of the success is a relatively straightforward task. A quantifiable indicator such as an increase in sales may be enough to convince a retailer that the activity has been worthwhile; it certainly will tell a supplier whether they have achieved their particular aims. However, this is a somewhat simplistic way of evaluating promotional activity. A deeper analysis might wish to know for example how long does an uplift in sales last? Was the sales increase restricted to one product line or did other products or categories benefit? Promotional activity requires time and resources input; was the investment worthwhile from the point of view of the increase to the retailer's profitability driven by the rise in sales?

Referring once more to the principles of ECR, outlined in Chapter 3, the notion of an efficient promotion is important here. This suggests that only those promotional activities that contribute a higher level of profit than that which could be generated without the promotional activity should be undertaken. It is not easy, however, to predict exactly the outcome of a promotion, and only those retailers who have the information management systems to calculate both the resources input and the profit output are able to conduct such an evaluation. Nevertheless, all retailers should beware of undertaking promotions that do not have clear and sound commercial retail objectives.

SUMMARY

In order to maximise product opportunities retailers need to inform customers about what is available. Although a good location and / or an attractive selling environment will help to persuade customers to sample the product range, it may be necessary to generate footfall to the outlet. Out of store communications including advertising, public relations activities and publicity can convince customers to make a visit. Promotions and personal communication take over within the retail outlet, helping the customer to finalise a purchase decision. One of the significant challenges retailers face when it comes to sending out messages about their products, is how to represent the range of items on offer using available media. Retailers use a variety of creative approaches, and are becoming adept at customising promotional activity via customer databases, and sending integrated messages using out-of-store and in-store communication channels.

CASE STUDY BODEN

The case study at the end of Chapter 13 provides the opportunity for reflection on retail communications. Some questions that relate to the Boden case are therefore included here:

Case study questions

1   How is product presentation within the catalogue used to send messages to target customers?

2   Who is Johnnie Boden, and what does he say about the company?

3   Draw up a list of customer communications objectives that would be applicable to Boden: (a) generally and (b) for their store opening.

QUESTIONS

1   Using examples, make a distinction between short-term promotional objectives and longer-term strategic communications objectives.

2   To what extent is the use of a 'personality' effective in getting across messages about a retailer's product positioning?

3   Analyse the relationship between sales promotions, point of sale initiatives and visual merchandising. Use examples as an aid within your analysis.

4   Referring to Box 11.2, evaluate the 'Birthday celebration as a form of strategic retail communication.

REFERENCES AND FURTHER READING

Davis, G. (2004) 'What's In It For You?, *Retail Week*, 19 March.

Dennis, C., Fenech, T. and Merrilees, B. (2004) *e-Retailing*, Routledge, London.

Dowding, S. (2002) 'POP Goes the Marketing Budget', *Grocer*, 9 November.

Harrington, S. (2002) 'Visual Consistency Aim as POP Gets Rethought', *Grocer*, 5 October.

Hemsley, S. (2004) 'Supplier Demands', *Marketing Week*, 12 February.

Martinez, E., Montaner, T. and Pina, J.M. (2003) 'Influence of Promotions on Brand Image of Hedonic and Utilitarian Products', Proceedings of the 12th EAERCD Conference, ESCP–EAP European School of Management, Paris, July.

McGoldrick, P.J. (2002) *Retail Marketing*, McGraw Hill, Englewood Cliffs, NJ.

Mintel (2000) *Sales Promotion UK Report*, Mintel International Group, London, January.

Morrell, L. (2004) 'Any Excuse to Party', *Retail Week*, 10 September.
Wood, Z. (2003) 'Boots to Push New Lines with £3m Ad Campaign', *Retail Week*, 12 September.

Web site

Larner, D. (2004) 'Comment: Taking a Hard Look at Digital Media Networks', www.theretailbulletin.co.uk?index.php?page=5&cat=rese&id=3827, accessed 28/04/04.

Chapter 12

Evaluating retail product management performance

LEARNING OBJECTIVES

The purpose of this chapter is to:

■ Introduce key terminology related to retail product management performance evaluation.

■ Develop an understanding of how the level of detail in retail product performance analysis will vary between different types of organisation.

■ Appreciate the contribution that cost and shrinkage control can make to financial performance.

■ Provide an insight into how customers evaluate a retailer's product performance.

■ Introduce the concept of qualitative performance measures, and appreciate how important these are from a consumer's perspective.

INTRODUCTION

In a competitive market, retailers must ensure that products are being managed in a way that is consistent with their overall objectives; product ranges that appeal to customers and provide good levels of return for the retailer, both on a short-term as well as a long-term basis, are the desirable outcome of the product management process. The aim of this chapter is to explore the crucial aspect of monitoring and evaluating product management performance. If operational and strategic objectives are not being achieved, the product management processes being implemented will need to be revisited.

PRODUCT PROFIT

One of the most straightforward concepts in product performance evaluation is the idea of a profit margin earned on each product item. The most simple profit analysis is the gross margin. This is the difference between the cost price (what a retailer pays a supplier) and the selling price (what a customer pays a retailer) for the same item. The gross margin in retailing is sometimes referred to as the 'markup'. A markup can either be expressed in terms of the actual monetary value of the gross margin, or it can be expressed as a percentage of the cost price or as a percentage of the selling price.

Example:

A retailer buys chocolate bars in at a price of £2.00 for a box of ten. Each chocolate bar is sold at a price of 24p.

The cost price for each bar is 20p.

The markup is 4p. This can be expressed as a markup on cost (20 per cent), or as a per cent of the selling price (16.7). As there is no defining rule about what the expression 'markup' refers to, it is more logical to only use the term 'gross margin', and express it as a percentage of the selling price.

Having mentioned the term markup, it is perhaps appropriate at this stage to also mention the term markdown. This retail term is used to express a reduction in price, and refers to the difference between an original selling price and a new selling price. A markdown can be expressed as a monetary figure or as a percentage of the original selling price. It would not be useful to express a markdown as a percentage of the cost of the product, however when a markdown has been taken the new selling price will have a reduced markup (or gross margin).

SALES

Another important indicator of good product performance is the amount it sells. Selling large amounts of products has the benefit of generating plenty of cash flow for the retail organisation, so that any immediate payments required can be met (such as paying suppliers' invoices and the wages of the sales staff). Selling products fast has the added benefit of moving stock quickly through the organisation, which stops products becoming obsolete, and allows a retailer to change their stock according to seasonal demand. Retailers often use sales figures (expressed either in volume or value terms) to make performance comparisons over time. However, anyone can sell products fast at low prices. The important balancing act is to ensure that products are selling fast and generating acceptable levels of profits.

The effect of price sensitivity on sales

Price elasticity is a key principle to be observed in the setting of prices. This is the extent to which demand for a product responds to change in price. As a guiding principle, the more discretionary a purchase, the more opportunity for retailers to use price elasticity in their pricing strategy; on the other hand, today's complex shopper does not act as a rational economically driven consumer (see Chapter 4), and the demand for products is affected by a whole host of variables other than price. It is not the intention of this chapter to explore the variables that influence price sensitivity, a discussion of which can be found elsewhere (for example Brassington and Pettit, 2003: 401), but to accept that demand for products will vary. This variation can occur at the SKU level, for example a well-known manufacturer's brand compared with an own-label variant; at category level caused by, for example, the effect of seasonal variation; and at product department level where demand for staple products like foods have more stable demand than discretionary household purchases such as carpets.

PROFITABILITY

The profit that a product generates to contribute to the costs of running a retailer's business depends on two important variables. The first is the gross profit margin that is applied per item according to the selling price set. The second is the amount of products of a particular type that is sold; this is referred to as the sales volume, and is often expressed as the number of items sold in a particular time period (rate of sales).

At one time it was fairly common practice for retailers to apply a 'uniform markup policy' throughout the store, so that every item had the same percentage gross margin. However, whilst simple to administer, this method did not allow the retailer to exploit the opportunity to charge higher margins where the market would stand it or to accept lower margins in the face of competition. Now, most leading retailers are able to conduct profit margin analysis at the SKU level, so the contribution to profits of every single item within the store is known and prices are set individually for each item.

Some products sell very frequently and only generate a very small profit margin, while others are much slower sellers, but have a bigger profit margin. In order to compare the overall profitability of products with differing rates of sale and profit margins a measure called the 'gross margin return on investment' (GMROI) can be calculated. This is a simple calculation where a product's gross margin is multiplied by its rate of sale within a time period (sales turnover), and it allows retailers to compare the amount of profit generated on a product line with the level of investment made in the stock (see Table 12.1). The higher the GMROI, the more 'work' an item of merchandise is doing for the profitability of your business. GMROI calculations can be made at different levels within the retail organisation, for example at SKU (stock keeping unit) level, product category level, or at department level.

The GMROI calculation is a simple analysis that will indicate to the retailer those products that are making the largest contribution to its overall gross profits in relation to the financial investment made in that stock. However, not all products within a retail offer require the same amount of resources in order to sell. Some products require special storage facilities (frozen or chilled foods, for example); some products require much larger amounts of space (a pack of toilet roll compared with a jar of honey, for example); other products require a high level of personal service to sell (musical instruments compared with stationery for example) and with these resources go costs. More refined retail product profitability measures therefore take the costs that can be attributed to the various areas of product management that apply.

Table 12.1 *Illustration of GMROI (gross margin return on investment)*

Product category	Gross margin (%)	Turnover ratio	GMROI (%)
Baked beans	10	12	120
Biscuits	20	6	120
Boxed chocolates	40	3	120

In this example, product categories with different gross margins and different turnover rates result in the same GMROI value

Product category	Gross margin (%)	Turnover ratio	GMROI (%)
Baked beans	25	12	300
Biscuits	25	6	150
Boxed chocolates	25	3	75

Here, the gross margin is equal for all three product categories, and the resulting GMROI shows considerable variation

Direct product profitability (DPP)

The concept of DPP emerged in the 1980s and to a certain extent only began to be used in retail profitability analysis when direct product costs (DPCs) could be accurately calculated using computerised cost analysis programmes. These costs not only include the costs of selling within the store, but they also attribute direct charges to the product right through the supply chain, so that all transportation, warehousing and storage, and handling costs are analysed at SKU level. A DPP calculation will also include any additional 'revenue' that a product generates such as a contribution from suppliers for advertising.

Activity based costing (ABC)

Activity based costing is similar in principle to direct product profitability analysis, but whereas DPP allocates direct costs to individual products, activity based costing also includes allocations for indirect costs on an individual product basis. This approach has highlighted areas of significant 'internal spending', which may not be paid back by the resulting merchandise range. For example, buyers' salaries and the costs of running a buying office in the centre of a commercial capital are considerable indirect costs, which cannot be changed in the short term. In order to cover such indirect costs, many retailers will make a charge at a flat rate to each product sold. In actual fact, a flat rate may not be applicable; for example, developing own-branded merchandise will be costly in terms of buyers' time and effort, compared to selecting products from a branded supplier's range. The costs associated with overseas sourcing may be greater than those associated with using domestic suppliers, and so the view might be taken that the cost of overseas sourcing activities (such as buyers' travel costs, buyers' time on trips, and additional input from technologists) should only be charged to imported merchandise. Otherwise areas of significant 'internal spending' may not end up being paid back by the resulting product range that caused the costs to be incurred.

Clearly, such a detailed approach to cost analysis is beyond the scope of a small retailer, who is less likely to be in a position to alter any of the direct or indirect costs. However, this type of detailed analysis has made an important contribution to cost saving in the supply chain, and improvements in space productivity (see Chapter 8). These initiatives have allowed retailers to improve their operating profit levels without the need to raise prices. Activity based costing is commonly used as the basis of the measurement of efficiency in ECR systems, discussed in Chapter 3.

BOX 12.1 FACTORY GATE PRICING

Factory gate pricing (FGP) is a term that refers to the way a price is quoted by a supplier to a retailer. Quite simply, the price a supplier quotes is 'ex works' which means it does not include any transportation (for example, to a retailer's distribution centre or to a store). Retailers, particularly those in the grocery sector, have been moving towards this as a basis for price quotation and negotiation for some time in order to make logistics costs more transparent.

Many of these larger retail organisations have got involved with 'primary distribution' themselves. This is the movement of products from suppliers to the retailer's distribution network, using the same fleet of transportation vehicles that make deliveries to stores. While this adds more complexity to retail logistics operations it also provides further opportunities for efficiency drives and cost reduction. It also gives the retailer more control further up the supply chain. FGP also has implications for profit margin analysis because supplier's prices will be lower, but direct product costs will be higher.

Source: Fernie and Sparks, 2004; Aujla, 2004

THE IMPACT OF MARKDOWNS

In a retailing situation where the product range is relatively stable, profitable retail management is principally a case of fine-tuning prices in response to the trading environment and monitoring costs. However, as discussed earlier in the chapter, where the sales patterns are subject to fashion and seasonality, it is important to monitor prices with a view to clearing out the old season's goods to make room for the new season's stock arriving. If good buying decisions have been made and the trading environment is buoyant, markdowns will only be needed to clear broken ranges (odd sizes and colours) and the total markdown for any particular product line will be low. If on the other hand the total markdown value is high, a markdown analysis should be performed so that specific product problems can be identified (see case study at the end of the chapter).

PRODUCTIVITY

As we saw in Chapter 8, sales and profits in retail business are often expressed in terms of the productivity of space, the most commonly used measure being the amount of sales in value terms being generated by square measure of space (e.g. £ per square foot or euro per square metre). The matrix shown in Figure 8.5 recommends various product management actions according to individual product productivity performances. For example, a product that is generating good sales volume but low profit margin may require margin adjustment, or the introduction of an own branded version, whereas a product that is generating a good profit margin but is a slow seller might need to be displayed more attractively in a better location in the outlet.

SHRINKAGE

Shrinkage is the term applied to stock that is removed from a retail outlet without any payment to the retailer. In effect, the value of stock held 'shrinks' without any compensating income from sales. Selling at full price is to be recommended as part of a profitable profit strategy, but having to mark down is better than missing the opportunity to sell the product at all. Losing stock through theft is one of the least controllable aspects of retail management, yet in high crime locations, it could be the element that has the most bearing on a branch's profitability. Theft, whether it is external or internal, is the main contributor to retail shrinkage, but the term also encompasses damage to goods, which are either sold with a markdown as shop-soiled goods, or may have to be destroyed. Closed circuit television (CCTV) systems and electronic tagging operations are among a number of methods used to combat theft, although the method of product presentation itself, for example secure fixturing and open layouts, can help reduce opportunity thieving (see Box 12.2).

Reducing shrinkage rates is best tackled as an integrated approach. For example, high shrinkage might be caused by a number of factors including poor packaging or handling, inaccurate coding or recording of stock, and inadequate rotation of stock on shelves (Cuthbertson and Moore, 2000). A cut in a retailer's shrinkage level can make a real difference to its profit performance. For example in 2003, it was reported that variety retailer Woolworth's had cut its shrinkage rate from 2.1 per cent of sales to 1.8 per cent, and this represented an additional £7.5 million contribution to profits in monetary terms (Finch, 2003).

BOX 12.2 UNDERSTANDING THE CRIMINAL CONSUMER

Retail crime is big business. In 1999, retailers spent £612 million on crime prevention, which was 11 per cent more than the previous year. Some 4.17 million offences were recorded against retailers, and whilst the majority of these were external theft by 'customers', an increasing proportion of retail crimes involve retailers' own staff, at just over 32 per cent of the total cost of crime, which was calculated to be £1.61 billion in 1999 (BRC Retail Crime Survey, 1999).

One of the ways to help to prevent retail crime is to understand the 'customer' behaviour of the thief. For example, in December a large number of crimes involve 'typical' gifts, such as toys and nightwear. Many criminal customers use a 'shop and steal' tactic, purchasing some but not all items taken out of the store; they may even return to steal or buy later in the same shop. Like other consumer behaviour, aberrant consumer behaviour is influenced by external factors (Bamfield and Tonglet, 1999), for example in terms of demographics, a 'swell' in the under 25 age group is likely to increase crime rates, because male under 25s are the group most prone to steal. Also, shops that are well stocked with merchandise attract thieves. But it is also important to recognise potential problems within a store layout, such as displaying expensive merchandise near exits, and using tall and solid fixturing that prevents an open view.

Understanding customers' actions also helps retailers to spot criminal behaviour; for example, excessive handling of goods, over-careful trolley packing, gazing in an inappropriate direction, and adopting strange stances to conceal stolen merchandise, are all indications that might alert a retail manager to wrongdoings.

Source: Bamfield and Tonglet, 1999; Clements, 2002

COST REDUCTION

Although many of the ways in which a retailer might attempt to cut costs are out of the direct control of the retail product manager, there are a number of areas where costs can be reduced in buying and merchandising functions. These are emphasised in the four areas where efficiency gains can be derived in the pursuit of ECR (efficient consumer response, see Chapter 3), and are reiterated here:

- the costs of developing new products;
- the costs of undertaking promotional activity;
- the costs associated with poor replenishment;
- the costs associated with having a poor assortment.

Another way to improve profit margins without the need to raise prices is to reduce the buying-in price of a product or, from an alternative point of view, 'squeeze the supply base'. One of the key responsibilities of a buyer is to obtain the very best deals from their suppliers. As discussed in Chapter 5, the best deals do not often result from concentrating on short-term price-orientated battles; but the ability to negotiate well, even within the context of a partnership, is an attribute every retail buyer or product manager should possess.

NEGOTIATION

According to Bailey *et al.* (1998), negotiation implies a mutuality of wants, resolved by exchange, and it can be as specific in nature as the design of a pocket on a shirt or as multi-faceted as in the setting up of a supply programme of pre-prepared meals under a retail brand. Negotiations may take place between two people, each representing one organisation (a buyer and a sales manager, for example), or the negotiation may involve whole teams of people including product developers, product managers, and logistics and marketing managers.

Negotiation is generally regarded as having three stages. The first stage takes place before the two negotiating parties meet, and involves a large amount of formal and/or informal preparation, including gathering together relevant information (for example, costing and performance data from previous dealings), setting objectives for the negotiations, and preparing strategies and tactics that might be used, including the roles the various people will play. The second stage is the meeting itself; this will develop from the formalities of welcoming (this can be very important in some cultures); to exploration and debate regarding all the relevant issues; to bargaining; and finally agreement. The third stage takes place after the meeting stage (which may in fact include meeting more than once in order to reach agreement) and involves the implementation of the agreement, such as the modification of a prototype, drawing up a specification (see Chapter 4), and preparing contract documents. Any of these can be performed by either retailer or supplier, depending on their individual facilities and established procedures, but there must be a signature of acceptance by both parties to the agreement to conclude it. The absolutely final stage of the implementation of negotiations is the supply of the right goods, at the right time and place and with the agreed price on the invoice.

Everything is negotiable

Negotiation is not just about price, but the agreement reached should include an understanding between the retailer and the supplier on what a particular price represents. Negotiation therefore often revolves around alternative product features and the services a supplier may undertake. For example, a cheaper raw material or a different type of packaging may be a way of getting a price down to the level the buyer wishes to pay without any fundamental change to the product itself. It is, therefore, important in the preparation stage to be clear about those product features that are essential, and those that are desirable but not essential. In addition, a buyer should try to be as open-minded as possible during the meeting stage because a supplier may present an unforeseen solution.

In order to be able to evaluate a product's contribution to retail profitability in comparison to others in a range, the cost prices for all products must start on a 'level playing field'. Prices quoted by suppliers to a retailer can be subject to a great deal of variation. There may be a discount for prompt payment or a stepped discount for increasing quantities. Prices may be quoted in different currencies, which may cause price fluctuations, and they may or may not include delivery. Additional services might be included in the price that a retailer would otherwise have to pay for (delivery and installation at a customer's home, for example). There may be an allowance for promotional activity or for a particular shelf location. It is very important, therefore, that in any profit comparison exercise between products the cost price is calculated in the same way and the kind of pricing variables listed above taken into account in the individual product profit equation (see Box 12.1).

AVAILABILITY

In terms of evaluating product management, availability is a performance indicator that is becoming increasingly important to retailers in a saturated and competitive market. Availability can be expressed in a number of different ways. First, the number of product items that are available on the shelves within the outlet at any one time indicates the extent to which an intended product assortment is in stock for customers to buy from. The ideal availability target would be 100 per cent, with everything in stock at all times. However, a more realistic target would be in the high 90s. To a certain extent retailers can manage less than 100 per cent availability by offering customers substitutable products, but low availability across the product range on anything but a temporary basis will inevitably result in customer dissatisfaction and the retailer will risk losing customers to competitors with better availability levels. High levels of availability are particularly important (and particularly challenging) for promotional merchandise. The value orientated variety retailer Matalan for example, increased the availability of products advertised in mail shots to customers from 74 per cent to 94 per cent as a result of a restructured supply chain and more targeted marketing (*Retail Week*, 2004).

A second availability measure is what is often referred to as stock cover. This refers to the amount of stock of a product line that is currently on the shelf or in the supply chain (for example at a distribution centre) in comparison to the rate of sales. It is a way of expressing how long the current stock holding will last into the future based on the current rate of sale (Jackson and Shaw, 2001). For example, if a product is selling at a rate of 120 items per week (in all outlets) and a retailer has 240 items on shelves in stores and 360 in the warehouse, then the retail business as a whole has stock cover of 5. If stock cover levels are too low, there is a danger that holes may appear in the product range. If on the other hand stock cover levels are too high, there is a danger that stock may become outdated, and storage and handling requirements will increase. With fashion and seasonal merchandise stock cover needs to be managed to ensure good availability at peak selling times, but once the main selling period is over, stock cover should be cut back to reduce end-of-season markdowns.

QUALITATIVE PERFORMANCE MEASURES

Whilst sales and profitability are of central importance when judging buying and merchandising success from a retailer's perspective, these are of little concern to the customer. Availability, on the other hand is a performance measure that concerns both; poor availability will affect sales and profits in the short term, and customer loyalty in the long term. Availability, however, is not the only factor upon which customers judge a retailer. Many other attributes of a retailer's business contribute to a customer's overall impression of the places they shop. In order to ensure they are achieving the best possible levels of customer satisfaction, retailers must monitor their performance from the customer's perspective. There are different ways of expressing the customer perspective of retail performance; these include:

- the retailer's reputation;
- the retailer's image;
- the retailer's brand value (or equity).

What these terms have in common is the notion that performance from a customer's point of view is broadly defined and that it is measured on a number of attributes that contribute to the overall evaluation. In his review of store image studies, McGoldrick (2002: 188) found 90 different elements had been used, which could be grouped into 18 general areas of evaluation. Of these, three areas are within direct control of product management. These are:

- *price of merchandise*, including low prices, discounts and bargains, good value prices, fair or competitive prices, high or prestige prices;
- *quality of merchandise*, including good/poor quality products, good/poor departments or categories, branded/designer goods, well designed products;
- *range of merchandise*, including breadth of choice, depth of choice, carries items I like, choice of brands, good for gifts.

Others areas are indirectly associated with product management, including promotions and advertising, store atmosphere and layout, and reputation on adjustments (e.g. warrantees and returns).

Customer's impression not only needs to be considered in relation to the whole product range, but also on a category or department basis to assess consistency or to address problem areas. Customer impressions, unlike profit margins and sales figures are not easy to quantify and various consumer research techniques such as focus groups or surveys will help a retailer to develop an objective understanding of customer perceptions. Buyers, merchandisers and category managers work at the operational level within a retail business. The decisions they make about products, prices, quantities and suppliers are made within corporate guidelines drawn up within the framework of an overall positioning strategy. It is a product manager's responsibility to balance the achievements in one area of image elements with the others, within the context of the overall aims set by the corporation. Decisions concerning assortment and quality for example have to be made in the light of a retailer's price positioning within the retail market, whether premium or EDLP (every day low price) orientated.

BOX 12.3   PRICING: THE BIGGER PICTURE

Pricing decisions for each product in the retailer's outlet are taken within the context of the merchandise assortment plan and within the framework of a broader market positioning strategy. Although it may be the buyer's intention to have similar products at different price levels in the product assortment plan in order to broaden the appeal of the product range, consistency in the pricing level across categories and departments reinforces a positioning strategy, in the light of the variety and depth of assortment on offer. A brief reference to the alternative general price level strategies of retailers provides the context in which retail product managers make pricing decisions.

Premium pricing

Premium pricing is used in order to obtain maximum profit margins on products by selling at a high level. In exchange for a high price, customers will expect some added value in their purchase, such as a high service level, or an exceptional or highly convenient selling environment. Taken one stage further, prestige pricing is used for many branded products, whereby the high price reinforces the brand value. Department stores like Harrods, or Bloomingdale's in New York, have worldwide reputations for their premium pricing strategies, which combine with prestigious products and surroundings to maintain an up-market image. However, in consumer markets where increasing numbers of people are value driven in their purchasing decisions, premium-pricing policies are becoming harder to sustain.

High-low pricing

The objective of a high-low strategy is to sell as much merchandise as possible at 'full price' with a high profit margin, for as long a period as possible, and then reduce margins after a time in order to clear out older merchandise to make room for new. Clearly, this is an inappropriate strategy for staple products, but it is widely used for seasonal and fashion products. Timing is crucial for this strategy, because retailers who reduce their prices too quickly will lose the trust of their customers, who will wait for the next 'sale' and become reluctant to buy anything at full price. Being too cautious about reducing prices, on the other hand, runs the risk that competitors will get to the customer's purse first and the merchandise become outdated and stale. High-low pricing works well with prestige pricing, so that outdated prestige merchandise can be sold off as a bargain in order to keep the ranges looking fresh and innovative.

Every day low pricing (EDLP)

Every day low pricing has a considerable appeal for customers because they feel confident that they are buying at 'fair' and 'good-value' prices, reinforcing a feeling of good sense and judgement in the shopping process. A constant stream of offers and promotions might appeal to the bargain 'junkie', but a time-poor multiple-occupation 'striver' might consider that variable pricing is time consuming to evaluate. The EDLP strategy, where margins and prices are kept constantly low, makes customers feel that the retailer has done the price comparison exercise for them. For staple products this strategy makes good sense and helps a retailer gain customer loyalty.

Discounting

Discounting is a strategy whereby the retailer sells at prices that are 'lower than average' on a permanent basis. It is only sustainable if the retailer has other low-cost element(s) within their marketing mix, such as a low-rent location, merchandise that is procured on an opportunistic basis, minimal service and a 'basic' store environment. Discounting is a useful strategy for clearing end-of-line merchandise or 'seconds' stock, and is the underpinning of retail phenomena, such as factory outlets. Retailers like the Body Shop use factory outlets to sell off discontinued lines, allowing the 'high street' stores to sell the current ranges without old stock cluttering the store (Hall, 1999).

BLENDING QUANTITATIVE AND QUALITATIVE MEASURES

One of the greatest challenges for retail product managers is to interpret the various performance indicators, whatever form that feedback comes in. It might be a detailed set of sales figures, DPP reports, or it might be a letter of complaint from a customer because their favourite brand has been withdrawn. Product managers must have the analytical powers and objectivity to see the way to optimising product ranges so that both short-term and long-term performance objectives can be achieved. This supports the argument for, as outlined in Chapter 2, a considerable period of training in which experience, knowledge and understanding can be accumulated about not only the product market they are operating in, but also about the retailer's own strategic objectives.

SUMMARY

Retail product management activities are only worthwhile if they are generating a satisfactory return on investment of resources, including the space in the retail outlet used. Product performance can be evaluated in increasingly sophisticated quantitative measures; however, while customers evaluate products using price, they also use various qualitative measures including product quality, depth and width of the assortment, the choice of brands, and availability. A growing number of customers will also evaluate products according to how ethically they have been produced and sourced.

Retail product managers work within the overall price positioning of the retailer within its market, and they can use a number of tactics to achieve the 'right' price, including margin adjustment, negotiation with suppliers and operational cost reduction.

EXERCISE   MARKDOWN ANALYSIS

In these three grids, the numbers indicate the £ value of the markdowns taken on three different styles of women's trousers, broken down into colours and sizes.

Style A

	Size 8	Size 10	Size 12	Size 14	Size 16	Size 18	Size 20	Size 22
Pink				10	10	15	15	
Green	40	30	10	10	10	5	10	5
Red	40	40	20	20	10	20	25	25
Cream	20	15			10	10		10
Navy	30	35	10				10	
Black	20	20						10

Style B

	Size 8	Size 10	Size 12	Size 14	Size 16	Size 18	Size 20	Size 22
Pink	20	20	30	40	30	40	50	40
Green	80	70	50	50	50	40	50	40
Red	90	80	70	60	60	70	80	80
Cream	60	50	40	30	40	30	50	40
Navy	50	60	40	40	50	50	60	60
Black	30	30	20	20	30	30	20	30

Style C

	Size 8	Size 10	Size 12	Size 14	Size 16	Size 18	Size 20	Size 22
Pink	80	100	80	100	120	130	130	140
Green	40	30	10	10	20	10	10	10
Red	40	40	20	20	10	20	25	25
Cream	40	30	40	80	130	150	160	180
Navy	30	35	10				10	
Black	20	20						10

Exercise questions

- What are the total markdown values for styles A, B and C? Express this in value terms and as percentages of the total markdown value for all three styles.
- Which style was the best seller?
- Which style had the highest markdown value and suggest possible reasons for this.
- What does the pattern of markdowns tell us for future buying in terms of style and colour?

QUESTIONS

1   Evaluate sales and profits as indicators of product performance.

2   Describe the three stages of negotiation and for a product category of your choice, explain the expression 'everything is negotiable'.

3   Review the alternative price positioning strategies that retailers might use and suggest how these will influence product management evaluation.

4   Discuss the various ways in which customers will evaluate a retailer's product performance.

5   Explain the term shrinkage and suggest measures that retailers can take to reduce it.

REFERENCES AND FURTHER READING

Aujla, E. (2004) 'Gates Open Wider', *Retail Week*, 14 November.

Baily, P., Farmer, D., Jessop, D. and Jones, D. (1998) *Purchasing Principles and Management*, 8th edn, Pearson Education, Harlow.

Bamfield, J. and Tonglett, M. (1999) 'Understanding Consumer Behaviour: How Shoplifters Shop the Store', Proceedings of the Tenth International Conference on Research in the Distributive Trades, Institute for Retail Studies, University of Stirling.

Brassington, F. and Pettit, S. (2003) *Principles of Marketing*, Pearson Education, Harlow.

Clements, A. (2002) 'Light-fingered Staff Challenge the Shoplifters', *Retail Week*, 7 April.

Cuthbertson, R. and Moore, C.M. (2000) 'Sainsbury's – The Trifling Case of the Missing Trifle: Lessons in Stock Loss', in B.M. Oldfield, R.A.Schmidt, I. Clarke, C. Hart and M.H. Kirkup (eds), *Contemporary Cases in Retail Operations Management*, Macmillan, Basingstoke.

Fernie, J. and Sparks, L. (2004) *Logistics and Retail Management*, 2nd edn, Wiley, London.

Finch, J. (2003) 'Woolworth's Bounces Back', *Guardian*, 27 March.

Hall, J. (1999) 'Body Shop Set For Euro Outlet Stores', *Retail Week*, 29 October.

Jackson, T. and Shaw, D. (2001) *Mastering Fashion Buying and Merchandising Management*, Macmillan, Basingstoke.

McGoldrick, P.J. (2002) *Retail Marketing*, McGraw Hill, Maidenhead.

Retail Week, (2004) 'Matalan Increases Availability Following Supply Chain Shake-up, 10 September.

Part IV

Retail product management applications

Chapter 13

Product management in non-store retailing

LEARNING OBJECTIVES

The purpose of this chapter is to:

- Highlight the fundamental differences between store and non-store retailers, in terms of product management.
- Become aware of the implications of non-store retailing for product assortment planning, product presentation, pricing decisions and stock management.
- Appreciate the importance of integrating high levels of customer service in a non-personal shopping method, and the need for an efficient product management infrastructure to support the non-store retailer–customer interface.
- Introduce the concept of a multi-channel (or hybrid) strategy and the associated opportunities and challenges it presents to retail product managers.

INTRODUCTION

Since the start of the new millennium, shopping via a computer has moved from something indulged by a niche market to a commonplace activity amongst the population masses. The internet has provided the retail industry with a new and exciting way of enticing consumers to purchase products from the comfort of their own home, office or wherever else they gain access to the 'virtual world'. In fact, recent developments in the personal mobile communications industry would suggest that before long we will be able to go shopping literally anywhere at anytime. However, non-store shopping is not a new phenomenon. The home delivery option has evolved alongside stores as the retail industry has developed.

For product management, retailing without a store requires some fundamental differences in approach, whilst its characteristics can make this method of acquiring goods more or less attractive to consumers. Although store based shopping is still easily the most popular way overall for consumers to retrieve their product needs, a significant and increasing proportion of goods and services are being sold to consumers through distribution channels that do not include walk-in stores. For some retail sectors, the adoption of alternative shopping methods has really shaken up the established industry hierarchy. The purpose of this chapter is to explore the additional implications for retail product management imposed by non-store selling formats.

NON-STORE RETAIL FORMATS

Non-store retailers make ranges of products available to potential consumers in a number of different ways. Some retailers take the product directly to the customer, for example in the 'party plan' method of retailing made famous by the lingerie retailer Ann Summers, where a group of potential customers are invited into a friend's home in order to inspect a range of merchandise. However, the majority of non-store retailers offer their products via some form of product representation, whether on paper or screen-based visual display. Table 13.1 outlines the main non-store formats used in retailing.

Table 13.1 *Principal non-store retail formats*

The general catalogue	GUS, Grattans, LaRedoute, Sears Roebuck
The specialist catalogue	Lands End, Joe Brown, Screwfix, Toast, Waggers.
TV retailing	QVC, Home Shopping Network, Teletext
Internet retailing (Via PC, mobile device or TV monitor)	Amazon.com, Tesco.com, E-Bay.com

HOME SHOPPING

Non-store retailing has a long history. Catalogues and mail ordering are as old as retail stores and were originally devised in order to offer customers who lived in remote areas the opportunity to acquire the kind of products their urban counterparts were able to buy in their local towns and cities. They also offered a service to people who disliked shopping in stores, especially for more personal items such as clothes.

In the postwar period, catalogue retailing, often administered through an 'agent', entered a period of steady growth, because the mail order companies offered low income families a credit facility that most store retailers would not allow. The biannual tome is still a feature in many homes, but the agency mail order business has declined as disposable income has risen and credit facilities have become widely available.

Whilst generalist catalogue sales have stagnated, more specialist mail order businesses have thrived. Many of the larger catalogue retailers launched more targeted catalogue offerings as a defensive strategy against more narrowly focused mail order retailers such as Land's End and N. Brown, and high street retailers started to enter the home shopping market with their own store catalogues in the early 1990s, as retail trends predicted a convenience shopping boom. The large mail order retailers now generally accept that agency business will increasingly be replaced by one-to-one marketing activities.

Through the 1990s home shopping became a strategic option for many previously store-based retailers in a diverse range of product sectors. Consumer trends (see Chapter 4) towards the cash-rich, time-poor consumer seemed to favour an increase in home shopping, and many of the store-based retail giants entered this market, for example Tesco and Marks & Spencer, initially with specialised range catalogues such as schoolwear, home furnishings, and gifts. However, as the twentieth century drew to a close, the internet as a non-store retail format began to take over the interest of the retail industry as the probable home shopping format of the future, using either PC, digital TV or mobile phone access. E-retailing, defined by Harris and Dennis (2002) as the sale of goods and services via internet or other electronic channels, for personal or household use by consumers, has continued to grow and has made a significant impact in a number of product markets.

PRODUCT MANAGEMENT IMPLICATIONS

In order to begin exploring the challenges of non-store product management, it is perhaps useful to be explicit about the principal differences between store and non-store retailing. Table 13.2 compares store based retailing with non-store based retailing. For the purpose of this exercise we have concentrated on home delivery methods and not included direct personal selling methods such as party-plan, telesales and door-to-door selling.

Table 13.2 *Store and non-store retailing: a comparison*

Store retailing	Non-store retailing
Product presentation Real, tangible	Represented by image
Selling environment Use of store environment to enhance experience Store design can be matched to product	Difficult to create atmosphere, although web site better than printed media Product can be shown 'in use'
Pricing Flexible and highly visible, but time consuming to make comparisons	Easy to compare prices between competitive non-store retail offers Not always possible to administer price changes immediately (especially print based media)
Customer service Direct, personal	Detached, impersonal; product information (especially comparison price) is often easy to access; security concerns
Convenience May be low, depending on individual circumstances	High (in principle) Low for impulse purchases
Product delivery Usually immediate	Not immediate; arranged, if product cannot be posted

PRODUCT PRESENTATION

Non-store retailers have a real challenge when it comes to product presentation. If a product is largely standardised and its tangible features wholly understood, for example a CD or a book, then the presentation of the product is less problematic. If the benefits of a product are mainly functional rather than aesthetic, then again a photographic image and a wealth of product performance detail are likely to be sufficient. However, for goods where the aesthetics and the sensory elements of the product are important, for example, fresh food, clothing and cosmetics, then a two-dimensional image may not adequately represent its benefits. Nitse *et al.* (2004) found that fashion retailers run real risks of losing sales as a result of poor colour representation on web sites. Representing the product in use may help, for example, showing clothing modelled, or home furnishings in room settings, but problems concerning the match between customers' own self-image and that of the photographic image can arise. For some products, a photograph of the product in use can be much more appealing than the product itself; hosiery, swimming costumes and garden accessories are all examples of products that look much better in use. Some mail order companies are adopting magazine-type layouts, to offer a 'lifestyle' approach to product presentation, and to transfer media familiarity to shopping formats. The Joe Brown home shopping organisation, which sells casual clothing and gifts, does not show clothing on models at all. Rather, they are shown in stylish crumpled abandon on a backdrop of graphics that incorporate images and icons that are meaningful to their young surfing enthusiast customers.

Internet sites were considered by Din (2000) to be visually lacking in stimulation, with too much written text, and essentially to offer the customer little more than the pages of a catalogue. The product offer is often presented on web sites in a list type of format, and can be organised according to retail categorisation, rather than being consumer orientated. For example, Tesco once used the term 'dry goods' on their web site, which is a trade term for packaged goods like sugar and flour and not a term that would necessarily be understood by customers (Packshaw, 2000). However, unlike static pages, the internet does allow some moving imagery to be lodged in the web site, such as a fashion show or a live product demonstration. In addition, the opportunity to deal directly with internet customers offers the possibility of tailoring the web site image to individual customers. Home shopping retailer Land's End, for example, has experimented with displaying merchandise on different models that are matched to the demographics of the online customer.

Internet shopping via mobile communications, via a cellular phone or a personal digital assistant (PDA) clearly offers market opportunities, given the popularity of the hand-held device as a communication medium, with its convenience, easy access and low cost. The opportunity to shop anywhere as well as anytime bodes well for even more customer convenience, while the facility to 'read' customers via radio frequency identification will further customise retailing initiatives.

Even with the improving digital imagery, however, product presentation on a mobile handset is challenging: transmission bandwidth can make screen information slow to receive and limited in scope; however, with rapid advances being made in the field of 'micro payments' the mobile handset becomes not only a shopping centre, but a banking centre (Dennis *et al.*, 2004).

Retailing via a television set offers much more flexibility for product presentation, and in particular offers the potential to make links from TV programming and interactive advertisements to web sites. TV as an electronic medium is more familiar, and with a saturated penetration level, the opportunities for TV retailing should be very attractive. However, the embedded attitude of consumers towards the TV as a social and relaxing medium, together with industry complications concerning the boundaries between programming, advertising and retailing, has resulted in a slow adoption of interactive TV as a route to e-commerce.

PRODUCT ASSORTMENT

The size of a store, as we saw in Chapter 4, can place restrictions on the product range offered. A web site has no size limitation, other than the attention span of the customer, and so a more extensive product range can, in theory, be offered. Nevertheless, some products have better affinity for e-retailing, and some are problematic when it comes to delivery (see p. 239). From a customer point of view the web site should represent the best retail offer, which is the whole product range. However a retailing organisation may find some products to be unprofitable to sell direct to consumer's homes. The customer profile of the online shopper needs to be considered in relation to their propensity to buy particular products and the compatibility of the web site offer. This area of product management is currently undergoing research and experimentation as retailers gain experience.

In some retail situations, incorporating a kiosk, where customers can access the company web site while they are shopping in store can provide the means by which the quality and features of a product can be seen 'in the flesh' while endless variations and customisation opportunities can be illustrated via the kiosk; the web site therefore becomes a valuable additional sales tool for people who sell complex products.

THE SELLING ENVIRONMENT

Creating an atmosphere within the brick walls that represent the store is not easy (see Chapter 9), but creating an atmosphere on the flat and static page of a catalogue or on a web site is even more difficult. The principles behind a store design and a non-store format design are, however, essentially the same. Layouts should be logical and product categories should be easy to locate. Navigability, or the ease with which a customer is able move round a web site, is fundamental to successful internet retailing. Products should be easy to locate within the subsections of the format, there should be links between complementary merchandise, and there should be consistency between the merchandise and the retailer's brand image.

Dennis *et al.* (2004) suggest that store design for e-retailers could be the most important part of their retail mix because the design directly incorporates the interaction between customer and retailer. Non-store retailing generally allows a non-personal medium to guide the customer through the selling process, and so the personal encounter that the customer has when using the web site directly influences the quality of the shopping experience. They also acknowledge the role of web atmospherics, in the creation or support of a retail image. Sophisticated web atmospherics, such as audio and video clips, moving imagery and complex artwork can be used to differentiate a web site, but many of these additions are slow to download and can cause frustration to customers who want to move quickly through the shopping process. The demise of a number of early e-retailers were compounded by the use of web site designs that were only fully accessible via high specification PCs.

Like physical store design, a retailer's web site has to blend practical (navigation and logic) and aesthetic (artwork and effects) to produce an appealing yet easy to shop interface. Some retailers have introduced relatively simple visual effects to improve the online shopping experience. Magnet, for example have a 'virtual showroom tour' which allows the shopper to navigate their kitchen, bathroom and bedroom showrooms using the computer mouse, with a 'zoom in' button for viewing the products in detail (www.magnet.co.uk). Men's clothing retailer HopeandGlory uses instamatic photos and pages out of a note pad to add interest and style to the 'click on here to find out more' facility (www.hopeandgloryclothing.com)

PRICING

Home shopping retailers have the potential to offer goods at competitive prices because they do not have the expense of running a portfolio of stores. However, in traditional mail order retailing, much of this saving is offset by the need to finance the high stock holding level that is necessary to guarantee good service, as well as the funding of long customer credit terms. In theory, an internet retailer can reduce these two costs; payment is usually taken at the point of product dispatch (if not earlier, at the point of order) and arrangements could be made for direct delivery from a supplier. However, skimping on infrastructure has been one of the commonest reasons for internet retailing failure (as discussed later on in this chapter), and so virtual retailing at very pared down prices becomes a risky business. Nevertheless, price comparison is very easy to make

235

between alternative internet offers, with shopping portals such as Kelkoo and Froogle offering to undertake this process in an extremely convenient manner for the shopper, free of charge. It is difficult to justify a premium pricing policy without the benefit of the store environment as an arena for adding value to the shopping process.

One of the most complex issues regarding pricing is consistency when a retailer is using more than one shopping channel (see later section on multi-channel retailing). Next, the UK clothing specialist, for example, has tended not to discount products in its stores outside the strictly controlled end-of-season sales periods, in order to protect the integrity of its catalogue, which offers a high proportion of products that are identical to the range found in the stores. On the other hand, multi-channel retailers are conscious that they need to be competitive on price with alternative online outlets, and while web-exclusive discounts go some way to achieving this, it is an unsustainable pricing strategy in the long run in a competitive retail sector (Connon, 2003).

One further issue with home shopping media is pricing flexibility. Catalogues have a comparatively long lead-time, and price changes have to be communicated separately once the catalogue has been issued. Store retailing offers much more immediacy in terms of price changes, and discounted items can be visibly promoted in a much more effective way, for example by moving the goods to the front of the store. Internet retailing, again in theory, offers price flexibility, as an immediate medium, but promoting offers is more complex, with the need for flexibility in the web page design.

SERVICE

Both customer service and stock service are important when carrying out a retail transaction. Dealing with live people in real time is one aspect of store shopping that in time may be its own salvation. Information about the product, its applications and uses, demonstrations and trials are available on demand within a shop. Also the stock position is immediately apparent and if a product variant is not in stock, the position can be established immediately, and/or alternatives offered. Therefore, the store arena offers the opportunity as a stage for delivering an excellent standard of customer service. In addition, the quality of the service is relatively easy to measure in this environment. Poor-quality service can be detected through visible signs of customer dissatisfaction or via customer complaints. It is much more difficult and in many cases impossible to evaluate levels and frequencies of customer dissatisfaction with an impersonal medium.

Customer service through non-store channels is not only different, but provides more opportunities for service implementation. A customer has to make a contact, for example by telephone or email, in order to find out any information about the product that is not immediately apparent. The stock position may be communicated, but this information has to be accurate and therefore continually updated. If the communication is via email the customer has to wait for a response. Following transactions the customer waits for the product to be delivered whereas in store retailing the customer (usually) departs with the product. Again the delivery promise must be rigidly adhered to in order to prevent customer dissatisfaction. The infrastructure that supports the product communication is absolutely vital to the success of any non-store retailer. One of the most frequent causes of internet shopping dissatisfaction, ('cyber-shopping rage') is poor response times to enquiries and poor order fulfilment, and in such cases all the convenience advantage of the shopping format for the customer is lost. Some internet retailers who have become aware of these problems have taken steps to prevent customer loss by incorporating service orientation in the web site design, for example by including email contact points, and 'phone-me' options. Some sites also allow customers to access real-time stock availability and delivery information, so there is no need for them to wait for an order acknowledgement or delivery arrangement.

BOX 13.1 ONLINE AVAILABILITY

Allowing customers to check availability and choose how they want to buy a product would seem to be a logical customer service provision. Instead of embarking on a shopping trip to a store, only to find your size is out of stock, or going to the time and trouble of filling in an order online, only to be notified a day later that there will be a delivery delay, if customers could have delivery information prior to their purchase decision, they would perhaps feel better about the retailer concerned. At least, armed with availability information they would be in control over the choice of either waiting until the product was in stock or continuing their shopping to find something else.

A number of retailers have taken steps to empower customers with availability information. Argos, the UK catalogue showroom retailer have extended their in-store availability check to allow customers to do the same online, and in the US BestBuy goes a stage further by letting customers check availability online and then if they wish to they can collect the product from the store within two hours of an online order being placed.

Being able to manage this level of service depends on fully integrated and powerful real-time stock management systems. Stores effectively become a forward distribution system that is tied into the online business. However, without the ability to have a complete picture of exactly what stock is where in all parts of the retail network at any one moment in time, the information given to customers would not be accurate and customer service would collapse. The web site of Globus Office World, a 59-store office stationery retailer, will not show a product if it is unavailable, and if a product is low in stock, the web site will offer an alternative product.

Although some might take the view that showing a product out-of-stock might be off-putting to customers, other retailers consider that it is offering more choice and allows the customer to make an informed purchase decision based on realistic information, rather than a hope, which can be dashed next day when the shopping process has to be revisited. Many customers would, at this stage lose interest and abandon the purchase for good.

Source: Based on Morrell, 2004

One feature of home shopping that is attractive to consumers is the ease with which goods can be returned. Catalogue retailers accept that around one-third of customer purchases will be returned, and in some departments, like clothing and footwear, this proportion can be considerably higher, as the customer will order two or more sizes to try, only ever intending to purchase one. Reducing the amount of returns is a way of improving retail productivity, whether store or non-store based, but internet retailers have to accept that returns are a necessary evil of home shopping, and make adequate provision for this service, clearly setting out the returns policy to the customer. One of many problems cited in the demise of online clothing retailer Boo.com was an indiscriminate returns policy, and an inadequate infrastructure to deal with returned goods. Again, multi-channel retailers have to consider how flexible their various outlets will be in terms of offering a multi-channel service, as well as a multi-channel selling strategy. Some retailers allow catalogue returns to be taken back to their stores, but others are not able or prepared to offer this flexibility. As the use of home shopping formats grows, the operational challenge associated with returned merchandise may lead retailers to employ the services of a third party logistics specialist who has dedicated facilities for collecting and sorting returned merchandise. The sorted merchandise can then be sent back to the manufacturer (if faulty) or returned to stock (Ody, 2002). Stock control is made more complicated when the flow of merchandise is a two-way route, and the stock management system must be able to effectively cope with additions to stock other than those accounted for by deliveries from manufacturers. Multi-channel retailers may resort to using their own 'discount outlets' to clear returned merchandise that becomes obsolete.

The chief concern amongst consumers with regard to internet shopping is security. Shoppers perceive giving credit card and personal details as a risk, which may not be outweighed by the benefits of convenience and price. This has two implications for e-retailers. The first is that customers are more likely to internet shop with retailers that they trust; this gives multi-channel retailers a distinct advantage, allowing them to transfer customer goodwill across shopping formats. The second implication is that secure payment systems will help to reassure customers that their personal details will remain safe and their privacy be respected.

CONVENIENCE

One of the most oft-quoted sayings in the retail industry is the following: 'there are three factors for success in retailing; these are location, location and location' (anon.). Perhaps the most pleasant and convenient shopping location for a consumer is at home. Traffic jams, weather and crowds can be avoided, prices can be quickly compared between outlets, and heavy and bulky shopping is delivered, rather than having to be carried and loaded. In addition, the consumer gains privacy and personal efficiency as they browse through non-store outlets that are geared to their individual needs. In a convenience orientated society, home shopping clearly purports to offer a set of tangible benefits. However, home shopping is only convenient if it delivers its promised service; if it does not, then it is highly inconvenient and risks high levels of customer frustrations. The infrastructure behind the non-store outlet must therefore not only support the product offer, but also the stated or assumed service offer.

ORDER FULFILMENT AND DELIVERY

In theory, the benefit of use of a product representation to sell from rather than 'live' stock is that the retailer can effectively operate a stock-free order fulfilment system (see Chapter 7). Only when customer orders roll in are products ordered from the suppliers. If the supplier holds stock and the product is not subject to seasonal trends and potential obsolescence, then this type of order fulfilment system would be possible. However, in the case of seasonal goods and retail branded items, suppliers are unlikely to hold stock without some form of order commitment from the retailer, in which case the buying processes and operations are similar to store retailers, except for determining order quantities.

Determining order quantities in non-store retailing

As indicated above, non-store retailers will wish to commit themselves to as little stock investment as possible. They do not have the need for stock to fill stores, but may need a level of safety stock in order to guarantee a fast delivery service. For seasonal and fashion goods, however, it is much more difficult to forecast and respond to peaks in demand (as discussed in Chapters 6 and 7) and so the larger fashion catalogue retailers use a 'preview' catalogue in order to test-market the new season's products. Previous customers of the retailer are sent a catalogue early in the season, offering a discount for early ordering, and a longer delivery time. This allows the retailer to anticipate the season's demand based on the level of orders placed from the preview catalogue.

Repeat orders are then placed with suppliers accordingly so that their production can be geared up to produce the best sellers for the season and keep the mail order retailer in stock through the selling period. If a product does not sell at all in the preview catalogue, there may be an opportunity to delete the offending article from the main catalogue or modify it in some way to improve its appeal. Likewise, multiple channel retailers like Next can cherry-pick the best selling lines from the catalogue for the new season's ranges for the stores, or products that have good trial results can be planned into future promotional activity across all channels. Internet retailing also offers the scope to pre-test new products or product variations. This gives a retailer an opportunity to trial over a larger geographic area. However, retailers must consider how closely the profile of their overall target customer market matches that of the current internet using customer. In some circumstances these may be quite different customer groups; the socio-economic profile of the internet customer group may well be higher than that of the general customer population, and so this might inflate demand levels for higher priced merchandise.

Delivery

The product categories that have seen early adoption of internet retailing (such as books, music, videos, DVDs and tickets) all have the characteristics of being easy to distribute, either physically through the post or digitally downloaded. Catalogue retailers are already set up with an organisational structure that understands rapid order fulfilment, delivery and returns of bulkier products, and they have a customer base that is more likely to be at home during 'normal' working hours to receive the goods. Internet retailers must appreciate that the bulk of their clientele are people who are working long and irregular hours. Weekend or evenings are the periods in which deliveries are going to be acceptable to these customers, and these present increased operational costs. It is predicted that this may be less of a problem for interactive TV retailers, who are more likely to be selling to high volume TV watchers from the 'cash-poor, time rich' section of the population (Wills, 1999).

The costs to a retailer of delivering some products are high; bulky products require large transportation vehicles and teams of delivery staff to unload and unpack the goods. Other fragile and breakable products will result in high levels of shrinkage and returns unless the delivery arrangements are satisfactory. Again, the retailer is faced with a complex pricing dilemma; should these additional delivery costs be passed on to the customer in a variable delivery charge, or should the price of delivery be consistent across the product range. Some retailers empower their delivery staff to give refunds or vouchers, which can solve a delivery problem on the spot, and reduce the need to both customers and retailers to go through the time-consuming process of organising a replacement. Tracking and pro-active order management software can help retailers to give more precise delivery times, and update customers on the progress of their order (Clements, 2004).

The illustrations in Figure 13.1 show how the infrastructure of non-store retailers compares with that of a store retailer. The apparent simplicity of the internet retailer in itself is what seemed to bode ill for retailers in general, as it is as easy for a consumer to reach a producer's web site as a retailer's. The opportunity for direct marketing has not passed manufacturers by; for example, in the US a group of high profile branded goods manufacturers, including Procter & Gamble, launched Consumer Direct Co-operative in order to test the viability of direct delivery to consumers (Fernie, 1999). However for most manufacturers, and particularly for those of lower priced fast moving consumer goods, selling to individual consumers is not a viable proposition. In addition, efficient distribution networks are based on co-operative rather than adversarial relationships and so most manufacturers have not pursued the option of competing with their customers for retail sales. In the end it is the seller who presents the best brand identity and most accessible method of product acquisition that will win the customer's purse. For the time being,

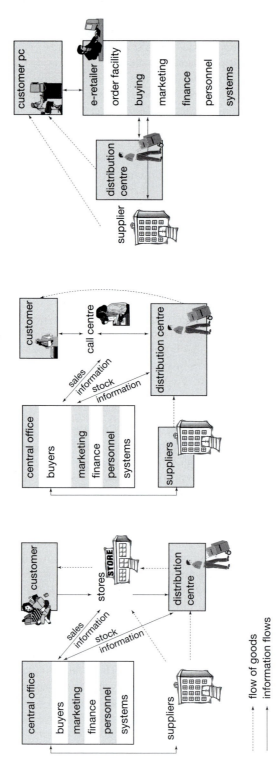

Figure 13.1 *Retail infrastructure: store based, traditional non-store and 'e-retail'*

retailers still have the advantage of being able to offer a product range that is understood and convenient for consumers to choose from, like Tesco.com online grocery shopping service. Consumers need simplification, speed and choice, which retailers, rather than branded goods suppliers, are able to offer. However, the internet does offer specialist producers a fast and inexpensive access to a potentially huge market of interested individuals.

BOX 13.2   MUSIC RETAILING: TECHNOLOGY INSTIGATED SIMULTANEOUS PRODUCT AND SHOPPING METHOD CHANGES

The shopping process for music has perhaps changed the most out of all product categories since the 1980s. Not only have the shopping channels expanded, as in other retail sectors to offer more convenience orientated routes to market, such as via supermarkets and online home delivery, but the product itself has changed from something fragile, tangible and tactile that had to be carefully cherished, to something that is now only heard and not even seen, let alone touched. Downloading music is changing the distribution channels and the nature of the product all in one. With the problem of piracy set aside, downloading onto a personal music system like an iPod or an MP3 player gives customers convenience, flexibility and choice; customisation is the expectation, rather than the exception and more control is handed to the consumer and ultimately the artist.

MULTI-CHANNEL RETAILING

After the initial excitement surrounding the possibilities for e-retailing and the vast amount of money invested in e-commerce ventures, the bursting of the dot.com bubble, which in the UK happened in the first half of 2000, brought internet retailing advocates back down to earth. Many traditional retailers, with their huge investment in their store portfolios, were criticised for their sloth in formulating e-retailing strategies. However, they appear to be somewhat vindicated as they have learned from other retailers' mistakes and have adopted multi-channel retailing at a more manageable pace. Retailers cannot ignore the internet. It allows businesses of all shapes and sizes new and different opportunities to communicate with customers. A general-purpose web site is these days almost a prerequisite for retailers and allows customers access to company information that was previously supplied by an extensive customer service provision for those who could afford the resources. Transactional web sites, however, are not an easy undertaking and if many of the errors that occurred in the early days of e-retailing are to be avoided, they should be organized as part of an integrated multi-channel strategy.

The integration of e-retailing has been easy for some retailers. In particular, traditional home shopping establishments, who initially appeared to be the most vulnerable to internet retail offers, have embraced the internet as a way of increasing the choice of route through which customers can order. Retailers like Next and La Redoute, who already had distribution centres, logistics networks and established supply channels for home shopping were in a good position to transfer their mail order business to an online catalogue. Customers already had trust in these retailers to handle their shopping requirements at a high customer service level. The home shopping retailer understood the importance of order fulfilment, had experience with forecasting

241

home-shopping sales, and had the facilities to deal with customer deliveries and returns (reverse logistics). Online ordering provided an opportunity to widen their customer base, and provide additional services.

Once the logistical challenges of home shopping were fully acknowledged and addressed, the transformation of many large retailers to multi-channel organisations has been highly successful, and has been central to a long-term survival strategy. The many various ways that retailers have incorporated e-retailing are beyond the scope of this text, but some significant opportunities and challenges, specifically related to product management can be highlighted.

CROSS-SHOPPING

One of the great benefits to customers afforded by multi-channel retailing is the ability to blend different modes of shopping as they see fit. In the early years of internet retailing consumers seemed to readily adopt the internet as an additional and very useful source when searching for information about products they wanted to buy. In particular, for products that were complex and high value, the internet provided a very convenient way of gathering specifications, information about customisation possibilities and prices. However, because of the high level of involvement the final purchase transaction was invariably carried out in the store environment, as a form of reassurance. This use of the internet is still important, but what customers are increasingly doing is going to shops to look at, touch and try out products, decide which item is their preferred choice, and then go home to order online. This presents a more leisurely shopping trip where choices are made, but the hard work involved with carrying products about is avoided. Shopping in this way is more conducive to making a day out, combining shopping with eating and/or some form of entertainment.

Although this type of cross-shopping is in the interest of the multi-channel retailer, which offers the choice of outlet in which customers carry out the various stages of their buying process, it requires the retailer to take a different attitude towards measuring profit contributions (see section below on cost allocation).

TRANSFER OF POSITIVE AND NEGATIVE IMAGE

No matter how many different shopping methods a multi-channel retailer offers, from a customer viewpoint they are all the same business, and so any new routes introduced must reinforce the image that has been built up over years of hard work within the framework of the traditional retail format.

Maintaining this image may require considerable investment in new product management skills. According to Ody (2000) 'clicks and mortar' retailers are able to accrue the benefits of cross-marketing that 'pure-play dot.com' retailers are unable to access. These would include better (more experienced) stock management, greater buying power, the opportunity to advertise in order to gain site awareness, and a better opportunity to track customer shopping habits by means of existing and new customer links. The importance of order fulfilment and delivery service in the support operations for a home shop 'front page' activity was highlighted earlier; whilst traditional catalogue retailers look most vulnerable to internet retail offers, they also possess assets and specialist management skills that new internet company start-ups are most keen to acquire. They have distribution centres, logistics networks and established supply channels; they also have experience in sales forecasting and responding to unpredicted demand, and supply market knowledge. Merging the skills of an innovative internet-based retail business and an established retail distribution organisation is an available and fast route to multi-channel retailing. John Lewis, the UK based department store and supermarket retailer acquired Buy.com for its internet retailing expertise, resulting in well designed and easy to navigate web sites for both sections of the business, which are now experienced hybrid retail concerns.

As indicated earlier in the chapter, pricing consistency across channels is an important issue; customers expect web site purchases to be cheaper, and competition from internet-only retailers can drive down online prices. However, selling goods under the same retail brand at significantly different prices runs the risk of causing customer confusion and resentment. As well as the need to react to online price competition, the long-term strategy of the multi-channel retailer will influence pricing tactics. For example, a retailer that is actively pursuing the strategy of encouraging customers to shop online can use price as a lure. On the other hand, retailers that see their online facility as a back-up service to a predominantly store shopping business are more likely to maintain price consistency. The use of 'online discounts' is a way of offering lower prices whilst maintaining the original price visibility across channels.

COST ALLOCATION

One of the most inhibiting factors in the process of multi-channel retail development is cost allocation. In Chapter 12, we examined the various ways in which product profitability can be approached. A new, and potentially important, retail format involves many start-up costs that seriously distort the finely tuned profit calculation used, for example, in activity-based costing. Cross-channel shopping behaviour compounds the complexity of sales and profit analysis because one medium may be used for the all important information search part of the purchase process, whilst an alternative medium may be used for the actual transaction. For example, consumers may conduct a considerable web-surf for product information, but prefer to see the product in the store before the final purchase. Other customers may prefer to browse in shops, spending time talking to sales assistants and using facilities to trial products but, rather than carry the goods home, order them via an interactive TV internet service. Knowing how consumers shop and how this can be profitably managed takes efficient consumer response to another level. Next, for example achieves its highest transaction values from customers who use a combination of internet and the Next Directory, selecting from the catalogues and ordering online (*Retail Week*, 31 March 2000). Tesco has found that their internet customers are concentrated in ABC1 socio-economic groups, and they tailor their product promotions to them accordingly. A wine promotion would have more resonance than one for instant noodles for this customer group (*Retail Bulletin*).

SALES CANNIBALISATION

Another cost involved with multi-channel retailing is sales cannibalisation. In all the complexity of multi-channel shopping, a retailer may not be gaining any more customers, in a similar way that opening more and more stores may just be providing more convenient outlets to existing customers. However, from a strategic viewpoint, cannibalisation is market share being protected, rather than market share being lost to retailers who offer more convenient product offers (Butler, 1999).

MARKETING

In spite of the various difficulties, multi-channel retailing as a strategic development offers some really important marketing opportunities. Retail brand positioning and reinforcement was a central theme of earlier chapters of this book when considering the relationship between product ranges and the selling environment. Making the retail brand more visible and more accessible to more customers will reinforce recognition and loyalty. Multi-channel retailing allows consumers more choice and flexibility so that the process of shopping can be blended into their busy and changing lifestyles (see Box 12.1). However, a multi-channel retailing strategy does not always develop in the 'brick to clicks' direction. Some retailers who have established successful home shopping based operations are realising that the more traditional retail formats can be used very effectively as a means of reinforcing their position in an increasingly competitive virtual marketplace. Gateway 2000, for example, began by selling computers on the internet, but later started a store portfolio development. Boden, the specialty catalogue retailer featured in the case at the end of this chapter, has also recently opened a store.

Other multi-channel operational complexities include how loyalty schemes transfer across channels, and how a comparable service is offered across all formats, as in the case of a returns policy, discussed earlier in this chapter. Multi-channel retailers have to appreciate that, from a consumer's viewpoint, the retail brand applies to all the alternative shopping formats and the internal structuring and financial reporting is of no interest to them. For example, an online purchase either adds to or detracts from the retail brand value built up by a store based retail operation, whilst an uninviting store environment is unlikely to encourage customers to visit a web site of the same retail fascia.

SUMMARY

New methods of retailing emerge and shopping processes evolve, but the product management issues associated with retail operations that do not enable customers to interact with the 'real' product will not disappear. Shoppers will adapt to the product offers made available to them in various forms, but the extent to which consumers accept the various home shopping methods available will determine the market size, not the amount of retailers subscribing to the new technologies. The developments in non-store retailing are as vital to traditionally store-based retailers as they are to those who have never relied on the physical presence of a product to help in the purchase process; and in the meantime, the role of the store is evolving from the point at which goods are distributed to consumers, to an arena where a branded retail identity is reinforced, through a blend of product presentation, information provision, access to retail services, and in-store interest and entertainment. In effect, the store becomes a showroom, while new technologies deal with sales transactions and order fulfilment. The final stage in the process, when the goods are delivered, is an opportunity to reinforce the retail brand, and should not be where it becomes irreparably damaged.

CASE STUDY BODEN

The UK retail mail order market was, for many years, dominated by a small number of large players, who traded from a large biannual tome of a general catalogue that covered a diversity of product categories. More recently, the mail order market has proliferated into a more fragmented market with many more specialised and targeted offerings, especially ones for the time poor dual income households and the less mobile elderly customer groups. Against this background, a retailer that exemplifies the growth of the specialist catalogue is Boden. Launched in 1991, and initially offering just eight menswear products, the immediate appeal of Boden products are their elegant casual style, blended with contemporary design twists. The company moved into the more lucrative womenswear market three years later, and into childrenswear in 1996. These three areas represent the core of the retail offer today, with the addition of a small range of footwear and accessories. Although Mintel (2003) described the Boden range as 'upmarket, targeted at customers with middle class lifestyles and high enough disposable incomes to be able to afford good quality clothing for their children as well as for themselves' prices are not *very* expensive. Through the emphasis on quality and durability, Boden aim to offer real value, loosely defined by the price of an item divided by the number of times worn (Mintel, 2003).

The company issues catalogues biannually. The adult catalogue is 240 pages, which is around 70 per cent womenswear and the rest menswear, although the womenswear section is also issued on its own for mailing to existing customers. The children's range has a dedicated 'Mini Boden catalogue', of around 200 pages, featuring boys' and girls' clothing up to mid-teenages. All products (including sale items) are featured on the web site.

Boden was ranked 22nd in the UK home shopping company table, ranked by sales, and has one of the strongest yearly increases in the whole sector. Financial performance is shown in Table 13.3.

Table 13.3 *J.P. Boden: financial performance, 2000–2002*

	2000	2001	2002	% change 2000–02
Sales (£000)	29,329	36,772	47,901	+ 63.3
Operating profit (£000)	145	1,791	4,463	+ 2,977.9
Operating margin (£000)	0.5	4.9	9.3	+ 8.8
Pre-tax profit (£000)	13	1,690	4,609	+35,353.8

Source: Annual Company Reports & Accounts/Mintel Home Shopping, 2003

The product range

A Boden product is not a fashion statement. The styling of garments for women, men and children is generally relatively simple and uncluttered. The materials used are predominantly natural fibre based and casual in nature. In the womenswear range, linen, cotton twill, needlecord and tweeds dominate whilst in the men's range corduroy, linen and moleskin is used extensively in outerwear and virtually all the shirts and T-shirts are 100 per cent cotton. Printed fabrics feature strongly, with antique florals, spots and stripes being favourite. Strong colours are used, but colour never takes over the retail offer as a highly co-ordinated colour 'story'; each product stands on its own and garment styles are often offered in quite diverse fabric types, increasing the individualism, and moving away from the 'colourway' product presentation method, so prevalent in catalogue retailing.

Perhaps the strongest and most unique part of the Boden product 'handwriting' is the attention to quality and detail in both the garments' base fabric and in the trimmings used. Although not used in all products, for example, where a patterned fabric is used as the main garment feature, the Boden design teams are adept at changing a very basic garment into a special one by the use of trimmings. Thus, T-shirts are trimmed with velvet or ruched ribbon, buttons, beads or patchwork section, while skirts are given pleating, appliqué and hem interest. Apart from very sparing usage in the Mini Boden catalogue, all products are free from external logos and badges.

Customer service

Boden attempt to make home-shopping from their catalogue as easy as possible for the customer. The catalogue contains full-size measurement detail, a personalised hemming service and an easy to complete order form. Trouser styles are compared on a full-page spread to show variation in fit and length (for example, wide leg, bootleg, cropped and so on). The exchange policy is generous, with a three-month time span in which returns are accepted, and loyal customers are offered free delivery and free returns on their first order of the season if they order within a specific time period. The return forms contain an optional tick box returns information section, so that problem garments can be diagnosed.

Outer packaging is brightly coloured plastic bags, or classic brown cardboard, with individual contents wrapped in high quality printed tissue paper, sealed with a Boden sticker. The way customers receive the parcel has been considered in fanatical detail: 'we consider everything from where the address labels will look best on parcels, to close examination of a single customer's complaint. We think about shopping from our customers' perspectives – from how they open parcels to why things have gone wrong. Scrutinising our mistakes keeps errors low' (Dreyer, 2002).

In 2002, Boden moved the distribution function from the original company base in London to Leicester in order to improve customer service to the rapidly expanding customer base. The company has taken steps to ensure that the excellent customer service that has been one of the founding principles of the company, does not get lost in the pursuit of higher volumes of product throughput. 'We encourage our customer service advisers to respond to callers as individuals. If the customer is feeling chatty, we are happy to talk. Busy customers will get brisk service. Letting our customer set the pace of the calls is costly, but it is part of the price of excellent customer service' (Dreyer, 2002). Although Boden consider systems and IT support as an integral part of good customer service provision, the company has preferred to rely on systems that are robust and practical; 'we constantly improve our systems to make them more effective, but never at the expense of reliability. Blaming technical glitches for poor service is guaranteed to annoy' (Dreyer, 2002).

Product presentation

The way Boden products are presented in the catalogue, and the photographic styling could be considered to be very 'atypical', within the mail order industry. The photographic locations have 'personality', for example a rambling stately home, moorlands and markets are used instead of the ubiquitous 'hotel balcony'. The models look like real people engaged in real activities such as having picnics, camping, splashing in puddles, and walking in hills. In fact, many of the children in Mini Boden are those of friends, as opposed to professionals: 'The models on these two pages (and most of the others in the catalogue) are friends or customers, not professionals. We have asked them all what job they would like to do when they grow up. You'll see their answers in the captions on the photograph' (Mini Boden catalogue, winter 2002). There is a dearth of make-up, and the feel is more of fun and informality rather than glamour. Many shots are like family album snapshots, with more apparent emphasis on the person and the situation than on the clothes. This theme is extended to irony in some cases, in a way of almost 'sending up' the catalogue photo-shoot. As a way of strengthening this unique aspect of product presentation, the reader is given extra snippets of information about the models: their name is always given, together with some frivolous personal detail such as: favourite actor, birthday, favourite sandwich, and their preferences such as 'Lennon or Jagger' or 'cinema or video'. The children charmingly divulge their aspirations of 'grown-up' life.

Customer communication

Imparting a brand identity through marketing communications is a well-established practice, and the use of a 'celebrity' or a 'personality' to give a brand recognition and identity is commonplace in retailing. This enables the retailer to avert the problems of extensive variety or seasonal changes in the product range (see Chapter 11). Boden use the 'voice' of the founder 'Johnnie Boden' in all customer messages, so that the customer feels that they are being written to, or talking with an old friend. 'Johnnie' explains customer service initiatives; 'Johnnie' introduces the products; 'Johnnie' implores you to order more. There is an assumed 'relationship' between Johnnie and the customer, which customises the business exchange in a way that is perhaps more effective than computer generated 'personalised' offers. One of the cleverest aspects of this communication is the fact that the tone avoids being patronising, and yet is familiar, at times almost cheeky.

> For his eyes only . . .
>
> Let me explain to you the 'all male' benefits of shopping with Boden: You will never again have to endure the experience of going into shop after shop and being offered a dizzying range of unwearable clothes before returning home exhausted . . .
>
> (Offer card, spring, 2004)

> Gigantic Offer[*]
>
> RRRRRROOOOOOAAAAAARRRRRRR!
>
> Welcome to Mini Boden
>
> Open your large powerful jaws and sink your mandibles of doom into our latest catalogue. Having already devoured our Adult collections, you are clearly a highly evolved Stylavore. As such, our fresh spring collection will prove to be wholly to your taste.
>
> To whet your appetite, we are giving you a dino sized 10 per cent off your next order.
>
> And as parcels can sometimes weigh as much as dinosaurs, we'll pay for your postage, packing and returns.
>
> Hurry though this offer is on the verge of extinction. Johnnie Boden.

Brand identity, personality and values

Although Boden rarely use external symbols or logos, there are a number of small details that help to create a strong brand identity. In particular, the Johnnie Boden signature, used on internal labelling, hanging loops, customer communication, the web site and packaging. However, what is perhaps the most important part of the Boden brand-building strategy is their use of story telling and humour, such as that used in the dialogue created with the models, and the friendly approach which shrouds fairly mundane, but important customer information. This approach is taken into the information imparted in the web site, such as the 'about us' section, which is brief, factual and humorous. The customer is made to feel involved with, perhaps even a personal friend of the company.

In a retail market characterized by high provision and only small opportunities for overall growth, Boden's success is notable. In 2003, the company opened their first shop, located in a vibrant, upmarket shopping district in London. The extent to which the Boden appeal can be translated into a store environment remains to be seen.

Source: Dreyer (2002), Mintel (2003); *mini Boden offer card, spring 2004 (on reverse of a picture of a dinosaur)

QUESTIONS

1   Review the developments in home shopping, highlighting the benefits and drawbacks of this retailing format to consumers.

2   Identify the main challenges in non-store retail product management, and suggest the steps that retailers might take to overcome these.

3   Referring to the case of Boden, analyse the product strategy that has contributed to the success of this non-store retailer.

4   Identify retailers that already successfully use multi-channel retailing, and make a critical analysis of their product offer across the different channels that they use.

5   Suggest retailers that you feel could benefit from alternative retailing methods, and the formats you feel are appropriate for them. Justify your recommendations.

6   The shopping medium may change, but the principles of retail product management remain the same. Discuss.

REFERENCES AND FURTHER READING

Berman, B. and Thelen, S. (2004) 'A Guide to Developing and Managing a Well-integrated Multi-channel Retail Strategy', *International Journal of Retail and Distribution Management*, 32(3): 147–156.

Butler, S. (1999) 'The High Street Heads for Home', *Draper's Record Focus*, February.

Clements, A. (2000) 'Clicks and Mortar and Customer Service', *Retail Week*, 4 February.

Clements, A. (2004) 'Stand and Deliver', *Retail Week Supply Chain Guide*, September.

Connon, H. (2003) 'Buying with Clicks is Better with Brick', *Observer*, 21 December.

Dennis, C., Fenech, T. and Merrilees, B. (2004) *e-Retailing*, Routledge, London.

Din, R. (2000) *New Retail*, Conran Octopus, London.

Dreyer, B. (2002) 'In the Bag', *Retail Week*, 1 November.

Fernie, J. (ed.) (1999) *The Future of UK Retailing*, Financial Times Retail and Consumer Reports, London.

Harris, L. and Dennis, C.E. (2002) in Dennis *et al.*, (eds), p. 2.

Kinnes, S. (2004) 'Women Start to Shop Like Men', *Times*, 29 February.

Markham, J.E. (1998) *The Future of Shopping: Traditional Patterns and Net Effects*, Macmillan, Basingstoke.

Mintel (2003) *Home Shopping UK*, Mintel International Group, London.

Morrell, L. (2004) 'With a View to a Sell', *Retail Week Supply Chain Guide*, September.

Nicholson, M., Clarke, I. and Blakemore, M. (2002) 'One Brand, Three Ways to Shop: Situational Variables and Multichannel Consumer Behaviour', *International Review of Retail, Distribution and Consumer Research*, 12(2): 131–148.

Nitse, P.S., Parker, K.R., Krumwiede, D. and Ottaway, T. (2004) 'The Impact of Colour in the e-commerce Marketing of Fashion: An Exploratory Study', *European Journal of Marketing*, 38(7): 898–915.

Ody, P. (2000) 'Channel-hopping is the Key', *Retail Week*, 5 May.

Ody, P. (2002) 'Returned Goods Open the Logistics Opportunity Door', *Retail Week*, 29 November.

Packshaw, H. (2000) 'Rational Balancing Act', *Retail Week*, 26 May.

Retail Week (2000) 'Next Customers Spend More Online', 31 March.

Reynolds, J. (2002) 'Charting the Multi-channel Future: Retail Choices and Constraints', *International Journal of Retail and Distribution Management*, 30(11): 530–535.

Rivett, D. (2000) 'Brands at the Mercy of the Killer Portals', *Retail Week*, 12 May.

Vrechopoulos, A.P., O'Keefe, R.M., Doukidis, G.I. and Siomkos, G.J. (2004) 'Virtual Store Layout: An Experimental Comparison in the Context of Grocery Retail', *Journal of Retailing*, 80: 13–22.

Wills, J. (1999) *Merchandising and Buying Strategies: New Roles for a Global Operation*, Financial Times Retail and Consumer Reports, London.

International retail product management

The purpose of this chapter is to:

- Identify the reasons why a retail product manager might need to take an international approach.
- Present arguments in favour of retailers keeping their product ranges standardised within international outlets.
- Understand the alternative to standardisation, which is to adapt product ranges for different international markets.
- Explore the relationship between international retail strategy and product management organisational structures.
- Consider the opportunities for sourcing internationally and appreciate some of the associated challenges for retail product management.

INTRODUCTION

Very few large retailers can ignore the opportunities afforded by an international approach to their business. As domestic markets become saturated and increasingly competitive, the attractions of serving emerging new markets become greater. In addition, competitive pressure to provide the best value in the product offer to the customer forces buyers to look further than their own domestic supply base for product sources.

For the product management team there are a number of important issues concerning international retailing, and these will be explored in this chapter.

INTERNATIONAL RETAILING AS A STRATEGY

For many retailers an international strategy has been central to their success; for companies like Woolworth's and Safeway, and more recently Ikea, Ahold, Tesco and Wal-Mart amongst many others, international operations have been a logical way to grow. Other retailers, like Next and Marks & Spencer, have taken a more cautious approach, and have met with varied success. The various entry and growth strategies have been well documented in other texts and sources (for example, Alexander 1997, McGoldrick and Davies, 1995), and so the discussion of internationalisation in this text is tailored to those specific retail operations that are concerned with product management.

PRODUCT RANGE: STANDARDISE OR ADAPT?

As a retailer opens more and more outlets in an increasingly diversified set of locations, it would seem logical to tailor the product range to the needs of the population. However, one of the attractions of an international market is to take a current successful retail format to a new set of customers who have similar characteristics and needs. Many retailers with a highly differentiated product range have had considerable international success without any great change to the retail identity or product range, for example, Body Shop, Ikea and (initially) Laura Ashley.

Salmon and Tordjman (1989) suggested that retailers either use a global strategy or a multi-national strategy for international operations. A global strategy is one that takes a successful retail formula from a domestic retail market and reproduces it around the world, whereas a multinational strategy involves setting up retail outlets that are owned or partially owned by the domestic retailer, but are adapted to the local market. A global strategy is said to concentrate on market similarities whereas a multinational strategy takes into consideration the differences. In fact, most successful international retailers' companies combine these two strategies to a greater or lesser extent. Adhering to a global strategy makes a retailer unable to react to local market opportunities and threats, so that once the novelty value of the new retail format has worn off, the formula becomes tired and vulnerable to local competition. The Spanish clothing retailer Zara, for example, has successfully adopted a product management strategy that allows it to adapt the product range within an operationally global business. They have a very fast turnaround of new products, with rapid replenishment and swift and deep markdowns of unsuccessful products. Once the bulk orders for a successful product have sold out, the original product is not repeated but the successful design features are incorporated into a new product. The replenishment and the allocation of the new product are made according to the sales of similar products sold previously in the individual outlets. Local preferences on colour, and local needs for different size ratios are also taken into consideration in the product allocation, and the stores are encouraged to speak to the company's product developers about popular designs in their region (Wills, 1999; Fernie and Sparks, 2004).

A multinational strategy generally takes longer and more investment from the parent company. A considerable amount of market research is required, followed by a programme of planning and implementation that may require new skills and approaches throughout the organisation. Scale economies may be difficult to achieve, given the diversity of marketing techniques and the tailoring of products to individual market needs. However, the opportunities for the transfer of knowledge and experience are much greater with a multinational strategy and the opportunities for international learning are also increased through the process of adaptation.

Treadgold (1990–1991) and Dawson (1994) developed the idea of a continuum of international retailing strategies, ranging from intensely global (no adaptation) to completely multinational (highly customised), with what were termed transnational companies in between. The transnational approach, which combines global operational efficiency while responding to national needs, opportunities and constraints, is the basis of the strategies of many successful international retailers. Even an essentially global retailer like Ikea has had to adapt 20 per cent of its product range for the US market; for example, European bed linen does not fit US beds (*The Economist*, 1994).

THE INFLUENCES ON DIFFERENT PRODUCT STRATEGIES

The differences in consumer behaviour in terms of product choice, brand preference, consumer economics, spending patterns and shopping methods, whilst challenging in a domestic market, become a myriad of changeable variables on an international scale. Some products, such as food, have a deep cultural relevance and localised interpretations, and so these products are more difficult to ascribe to a global strategy. US consumers, for example, generally have more storage space than their European counterparts and so are more inclined to buy groceries in bulk or large pack size.

On the other hand, if the target market is a narrow segment of the worldwide population, then the customer characteristics and product preferences may be more homogenous. Luxury goods traditionally have developed a universal appeal in the upper income brackets. Brands like Dunhill, Hermes, Gucci and Ralph Lauren have all 'travelled well'. With the increased globalisation of communications, the notion of 'international youth' has offered significant opportunities for retail brand globalisation, as shown by Gap, Levi's, and H&M.

UNAVOIDABLE ADAPTATIONS

Whilst the adaptation of the product range to a new geographic market is a matter of strategic judgement, there are some product modifications that are completely unavoidable. For example, product information in a dozen languages on one label may be necessary but render the information unreadable, and so the packaging or labelling design may need to be reformulated. Packaging and labelling requirements may also vary from country to country, and different climates may require alternative approaches to storage. Technical compatibility is often an issue in the electronics market. Likewise there is no escaping the additional documentation and administration that international trading brings, or barriers to trade that may be insurmountable, such as trade embargoes.

Retail pricing in the international market is a very complex issue with different currencies and exchange rates, import duties and taxes all having a bearing on the final pricing decision. In addition, a retailer needs to consider the different costs involved in retailing internationally, especially the distribution costs. In many cases, an international retailer will have a higher market positioning in non-domestic markets, in order to cover the additional costs. Marks & Spencer, for example, began with a more upmarket product positioning in their east Asian markets, where the clothes were considered to be 'designer wear', compared to the middle market position that they occupy on home ground.

ORGANISATION FOR PRODUCT MANAGEMENT

A retailer has the choice of adopting a centralised approach to its international activities or a decentralised approach. Earlier on in this text the benefits of a centralised buying organisation were presented and some of the drawbacks given (see Chapter 2). This discussion can be expanded to explore the issue on a global scale. A centralised approach has the advantage of retaining the significant economies of scale afforded by having a specialised team handling all sourcing operations from one base. However, one of the problems with simply extending the current roles to handling international outlets along with domestic ones is that the non-domestic outlets may not be given the attention they deserve. Reasons for poor performance may not be explored and product opportunities may not be optimised, because the domestic business (which will normally be larger at the start of international operations) takes priority.

Ultimately, the organisation that is adopted should reflect the product strategy being used. Where a high degree of standardisation is retained in the product range, with little adaptation to local markets, a centralised structure is more appropriate; but where a retailer adopts a strategy of adaptation, then a decentralised product management structure is more appropriate. A retailer may start its international expansion using the existing buying organisation, and then as the international operations grow and adaptations begin to appear necessary, a separate or decentralised structure may emerge. Body Shop, for example, introduced a decentralised structure in 1999, in order to gear their operations more closely to different international markets, in terms of both product development, and sourcing. The company split its international markets into four regions: UK, Europe, the Americas and Asia, and put a management team in place for each region. In this way it can identify and respond to product market opportunities more quickly and efficiently, rather than everything being managed from a UK base (Wills, 1999).

Where the entry strategy for a new geographical market is by means of acquisition, then it makes sense to retain the existing buying organisation, at least until the opportunities for consolidation can be fully explored. Local sources and existing relationships with suppliers may offer benefits that outweigh the efficiencies of increased buying power. The extent of synergy will depend on the similarities in the product range. Kingfisher, for example, undertook an aggressive international growth strategy by means of acquisition, predominantly in the European market. Whilst it retained separate management teams for the store fascias in the different locations, the teams work together to exchange best practice and achieve joint buying economies in some areas (Kingfisher company report, 1999).

BOX 14.1   B&Q: GLOBAL SOURCING FOR A GLOBAL RETAIL CHAIN

B&Q has been involved in international retailing for some time, in terms of both the direct sourcing of products and operating outlets. The UK's largest hardware and home improvement retailer, it has recently taken steps to increase direct overseas sourcing by opening a buying office in Jaipur, India, and appointing exclusive agents to source products in South Africa. This adds to a global supply network that already includes sourcing teams in Asia, with buying offices in Hong Kong and Shanghai. B&Q is reported to have doubled the number of products sourced directly over two years to 2004, with the aim of reducing product costs and developing new supply links by cutting wholesalers out of the supply chain. Direct sourcing allows the retailer to take more control over supply issues, such as product development and quality assurance. With stores operating in China, Taiwan and Turkey, B&Q is rapidly becoming a retailer that views the globe as its market, both in terms of supply and demand. As well as being one of the founding organisations of the worldwide non-profit making Forest Stewardship Council (FSC) which certifies well managed timber sources, B&Q has also helped to support communities in developing countries in their efforts to use safer and more socially responsible manufacturing methods. B&Q grade suppliers on environmental performance in a number of areas, which encourages them to make incremental improvements.

Whilst consistency in the international supply market provides challenges for sourcing, inconsistency in consumer demand provides challenges for product range development. Recent moves into China forced B&Q not only to take into account the differences between the UK and China, but also the differences between Chinese regions. The country has a cooler climate in the north, so they had to stock more radiators, whereas in the south of China they had to offer more air conditioning units. In Shanghai the customers like wooden floors, in Shehen they prefer tiles. As the country does not have a DIY (do it yourself) background, new services had to be offered, including links with local contractors to carry out work in customers' homes. B&Q also developed 'lifestyle' which gives customers the finishing touches and helps to prevent customers going to Ikea for the softer home improvements. The gardening offer was also reduced as this was of less relevance to the Chinese customer.

Source: *Retail Week*, 2004; *Retail Week*, 7 October 2002; and company literature

LOCAL SOURCING

Local sourcing can help an international retailer in a number of ways. Local sources will be in touch with local tastes and preferences and may be already integrated into the retailer's own supply chain, as in the case of an international acquisition, for example. Supporting local industries can have a positive effect on the local economy and can help a retailer develop a positive image with local customers. In some cases, the host country may even insist that a retailer purchases local supplies as a pre-requisite for trading. Toys 'Я' Us for example tend to purchase around one-third of their product range from local suppliers which helps them integrate into the new economy as well as respond to local preferences (Berman *et al.*, 1996).

GLOBAL SOURCING

Operating outlets 'abroad' is the most common interpretation of international retailing; nevertheless, importing goods from other countries is often the first step a retailer takes towards being an international player. Whilst many retailers never get beyond this step, there can be no doubt that an international outlook and transfer of expertise on a global scale has contributed to the growth in international retailing activities.

Improvements in technology, transport and logistics, and communication have made global sourcing a viable option for more retailers, whilst consumer demand and competitive pressure have pushed retail buyers to all corners of the earth to find producers for a wide and consistent selection of keenly priced goods. We are gradually losing the notion of seasonal produce; to the supermarket operator, the more months in which customers can be offered premium products like fresh strawberries the better.

The manufacturing of labour intensive products is a key feature of a nation's industrialisation and economic development, and as a new region enters the frame as the lowest cost producer, international buyers change their travelling routes. Training shoes, for example, are now sourced from Vietnam, having moved from Hong Kong to China and Korea previously.

As consumers travel more, both for leisure and in business, their knowledge and experience of 'foreign' products widens. In addition, the influence of more confident ethnic communities becomes more widespread, and so markets in developed countries have become keenly international in their tastes. At the same time, consumers are deepening their interest in their own cultural heritage, and so product diversity is an ever-increasing trend in retailing, in spite of the dangers posed by the need for product rationalisation in order to achieve efficiency (see Chapter 3).

Lui and McGoldrick (1995) note that international sourcing is different to importing. Often retailers sell imported goods without trading internationally, by purchasing goods from agents or distributors, and in many cases even large retailers prefer to deal with a domestic supplier who imports from its own global network of factories. However, as retailers become increasingly international in terms of outlet operation, it makes sense for them to develop supply and distribution networks that reduce the time that products have to spend in costly transit. The retail industry is consolidating on a global basis, giving rise to an international league of mass-market retailers; and so global scale competition will force international trading to become central to a competitive worldwide operation. In its bid to become a player in this field, Tesco has established buying teams around the world, adding India, Thailand and Europe to its established operations in Hong Kong. This network of buyers are to source in particular non-food ranges for both the domestic stores and its increasing number of international outlets, which cover central Europe, Ireland and the Far East (Riera, 2000).

Although not the only consideration, the fact that products can be bought in at lower cost prices means that retailers will continue to source from abroad. Improvements in product quality, communications and customer service (such as product development and sampling) have made the overseas buying trip all the more viable. International logistics have decreased lead-times and improved the reliability of delivery, so many of the traditional problems associated with global sourcing have diminished. Global sourcing requires a global set of selection criteria, but to operate efficiently the activities that it entails should be costed. What might appear to be an excellent profit margin could quickly diminish if additional time spent controlling quality and chasing deliveries were taken into account. Box 13.1 describes how information technology applications have helped US retailer Petsmart to source efficiently on a global scale. In selecting suppliers from a global supply base retail product managers may use some or all of the following strategies:

- *limit the percentage of internationally sourced goods*, using domestic suppliers for specific product or service requirements (for example, to repeat fast-selling merchandise);
- *spread the risk* by sourcing from a number of different countries and different manufacturers;
- *limit buying to certain geographical regions* to keep sourcing travel costs under control, possibly sourcing other regions through agents.

Locating sources around the world is another challenge for the retail buyer. As in domestic supplier selection, trade journals, directories, web pages, trade conventions and trade associations are useful points of information. Retailers will want reassurance that the supplier is experienced in international trade, is financially sound and has an established network of raw material suppliers and transporters. Some retailers, usually the larger groups, have buying offices located in the global supply markets. Otto Versand, for example, have a network of offices in Europe and the Far East through which buyers from all their mail order companies can source products. Smaller retailers may be able to tap into global markets by becoming affiliated to an international buying office organisation. The buying office may undertake a number of tasks, including the identification and recommendation of suppliers according to the retailer's needs, obtaining samples and price quotations, organising buying fairs, contract negotiation, collating orders, arranging payments, progress chasing and overseeing shipments.

Increasingly, e-commerce trading networks such as GNX (GlobalNetXchange) and Worldwide Retail Exchange are becoming a feature of the global supply market (see Chapter 5). The benefits that retailers are likely to accrue from electronic trading are principally concerned with lower order processing costs and obtaining price transparency, but they also allow retailers to easily compare suppliers on a global scale, whilst entering new supply markets cautiously on the back of a larger organisation or an experienced partner. Order processing is potentially much faster, which will help retailers and their suppliers. Other opportunities for suppliers include the means by which excess product can be sold off quickly and easily, and the exchange provides smaller, remote suppliers access to large retail buyers.

BOX 14.2 PETSMART

Petsmart, the US-based category killer retailer, sources products around the world from its buying office in Phoenix, Arizona. Suppliers are based in the USA, Asia and Europe, and range from small-scale specialists to multinational producers. The internet has given Petsmart the opportunity to create a standardized sourcing system, allowing all suppliers to be linked into a single buying network. The information technology solution, supplied by SourcingLink.net, provided a tailored retail-supplier procurement system that allows buyers to build up contact information, gather product source information, and then place and track orders with suppliers. The system is capable of producing digital imagery to help with product development at suppliers across the globe. Benefits from using such systems include a reduction in buyer's travelling time and costs, improved and cheaper communications with suppliers and more product innovations at a reduced time to market.

Source: Ody, 2000

ETHICAL SOURCING

One of the difficulties associated with global sourcing is that the distance away from the supply source makes it more difficult for buyers to assess suppliers. A buyer may be placing orders with a sourcing agent or with a trading company that uses a network of manufacturing units, and so it is often difficult to establish exactly how and where the products are actually manufactured. Buyers may be unaware that their products are being made in factories where the working conditions fall short of what would be considered satisfactory. Of course, different countries have different laws and regulations concerning working hours, age limitations and working conditions, but the international trading community has a collective social responsibility to ensure that international trade does not result in the exploitation and abuse of humankind.

Retailers have recently been under increasing pressure by both consumers and human rights organisations to be more concerned about the way they conduct trade. As consumers become increasingly knowledgeable, experienced and sophisticated, the more concern they have about what goes into the products they buy and the way they are produced. Many large international retailers have borne the brunt of unwelcome publicity concerning the production of their goods, including Gap, Eddie Bauer, Toys 'Я' Us, Sears, Nike and Wal-Mart (Lavin, 1999). In response to this ethical concern, retailers have introduced codes of conduct, backed up by supplier development and monitoring procedures. The Ethical Trading Initiative is an example of this kind of retailer response (see Box 14.3).

In a similar vein, there has been a growing interest in 'fair trade'. According to FINE, a network of organisations promoting fair trade in Europe, fair trade is defined as 'an alternative approach to conventional international trade. It is a trading partnership that aims at sustainable development for excluded and disadvantaged producers' (Fair Trade Fact Sheet, 2000). The move towards trade rather than aid is a hopeful sign for developing countries in an international society that provides low levels of aid and investment into these areas. Affiliated to FINE is the Fairtrade Foundation, a trading organisation which endorses products that are produced by suppliers in need of investment and support. The Co-op in the UK for example consider Fairtrade tea and coffee to be profitable and innovative additions to their beverage range, but one of the complications with the Fairtrade brand goods is that they only apply to products that are produced in parts of the world where suppliers need assistance; the label is not applicable to all types of produce, and so branding consistency is not achievable. The Co-op nevertheless are extending their involvement with Fair Trade by using these sources for some key own-branded products, like chocolate bars and wine. Fair trade has been at the heart of Body Shop's supply policies for a number of years, where sustainable trading relationships have been established with 36 supplier groups in 21 countries through its growing Community Trade Programme (Clements, 2000b).

BOX 14.3 THE ETHICAL TRADING INITIATIVE

The Ethical Trading Initiative (ETI) was launched in 1998, with the backing of Christian Aid, an official aid and development agency of forty British churches. It was formed as a result of co-operation among campaigning groups, trade unions, major retailers, manufacturers and the British government, with the view to enabling third world workers to get a decent deal for producing the foods that we shop for in our supermarkets. One of the first grocery multiples to get involved was J. Sainsbury, which presented its ethical policy to the press in 1996, and by 1999 Asda, CWS, Somerfield, and Tesco were all members of the ETI.

To become a member, a company must agree to a set of commitments. This includes adopting a 'base code' of labour practice that incorporates relevant internationally agreed labour standards. They then work with suppliers to move towards these standards. The ETI believes that a retailer should not have to choose between trade and ethics, and provides a forum at which the overlap between these interests can increase. Although a majority of leading UK retailers have expressed an interest and many have become members of the ETI, the success of this initiative will be dependent on how quickly the code of practice is implemented by the retailers, how well it is adopted by suppliers, how rigidly it is enforced. This calls for extra resources to be invested by the retailer. The extent of consumer pressure will influence the level of investment retailers are prepared to make and the speed of adoption of the new practices.

Full implementation of the Ethical Trading Initiative would mean that consumers could shop in their supermarkets in the knowledge that what they buy comes from suppliers who offer working conditions which meet internationally accepted standards.

SUMMARY

International activities are no longer an 'add on' in a retail strategy; the vision of the globe as the market, both in terms of demand for the retail offer, and supply of products to sell in the retail outlet, is one that is taken by an increasing number of retailers. International consolidation is taking industry leaders out of domestic markets and putting them into an international premier league. The opportunities for international retail expansion are becoming increasingly attractive as established markets tighten up and new markets open. However, product management is fundamental to the formulation of an appropriate strategy for the individual retailer, and the extent to which ranges and sources remain the same, or are adapted, will depend on the retail formats used and the product sector being developed. A global approach to product sourcing can help a retailer to maintain an innovative and price competitive product offer. However, planning and control and measuring results, remain at the crux of product management on an international scale, and must increasingly need to incorporate ethical issues that have a bearing on the customer's evaluation of a retailer's brand.

CASE STUDY GONE BANANAS?

The banana, with its sweet tasting and nutritious appeal and distinctive and convenient packaging, is the product that brings the highest sales value to British supermarkets, apart from petrol and lottery tickets. Every EU citizen is said to consume about 10 kilos of bananas each year. As an indigenous product, these huge quantities of bananas have to be imported and the international trading of this fruit is part of the UK's economic history. More recently, however, wrangles between the US and the EU have caused disruption within the banana trading community and highlighted some of the issues retailers face when managing a remote supply base.

At the heart of the 'banana war' was an objection by the US to a long-standing European quota system that was deemed to be detrimental to multinational banana distributing companies such as Chiquita. The quota system had been introduced in an attempt to sustain banana growing in poor countries like the Caribbean Windward Islands and prevent farmers resorting to more profitable, but illegal crops. However, by 2000 only a third of the Windward Island's farmers were still in business.

Being such a popular product, bananas are often the focus of supermarket price comparison exercises, which inevitably drives prices down in a highly concentrated and competitive retail market. Supply partnerships, such as the one between Wal-Mart and Del Monte help to make the banana a price-driven product category. Paradoxically, lower prices for bananas make little difference to sales volume because consumers are not able to stockpile them, so the losers in this situation were the growers who ended up with rock bottom prices for their products. Eventually, after considerable media coverage, the plight of the Windward Isles farmers reached the awareness of the UK consumer, who in the meantime had become interested in the concept of Fair Trade products, promoted heavily by the Co-operative retail group. In 2002, it was reported that yearly demand for Fair Trade bananas was rising by 53 per cent. In addition, Windward bananas now have their own trademark, so that supermarket shoppers who wish to, can support the efforts of the Caribbean island community to continue its banana growing industry.

Source: Based on Ryle (2002)

QUESTIONS

1   Outline the differences between a global product strategy, a multinational product strategy and a transnational product strategy, and discuss how the retail product sector might determine which strategy is used.

2   Examine the reasons why an international retailer might adopt a decentralised international buying organisation.

3   Suggest reasons for the increasingly global approach to product sourcing by retailers.

4   Explain what is meant by the terms fair trade and ethical trading, in the context of international retailing, and suggest steps that retail product managers can take towards socially responsible sourcing.

5   Discuss the additional selection criteria that might be necessary to consider when assessing non-domestic suppliers.

6   Discuss the reasons why retailers are under increasing pressure to ensure that the products they are supplied with are the result of fair and ethical trading. Referring to the case study, suggest initiatives that retailers can take to increase consumer awareness of these products.

REFERENCES AND FURTHER READING

Alexander, N. (1997) *International Retailing*, Blackwell, Oxford.

Berman, B., Evans, J.R., Berman, L.N. and Berman, G.L. (1996) 'Toys ЯUs Inc.: Analysis of a Global Strategy', Proceedings of the 4th International Conference of the European Association for Education and Research in Commercial Distribution, ESCP, Paris, 4–5 July.

Clements, A. (2000a) 'Chains Hope to Net the Benefit', *Retail Week*, 14 April.

Clements, A. (2000b) 'A Fair Chance for the Third World', *Retail Week*, 10 March.

Dawson, J. (1994) 'Internationalisation of Retailing Operations', *Journal of Marketing Management*, 10: 267–282.

Economist (1994) 'Furnishing the World', Management Brief, 19 November.

Fernie, J. and Sparks, L. (eds) (2004) *Logistics and Retail Management*, 2nd edn, Kogan Page, London.

Lavin, M. (1999) 'Press Accounts of Sweatshop Atrocities: The Potential for Consumer Negative Evaluation of Retailers', Proceedings of the 10th International Conference on Research in the Distributive Trades, Institute for Retail Studies, University of Stirling, 26–28 August.

Lui, H. and McGoldrick, P.J. (1995) 'International Sourcing: Patterns and Trends', in P.J. McGoldrick and G. Davies (eds), *International Retailing, Trends and Strategies*, Pitman, London, ch. 5.

McGoldrick, P.J. and Davies, G. (1995) *International Retailing, Trends and Strategies*, Pitman, London.

Ody, P. (2000) 'Smarter Sourcing of Supplies', *Retail Week*, 5 May.

Riera, J. (2000) 'Tesco Sourcing Teams to Drive Down Global Costs', *Retail Week*, 17 March.

Ryle, S. (2002) 'Banana War Leaves the Caribbean a Casualty', *Observer*, 24 November.

Salmon, W.J. and Tordjman, A. (1989) 'The Internationalisation of Retailing', *International Journal of Retailing*, 4(2): 3–16.

Treadgold, A. (1990/1) 'The Emerging Internationalisation of Retailing: Present Status and Future Challenges', *Irish Marketing Review*, 5(2): 11–27.

Wills, J. (1999) *Merchandising and Buying Strategies: New Roles for a Global Operation*, Financial Times Retail and Consumer Reports, London.

Web site

Fair Trade Fact Sheet on www.traidcraft.co.uk, April 2000.

Index

Routledge Retail

Retailing Reader

Edited by **John Dawson**, University of Edinburgh, UK and **Anne Findlay** and **Leigh Sparks**, both at the University of Stirling, UK

June 2006: 246x174: 320pp
Hb: 0-415-35638-5: **£85.00**
Pb: 0-415-35639-3: **£24.99**

Presenting an international and multidisciplinary collection of articles, case studies, histories and readings, this text captures the core functions, behaviours and approaches within retailing. The editors have compiled a collection of readings from books and journals which will interest all those who study or work in retailing.

The text's emphasis is on research that informs the current debates about, and practice of retailing. It draws on recent and classic articles and readings published in leading journals and written by experts in the field. Each of the six sections is prefaced with an editorial introduction - a contextual and interpretive chapter, setting the selected material in the overall context and direction of retail change. Each individual reading is then introduced by a brief discussion of the author and the criteria for the selection of their work. Each section of the text is supported by an extensive further reading / bibliography, and by a case studies section which provides both specific illustrations of significant retail change and also allows readers to investigate issues through the cases.

This text collates an extensive body of topical work in one volume and will be a valuable resource for students of retailing, marketing, business and management.

Contents

Section 1: Consumers and Shoppers   Section 2: Buying, Supplying and Merchandising   Section 3: Retail Branding and Marketing   Section 4: Retail Strategy   Section 5: Internationalization

Routledge books are available from all good bookshops, or may be ordered by calling Taylor & Francis Direct Sales on +44 (0) 1264 343071 (credit card orders) For more information please contact David Armstrong on 020 7017 6028 or e-mail david.armstrong@tandf.co.uk

2 Park Square
Milton Park
Abingdon
Oxfordshire OX14 4RN
www.routledge.com

Strategic Issues in International Retailing

Edited by **John Dawson**, University of Edinburgh, UK, and **Roy Larke** and **Masao Mukoyama**, both at UMDS University, Kobe, Japan

May 2006: 234x156: 256pp
Hb: 0-415-34370-4: **£75.00**
Pb: 0-415-34371-2: **£22.99**

As retailing becomes a globalized sector, the existing concepts and theories of international business fit uneasily with it. This significant book takes a strategic approach to this topic, examining in-depth studies of several retailers, and marrying theory with practice to clearly present material for students at every level.

Illustrating and evaluating the strategies of international retailers, developing concepts and theories that enable an understanding of international retailing and showing the contrasts in the approaches adopted by major firms in their international operations, this important text is a must-read for all those studying or working in international retail.

Contents:

Routledge books are available from all good bookshops, or may be ordered by calling Taylor & Francis Direct Sales on +44 (0) 1264 343071 (credit card orders) For more information please contact David Armstrong on 020 7017 6028 or e-mail david.armstrong@tandf.co.uk

2 Park Square
Milton Park
Abingdon
Oxfordshire OX14 4RN
www.routledge.com